THE ECONOMIC DEVELOPMENT OF
THE PACIFIC BASIN

WILLY KRAUS
WILFRIED LÜTKENHORST

THE ECONOMIC DEVELOPMENT OF THE PACIFIC BASIN

Growth Dynamics, Trade Relations and Emerging Cooperation

ST. MARTIN'S PRESS, NEW YORK
C. HURST & COMPANY, LONDON

87 -434

St. Martin's Press, 175 Fifth Avenue, New York, NY 10010
Printed in England on long-life paper
First published in the United States of America in 1986
ISBN 0–312–00452–4

Library of Congress Cataloging-in-Publication Data

```
Kraus, Willy.
    The economic development of the Pacific Basin.

    Bibliography: p.
    Includes index.
    1. Asia, Southeastern--Commercial policy.
2. Japan--Commercial policy.  3. General Agreement
on Tariffs and Trade (1947)  I. Lütkenhorst, Wilfried.
II. Title.
HF1591.K73  1987      338.95           86-26292
ISBN 0-312-00452-4 (St. Martin's Press)
```

PREFACE AND ACKNOWLEDGEMENTS

This book is published at a time when development trends and economic strategies in the Pacific region in general and in Japan in particular have kindled an intense discussion in the developed countries. For many years public opinion in those countries had neglected the structural changes in the world economy emerging from the increasing importance of the Pacific area. Now, however, the slogan of the 'Pacific challenge' is on everybody's lips, and a mood is spreading which Newsweek (7 May 1984) rightly referred to as 'Europe's Pacific nightmare'. We are aiming here to provide background studies on this important subject, the history of which has received too little attention. Furthermore, it has not been placed to a sufficient extent in the general framework of international economic relations and trade policy.

The first chapter provides an introduction into the basic problems of current international trade policy and the GATT framework of rules, and we argue here that the concept of a globally valid trade policy has entered a fundamental crisis. This in turn has created a strong interest in regionally limited trade policy approaches, but without being able to guarantee their superiority and success. Chapter II.A turns to recent developments in the trade policy of the Pacific developing countries, and Chapter II.B presents a critique of the controversial Japanese trade policy, a topic that has often been dealt with in the past by sweeping, prejudiced statements. Chapter III — in a sense the book's core — provides a detailed description and analytical assessment of the preconditions, prospects and limitations of various concepts of economic cooperation in the Pacific Basin.

The authors thank all those colleagues who have contributed to the study both by providing access to their own related research and by patiently taking part in numerous discussions. Special thanks are due to the Institute for Development Research and Development Policy at the Ruhr-University in Bochum for its encouragement of our project and for its generous financing of the necessary field research.

Bochum/Vienna, August 1986   WILLY KRAUS
                                                 WILFRIED LÜTKENHORST

v

CONTENTS

CONTENTS

TABLES

FIGURE

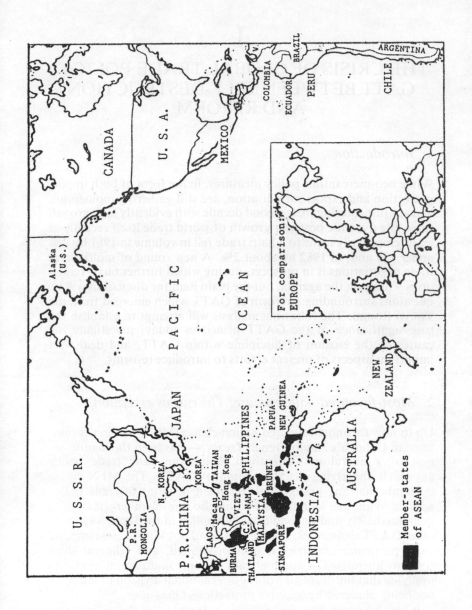

I

THE CRISIS OF GLOBAL TRADE POLICY: GATT BETWEEN SELF-DESTRUCTION AND REFORM

1. Introduction

While neo-mercantilist policy measures, in the form of both import protection and export subsidisation, are still gathering momentum and are just entering their second decade with evidently high growth rates, the dynamic post-war growth of world trade itself recently at least temporarily came to a halt: trade fell in volume in 1981 by just under 1% and, in 1982 by about 2%. A new round of multilateral trade negotiations is in prospect, during which further tariff reductions will be on the agenda, but the main item for discussion will be questions surrounding a reform of GATT which emerged from the Tokyo Round. The following analysis will attempt to establish the true significance of the GATT principles today, investigate the causes of the erosion of discipline within GATT, and deal with important aspects of present efforts to introduce reforms.

2. Most-favoured-nation clause: The rule as exception?

Up to now the most-favoured nation clause (MFN) — first formulated in Cobden's Anglo-French Treaty — has been the manifestation of a liberal multilateralism, being the basic trade policy approach underlying the foundation of GATT. The MFN clause demands that any preferential treatment in terms of trade policy applied to another country (including also non-members of GATT) be immediately and unconditionally applied in the same way to all other GATT signatories. Discrimination of any kind against imports from particular countries is thus prohibited, and bilateral steps towards liberalisation automatically become multilateral in effect, implying that the deepening of the international division of labour is not being hindered by selective protectionist measures.

It has, however, become apparent in recent years that a large and rapidly increasing proportion of world trade is taking place outside the most-favoured-nation framework:

(a) From the start, exceptions to the fundamental MFN principle were made for preference systems already in existence before GATT came in force and also, under certain specific conditions, for free trade areas and customs unions. The intention was to support regional approaches towards trade liberalisation as second-best solutions compared with global liberalisation.

(b) Further exceptions to the MFN principle emerged in 1971 with the General System of Preferences (GSP) which, based on a GATT waiver, is now in force in most industrial countries with the aim of selectively supporting the exports of developing countries. While the GSP's impact in terms of additional LDC exports is still subject to controversy compared to the impact of further MFN tariff reductions,[1] in terms of its impact on trade policy in general and the MFN principle in particular, the GSP should not be considered a major blow against the spirit of GATT: a particular group of countries was awarded preferential status according to the consensus of the contracting parties in order to give the former easier access to export markets, i.e. following trade liberalising motives with a development policy orientation.

(c) Certainly the severest blow suffered by the MFN principle in recent times has been the unfettered growth of non-tariff barriers to trade (NTBs). It has to be pointed out strongly that tariffs hardly count any more as trade barriers in the industrialised nations: as a result of the Tokyo Round, the weighted average of nominal tariffs on industrial goods is now 4.4% for the USA, 2.8% for Japan and 4.7% for the European Communities (EC).[2] It may thus be a considerable waste of resources to devote still more negotiating energy to further tariff reductions which in the future will only be of symbolic value. In contrast to this — and the link is obvious — NTBs are showing rapid increases both in the various forms they take and in the scope of their effect, to the extent that 34% of industrial production in the USA is now protected in this way, 32% in France and 20% in West Germany.[3] A more precise overall view of the relative frequency of price and volume-related NTBs in various product

---

[1] Cf. A. Sapir, 'Trade Benefits under the EEC Generalized System of Preferences', *European Economic Review*, vol. 25 (1981), p. 339 ff.; R.E. Baldwin, T. Murray, 'MFN Tariff Reduction and Developing Country Trade Benefits under the GSP', *The Economic Journal*, vol. 87 (1977), p. 33 ff.

[2] Cf. GATT, *The Tokyo Round of Multilateral Trade Negotiations*, vol. II, Geneva 1980, p. 33

[3] Cf. R.B. Reich, 'Beyond Free Trade', *Foreign Affairs*, vol. 61 (1983), p. 786. This excludes of course the whole area of "hidden" NTBs. Cf. Chapter II.B(3) on their importance in the case of Japan.

categories is provided by a recent UNCTAD study. As might be expected, it points to the overriding significance of agricultural and textile protectionism (see Table 1).

A crucial aspect for the future role of the MFN clause is the fact that a large proportion of NTBs are discriminatory, i.e. imports from particular countries are selectively restricted. For instance, the Multi-Fibre Arrangement (MFA), which may be expected to be renewed for a third time, has accomplished the remarkable feat of tying a dense, comprehensive restrictive net of bilateral "voluntary" self-restraint agreements under the GATT label of multilateral negotiations: MFA III now controls about 84% of world trade in textiles and clothing, and contains more than 3,000 quotas applying to specific countries or products.[4] Moreover, the higher the competitiveness of the exporting countries has been in the past, the more restrictive these quotas have become. Although other sectors have a long way to go before they can achieve the systematic, precise application of the protective measures in the textile sector, the proliferation of "voluntary" export restraints (VERs) and orderly marketing agreements (OMAs) is now also proceeding to the steel and automobile industries, consumer electronics etc.

(*d*) The effect of NTBs in violating the most-favoured nation principle has long been obvious, whereas other developments are taking place less visibly. This applies in particular to the increasing significance of counter-trade in all its forms.[5] Although there is some discussion concerning the proportion of world trade this embraces (estimates vary from 10% to 25%), its development shows a clear upward trend. Various motives can spur counter-trade deals (securing particular sources of raw material imports; saving scarce foreign exchange), and they can assume a variety of forms. In the past they have tended to be in the forefront in the context of trade with the Eastern bloc countries which have been chronically short of foreign exchange. At present, though, it has to be said that counter-trade is being practised along a broad front, including a large number of developing countries, no small factor in this latter development being the serious deterioration in raw material prices and the

[4] Cf. UN, *World Economic Survey 1983*, New York 1983, p. 31
[5] For a general overview, see J. de Miramon, 'Countertrade: A Modernized Barter System', *OECD Observer*, no. 114/1982, p. 12 ff.; J.I. Walsh; 'Countertrade; Not just for East-West any more', *Journal of World Trade Law*, vol. 17 (1983). p. 3 ff.; G. Banks, 'The Economics and Politics of Countertrade', *The World Economy*,' vol. 6 (1983), p. 159 ff.; I. Outters-Jaeger, *The Development Impact of Barter in Developing Countries*, OECD, Paris 1979; OECD, *Countertrade: Developing Country Practices*, Paris 1985.

Table 1.   INCIDENCE OF PRICE AND VOLUME NTBs BY
PRODUCT CATEGORIES^a (%)

CCCN product groups	Developed market economies				Developing countries
	Total	U.S.A.	E.C.	Japan	
1. Live animals; animal products	47.1	38.2	58.4	41.2	36.4
2. Vegetable products	32.6	9.7	41.7	25.8	35.5
3. Animal and vegetable fats and oils	24.8	13.3	22.9	–	24.9
4. Prepared foodstuffs, beverages, spirits, tobacco	37.3	18.9	48.3	17.0	37.6
5. Mineral products	8.2	4.1	7.3	16.3	16.8
6. Products of chemical and allied industries	11.2	9.4	13.4	14.5	19.6
7. Artificial resins and plastic materials	15.2	17.4	15.5	8.7	27.5
8. Rawhides and skins, leather, fur skins	10.8	10.5	9.8	15.8	27.5
9. Wood and wood products; manufacture of straw	9.9	3.2	12.9	–	30.4
10. Paper-making material, paper and paperboard	7.4	6.7	5.2	–	30.9
11. Textiles and textile articles	44.6	25.2	79.9	7.8	33.7
12. Footwear, headgear, prepared feathers	23.1	70.0	24.3	5.0	33.5
13. Articles of stone, ceramics	15.7	14.3	19.0	–	27.3
14. Pearls, precious and semi-precious stones	13.4	–	14.3	5.9	42.7
15. Base metals and articles of base metal	13.5	20.2	20.9	2.4	25.5
16. Machinery and mechanical appliances	11.5	9.8	11.5	2.2	32.0
17. Vehicles, aircrafts, vessels	17.0	18.2	17.8	21.2	29.8
18. Optical, photographic, cinematographic	8.0	3.8	13.4	1.9	25.9
19. Arms and ammunition, parts thereof	25.4	42.9	20.4	100.0	62.3
20. Miscellaneous manu- factured articles	8.8	5.8	11.2	3.1	33.8
21. Works of art, collectors' pieces, antiques	0.9	–	–	16.7	35.6

^{a} The incidence of NTBs is measured at the 4-digit CCCN product group level. The price restraints cover variable levies, minimum prices, anti-dumping and countervailing duties. The volume restraints cover quotas, prohibitions and discretionary licensing. Instances of two or more NTBs applied to one product were discounted and such products enter the calculations only once.

Source: Protectionism, Trade Relations and Structural Adjustment. Report by UNCTAD Secretariat (TD/274), Jan. 17, 1983, p. 17.

resultant balance of payments problems. The most prominent current example is without doubt the counter-purchase policy being conducted by Indonesia, initiated in early 1982 with the aim of encouraging non-traditional exports.[6]

Although, in contrast to NTBs, counter-trade arrangements do not imply a clear violation of the principles of GATT, they do of course run counter to its *multilateral* trading philosophy. They are frequently used as an instrument for bringing some balance to *bilateral* trading relationships, which will certainly jeopardise the flexibility and ultimately the growth potential of the international division of labour. Counter-trade deals make both the volume and direction of any country's foreign trade dependent on *bilateral* balance of payments criteria, and in this respect are at least indirectly opposed to the basic MFN principle. On the other hand it is understandable that arguments centred on optimising the system of the international division of labour find little sympathy in the countries affected. Indeed one of the reasons given to justify counter-trade measures in economic policy terms is that they are intended to compensate for the protectionist measures taken by the industrialised nations.[7] The trade policy approach now adopted by industrialised countries may therefore play a part in determining whether the growing move towards counter-trade arrangements will be remembered as a temporary phenomenon or whether it will become a long-term trend in international trade relations.

Taking together the effects so far outlined — and still ignoring the fact that a substantial portion of world trade is by now intra-firm trade within the multinationals — one is forced to draw the conclusion that at most just over one-third of world trade is still conducted on a non-discriminatory basis.[8] More than half, on the other hand, falls into the category of managed trade or trade involving preferential treatment.

3. *New interpretation of reciprocity*

Another fundamental GATT principle, that of reciprocity, seems to be losing its significance, particularly by being re-interpreted with a

[6] For details see W. Lütkenhorst, *Trade Policy Approaches of Pacific Basin Developing Countries* (Institut für Entwicklungsforschung und Entwicklungspolitik, Materialien und kleine Schriften, no. 96), Bochum 1984, p. 22 ff.
[7] Cf. the remarks made by the Malaysian Premier Mahathir in *Far Eastern Economic Review*, March 17, 1983, p. 8.
[8] Cf. also L. Dunn *et al.*, *In the Kingdom of the Blind: A Report on Protectionism in the Asian-Pacific Region*, London 1983, p. 69.

protectionist bias. The rule of reciprocity, not actually codified within GATT, has hitherto been mainly used in connection with the rounds of multilateral trade negotiation; it was applied to ensure that tariff reductions conceded by the contracting parties were felt to be balanced. Reciprocity, in this sense, refers to the *overall* effect of the *reduction* in tariff protection. By thus combining the idea of *unconditional* adherence to the MFN principle on the one hand with that of maintaining *overall* reciprocity on the other, GATT managed in a rather novel way to uphold two essentially incompatible fundamental principles simultaneously.[9] Although it was recognised then that tariff reductions represented concessions to trading partners for which equivalent concessions might be sought in a process of negotiation, any renewed propagation of a narrow, bilaterally oriented interpretation of reciprocity was successfully prevented.

During 1982 and 1983, however, the Reagan Administration in the USA supported a series of bills still (at the time of going to press) under dispute in Congress which give fresh impetus to precisely such a bilateral interpretation of reciprocity. The proposals envisage raising US exports "through the achievement of commercial opportunities in foreign markets *substantially equivalent* to those awarded by the United States".[10]

One of the main roots of this new bilateralism has been the perception — widely shared among politicians — that the large US trade deficit with Japan can be attributed to differences in protection levels between the two countries which should by now be balanced out. Reciprocity has thus been redefined to a demand that the *level* of protection within *individual* sectors should be *equalised* between the USA and its trading partners.[11] If this concept were to be passed into law and become regular practice in trade policy, it would bring with it an especially severe violation of the unconditional MFN treatment. Instead of being an instrument of liberalisation, reciprocity would again become what it was in the 1930s, namely the basis for the *unilateral* declaration of trade policy measures

[9] Cf. UNCTAD, op.cit., p. 31, and the remarks made by the Director General of GATT, Arthur Dunkel: 'In the 1920s, the words "reciprocity" and "non-discrimination" . . . denoted contradictions . . . The fact that the GATT countries have been negotiating and contracting with each other on the basis of reciprocity and non-discrimination is due to their understanding that reciprocity is always a subjective notion which cannot be looked at in bilateral terms' (GATT Press Release, no. 1312, March 5, 1982).
[10] Reciprocal Trade and Investment Act (Draft), quoted from P. Dymock, D. Vogt, 'Protectionist Pressures in the US Congress', *Journal of World Trade Law*, vol. 17 (1983), p. 507 (emphasis added).
[11] Cf. W.R. Cline, *'Reciprocity': A New Approach to World Trade Policy?*, Washington DC 1982, p. 7 ff.

which abandon the principle of multilateral decision-making and remain in the bilateral camp, thus creating a large potential for retaliatory measures.

Quite regardless of whether or not such tendencies will become stronger in the future, anyone making a realistic examination of GATT is bound to conclude that the hallowed pillars of the agreement are not just showing superficial signs of rust — they may already have lost the capacity to hold together the whole GATT system: 'To sanction long-term quotas, as for example via a series of textile agreements, without proof of serious injury and in the absence of some agreed-upon definition of a disrupted market amounts to a major revision of the trading framework in a protectionist direction. The GATT has now accepted, in effect, the freedom of the importing countries to impose quantitative restrictions whenever important domestic industries deem it in their interest to prevent "too much" import penetration into their own markets.'[12] There is no longer any such thing as a commonly binding international trade policy, nor — even more important — can it be restored retrogressively: 'A return to the classical order of international trade . . . as still embodied in GATT, appears to be out of the question in a world in which national states cannot be compelled to waive their right to an autonomous growth and employment policy.'[13]

4. *Dominance of national economic policy goals*

Before going into the reasons for the gradual self-destruction of GATT in more detail, the general observation must be made that it is not so much the *attitude* of the major trading countries towards a liberal system of trade which has changed; rather, the main change has been in the overall *conditions* set by the world economy, and hence in the relative distribution of the advantages gained from international trade. Generally speaking, a liberal order of world trade remained in force for as long as, and to the extent that, the powerful nations could profit from it. In those sectors where disadvantages were perceived as caused by a liberal trading system, protectionist exceptions were quickly made: it took only till the beginning of the 1950s before a cry went up from the one-time bastion of free trade, the USA, for a GATT waiver for agricultural trade,

---

[12] H. Kitamura; 'International Division of Labour and Industrial Adjustment: Relevance of Theory to Policy Analysis', *The Developing Economies*, vol. 18 (1980), p. 384.
[13] H. Körner, 'The New Protectionism and the Third World', *Intereconomics*, vol. 17 (1982), p. 183.

which was duly granted in 1955, delivering a severe blow both to the USA's credibility in trade policy terms and to GATT's overall standing in the eyes of many countries.[14] Textile protectionism first began to take hold almost as early; 1957 was the first year in which Japan had to accept the need to exercise self-restraint in its textile exports to the USA. It was only another five years before the Long-Term Arrangement Regarding International Trade in Cotton Textiles was concluded. In 1974 it was replaced and broadened by the Multi-Fibre Arrangement, which in the mean time has been renewed twice and needs no further elaboration here.[15] The orientation towards free trade has obviously always run up against its own narrow limits whenever it threatened to damage the national economic interests of the USA as the *'économie dominante'*. As long as the USA was able to derive benefit from liberal world trade in most economic sectors and to preserve that liberal order by virtue of its overriding political influence, the constituent principles of GATT remained valid for the greater part of world trade. However, this position changed as (*a*) an increasing number of sectors were subjected to pressure from new competitive suppliers,[16] and (*b*) the *Pax Americana* was gradually transformed into a polycentric system of economic and political power where other parties (not least the EC) were also able to assert their needs for protection in particular sectors.

The idea that the leading industrialised nations had given their lasting agreement to a liberal order of world trade because of some higher economic ideal was therefore never anything other than an illusion. The right assessment, in fact, is that the post-war period created atypical conditions with structural problems remaining concealed beneath high growth-rates, and that under those conditions the targets of national economic policies were in harmony with a liberal foreign trade regime.[17] This realistic perspective may be the

---

[14] Cf. K.W. Dam, *The GATT Law and International Economic Organization*, Chicago 1970, p. 270 ff.; G. Curzon, *Multilateral Commercial Diplomacy*, London 1965, p. 168 ff.; R.B. Reich, op. cit., p. 779 ff.

[15] Cf. M. Wolf, 'Managed Trade in Practice: Implications of the Textile Agreements' in W.R. Cline (ed.), *Trade Policy in the 1980s*, Washington DC 1983, p. 455 ff.

[16] In the case of the USA, the country's growing interdependence with the world economy should be noted. This raised the proportion of imports in GNP from 3% at the start of the 1960s to 10% at the start of the 1980s. This was accompanied by a substantial rise in the proportion of total imports taken up by manufactures, hence the increasing influence of manufacturer lobbies. For a general account of trade policy decision-making processes in the USA, cf. H. Müller-Godeffroy *et al., Der neue Protektionismus*, Bonn 1983, p. 50 ff.

[17] Lorenz appropriately describes this phase as 'international specialization without tears'. Cf. D. Lorenz; 'On the Crisis of the "Liberalization Policy" in the Economics of Interdependence', *Intereconomics*, vol. 13 (1978), p. 169.

only way of explaining how any sort of GATT principle could be toppled with so little inhibition the moment it threatened to collide with national targets.

5. *Reasons for the decline of self-discipline within GATT*

There are many different reasons for the rapid decline in GATT discipline and the revitalisation of mercantilist elements in policy-making, but they can be traced back to a small number of primary causes:[18]

(*a*) Causes must first be outlined which are inherent in GATT itself. The GATT-MTN system was regarded for too long, i.e. right up to the Tokyo Round, as a straightforward 'tariff-lowering device'. The complex of different objectives of international trade policy was one-dimensionally reduced to achieving maximum reductions in trade barriers, and insufficient attention was paid to the fact that workable mechanisms for dealing with the resultant structural changes ought to have a central significance. A symptom of this deficit is the controversy which has persisted to this day over the need to reform the safeguard clause in Article XIX (see below) which has proved inadequate for trade policy purposes and which, above all, has brought about 'mercantilist innovations at the margins of legality'.[19] Furthermore, it is evident that in particular the chief protagonists (USA, the EC, Japan) make their adherence to GATT rules, or any resort they have to GATT in its role as arbitrator on trade policy matters, dependent on the gains they expect to make from taking such action. Unpalatable GATT decisions are widely ignored, or else solutions to conflicts are negotiated bilaterally and the remaining signatories have no choice but to add their agreement after the event.[20]

(*b*) There are a number of other reasons why past increases in the demand for protective measures have been so strong, apart from weaknesses in the GATT system. One of these is the general tendency of Western industrial countries to develop into societies which are fundamentally oriented towards a more or less extensive welfare state. This trend is accompanied by a strong element of corporatism,

---

[18] On the following point, cf. chiefly D. Lorenz, 'Ursachen und Konsequenzen des Neomerkantilismus' in A. Woll (ed.), *Internationale Anpassungsprozesse*, Berlin 1981, p. 16 ff.

[19] D. Lorenz, 'Ursachen und Konsequenzen', op. cit., p. 17

[20] Cf. H.B. Malmgren, 'Threats to the Multilateral System' in W.R. Cline, *Trade Policy*, op. cit., p. 196 ff.

i.e. powerful interest groups have emerged which participate in the political decision-making process and which readily assert their sectoral needs for protection against the interests of the politically diffuse majority of the consumers. This has been accentuated because a certain preference for the *status quo* (as far as both place of residence and standard of living are concerned) has taken on a high priority in more and more sections of the population, meaning that the mobility requirements posed by rapid structural change are largely perceived as a threat.

(c) The deepening of the international division of labour has become all the more explosive a topic now that comparative cost advantages — in an age where high-technology goods are traded on an intra-industry basis — have finally lost their 'political innocence'. The sectors of trade between industrial nations and newly-industrialising countries (NICs) which are now gaining significance are determined neither by availability of natural resources ('Ricardo goods') nor by relative factor endowments ('Heckscher-Ohlin goods'). Cline very appropriately gave this sphere the label of 'arbitrary comparative advantage'.[21] What he means is that the patterns of specialisation emerging in particular areas of production are not determined *ex ante* by economic structural parameters, but are a quite conclusive result of political intervention: 'In a very real and immediate way, a nation *chooses* its comparative advantage.'[22] This applies not only in the stricter sense that specific lines of technological development are given priority and are deliberately promoted (subsidised). It also applies in the broader sense that, in view of the increasing significance of human capital as a factor of production, a country's educational system and entire social infrastructure determine its overall competitiveness more strongly than ever before. This is a situation where the opportunity costs of refraining from political action are ever greater; a premium is placed on the earliest possible promotion of *potentially* competitive technologies and products. Considering that governments have a *de facto* responsibility for growth and employment (which one may or may not believe to be a good thing), a new type of international competition has emerged which could lead during the 1980s to a subsidy war no less dangerous than the devaluation and protection war of the 1930s. Hager deserves complete agreement when he says that 'in a world where all governments accelerate or retard adjustment in pursuit of national targets, the market as a coordination mechanism cannot function.'[23] If this

[21] Cf. W.R. Cline, 'Reciprocity', op. cit., p. 38 ff.
[22] R.B. Reich, op. cit., p. 782
[23] W. Hager; 'Free Trade means Destabilization', *Intereconomics*, vol. 19 (1984), p. 30.

problem is not quickly brought under control (especially regarding production and export subsidies), then he may also be proved right in his thesis that 'managed trade is . . . a logical necessity for achieving balance between managed domestic factor and goods markets.'[24]

(*d*) Although the preceding point refers mainly, if not exclusively, to trade between industrial nations, it has also been evident for some time that the economic rise of the NICs has been one of the chief causes of neo-mercantilist trade policy. Of course, no one can deny that successful export diversification, especially in the East and South-East Asian NICs, is putting the industrial nations under severe pressure to make structural adjustments. Nevertheless a marked overemphasis of the phenomenon in political discussion is in evidence: while structural change fuelled by *domestic* factors (changing consumer preferences; divergent rates of productivity growth from sector to sector) is largely accepted, there is a contrasting tendency to block out structural change *induced by external trade*, which obviously is not regarded as of equal legitimacy. Third World exporters of competitive manufactures have normally found themselves in a particularly unfavourable position. This is partly due to economically rational reasons, because the division of labour between industrial and developing countries (including the NICs) continues to be *inter*-industrial in nature much more than *intra*-industrial. This makes structural adjustment a particularly difficult task. The problem is intensified, however, by the NICs' limited bargaining power in the international system, which makes the political cost of unilaterally declared defensive measures appear very low for the industrial nations. These two factors taken together explain the highly *selective* nature of protective measures against those countries with the least potential for retaliatory action: in the three years 1975–7 alone, Taiwan and South Korea respectively saw 26 and 52 new discriminatory measures brought into force against them by various industrial nations.[25] Bilateralism is hence no longer merely a danger; it has once again become a reality and is mainly being used to bar market entry to those countries which might be successful in carrying out their belated industrialisation.

To our knowledge the only authors who have managed to see positive features in this bilateralism are Yoffie and Keohane. They believe there are advantages to be gained for the NICs in that (*a*) the short-term, uncoordinated and *ad hoc* measures being taken by the

24 Ibid.
25 Cf. B. Nowzad; *The Rise in Protectionism*, IMF Pamphlet Series, no. 24, Washington DC 1978, p. 108 ff.

industrial nations are likely ultimately to be less restrictive in total than measures conceived in a multilateral framework might be, and (*b*) bilateral measures could at least open up small negotiating opportunities for the NICs affected: 'The ADCs [advanced developing countries] have an interest in keeping trade low-key, minimizing the significance of any particular agreement, maintaining flexibility and trying to keep the United States Government [and other governments] from adopting a coherent and comprehensive long-term trade policy.'[26] However, this is an extremely risky line of argument, not least because it neglects the immense significance of *long-term stability* in the trade policy setting if export production is to be efficiently built up.

6. *Differing recommendations for economic policy*

Although the diagnosis offered at present is unanimous, namely that GATT has to a great extent lost its normative power as a regulatory mechanism and that 'general trade policy . . . has virtually ceased to exist',[27] a reliable prognosis as to the future direction of international trade policy can hardly be given. Not only does Friedrich List's statement still hold true that 'in no other branch of political economy . . . is there such a divergence of opinion between theoreticians and practitioners as in matters of *international trade* and *trade* policy'.[28] It can furthermore be observed that — how could one expect it to be otherwise? — even in the realm of academic debate the most varied recommendations are made.

At one end of the spectrum of opinion we find appeals to governments — obviously apolitical in nature — finally to renounce protectionism, depoliticise the world economy and allow it to be governed by market forces. According to this point of view the problem of finding acceptance for this approach could readily be solved simply by making the public aware of the high macroeconomic

---

[26] D.B. Yoffie, R.O. Keohane, 'Responding to the New Protectionism: Strategies for the Advanced Developing Countries in the Pacific Basin', in W. Hong, L.B. Krause (eds), *Trade and Growth of the Advanced Developing Countries in the Pacific Basin*, Seoul 1981, p. 583 ff.

[27] J. Tumlir, 'International Economic Order — Can the Trend be Reversed?', *The World Economy*, vol. 5 (1982), p. 30

[28] F. List, *Das nationale System der politischen Ökonomie*, Basel/Tübingen 1959 (first published 1841), p. 30.

[29] Cf. for example *Global Strategy for Growth* (A Report on North-South Issues by a Study Group under the Chairmanship of Lord McFadzean of Kelvinside), London 1981, p. 78 ff.

costs of protection.[29] At the other end of the spectrum there is dangerous talk of comprehensive European protectionism.[30] The most unequivocal proponent of this approach, Hager, quite rightly draws attention to the fundamental significance of the threat to the 'old' industrial nations coming from the Pacific region — both from Japan and from the NICs.[31] However, because he believes that for the countries of Europe actually to withstand such competition they would have to pay the price of abandoning their whole present social organisation, he advocates a comprehensive system of quotas, minimum prices and market share regulations for substitutive imports of manufactured products. According to this approach, such measures would be the only way of at least upholding liberal foreign trade *within* Western Europe. Evidently what has happened here is that the senescent-industry argument has grown straight into a senescent-country argument, demanding that the whole of Western Europe withdraw from international competition and the division of labour.

Neither of the approaches outlined above proves particularly helpful in the central task of trade policy in the 1980s, namely that of reforming the GATT rules in such a way as to ensure that they will find stronger political acceptance among the agreement's contracting parties: 'The issue is . . . whether we will have a GATT which applies to world trade versus one that increasingly does not . . . by our insisting that the GATT must remain pure, and therefore, irrelevant.'[32]

Of the numerous controversial questions surrounding the reform of GATT, the concluding parts of this chapter will therefore address three quite fundamental problem areas which bear particularly upon the relationship between industrial and developing countries within the GATT framework.

7. *Reform of safeguard clause in Article XIX*

Discussion of the safeguard clause as expressed in Article XIX of GATT has by now continued for more than a decade. In theoretical

---

[30] Cf. Hager, op. cit.; W. Hager, 'Protectionism and Autonomy: How to Preserve Free Trade in Europe', *International Affairs*, vol. 58 (1981/2), p. 413 ff.
[31] For a comprehensive account, cf. W. Kraus, 'Pazifische Zusammenarbeit und Europäische Gemeinschaft', *Aussenpolitik*, April 1984; E. Rhein, 'Die pazifische Herausforderung: Gefahren und Chancen für Europa', *Europa-Archiv*, vol. 39 (1984), p. 101 ff.
[32] A.W. Wolff, 'Need for new GATT Rules to Govern Safeguard Actions' in W.R. Cline, *Trade Policy*, op. cit., p. 391.

terms the discussion of alternatives has long since reached the point of exhaustion, but a political compromise has yet to be achieved. The issue of the safeguard clause was the most important item of "unfinished business" left over after the Tokyo Round, and the GATT Ministerial Conference in November 1982 also failed to reach a common position on it. What, then, lies at the heart of this problem?[33] The fact that Article XIX can only be invoked within the framework of the *most-favoured-nation principle* (in other words, against all the exporters of the goods in question), and that the exporters are then allowed either to require *compensation* or to take *retaliatory measures*, has meant that relatively little use has been made of the safeguard clause. Instead, countries have increasingly resorted to selective protective measures (Voluntary Export Restraints [VERs]; Orderly Marketing Agreements [OMAs]) outside the control of GATT; of the total of 114 protective measures taken since 1978, only 30 came within the terms of Article XIX, the corollary being that all the others ignored the GATT provisions.[34]

Only a small number of purists still maintain that Article XIX should be preserved unaltered[35] — virtually in the sense of a moral finger pointing out the compulsory, iron-clad principles of GATT — while all others agree that it is in need of reform. One point that is accepted without question is that one should aim to make all protective measures notifiable as a general rule, bringing them back from the twilight zone of trade policy and raising the political costs of selective protection by making it internationally more visible. A question that continues to be controversial, however, is whether Article XIX should itself actually permit selective protective measures, thereby abandoning the most-favoured-nation principle; this is what the EEC countries have demanded, and the developing countries in particular have rejected.[36] The proposals made in this direction have varied in scope, as they have linked a selective safeguard clause to different restrictive conditions. The particular restrictions suggested, which are not mutually exclusive, are as follows:

---

[33] On detailed aspects, cf. the precise and comprehensive account in Wolff, op. cit.

[34] Cf. UN, op. cit., p. 62 fn. 1; also, for a detailed account, S.J. Anjaria *et al.*, *Developments in International Trade Policy*, IMF Occasional Paper no. 16, 2nd Imp. July 1983, p. 122.

[35] L. Dunn *et al.*, op. cit., p. 120, voice their opposition to 'writing a rule in violation of a basic principle'.

[36] The controversy can actually be traced back to the mid-1950s when an ad hoc committee on the problem of the safeguard clause was formed in connection with Japan's accession to GATT. On this point, and on the overall history of Art. XIX, cf. R. Quick, *Exportselbstbeschränkungen und Art. XIX GATT*, Cologne 1983, p. 95 ff.

— the approval of the exporting country affected, or 'consensual selectivity', which is tantamount to a simple legalisation of VERs and OMAs;

— strict international monitoring of safeguard measures, coupled with firm limits on their period of effectiveness;

— compliance with objective criteria relating to the extent and the unpredictability of material injury, and the extent to which particular countries may be identified as being clearly responsible for that injury;

— simultaneous presentation of an adjustment plan (trade adjustment policy) to cut back productive capacity which is no longer competitive.[37]

Furthermore, irrespective of the selectiveness or non-selectiveness of Article XIX, it has been suggested that the right to take retaliatory measures (or the right to receive compensation) be suspended for a certain period, provided the country invoking the safeguard clause does not delay the necessary adjustment process.[38]

The central problem with all these reform proposals lies, of course, with their political trustworthiness, i.e. one may ask whether the NICs — the countries most affected — 'have good grounds for trusting the established industrialized countries to adhere faithfully to whatever criteria were agreed for selective action'.[39] It must be realised, on the other hand, that even if the new rules were to be violated again (as is to be expected), this could certainly not be worse than the *status quo* where successful exporters are discriminated against with total lack of control in a way which, under GATT, is illegal. Looked at in this way, some pragmatic reform of Article XIX would at least offer an opportunity, at no extra risk, to restore a little strength to GATT's dwindling authority. Protectionism,

---

[37] It must be noted with regret at this point that the discussion which went on intensively for a long period over the need for trade adjustment policy (cf. K. Glaubitt, W. Lütkenhorst, *Elemente einer neuen Weltwirtschaftsordnung*, Tübingen, Basel 1979, p. 125 ff.) has meanwhile come to a halt. Evidently the underlying political dilemma is that the necessity for an anticipatory structural adjustment policy related to foreign trade is not realised during the periods of satisfactory growth, while the deliberate contraction of individual sectors appears to be unenforceable during periods of general economic weakness.

[38] Cf. E. Minx, *Von der Liberalisierungs- zur Wettbewerbspolitik*, Berlin, New York 1980, p. 205. This proposal is fundamentally convincing, but putting it into operation could be expected to raise problems which would be difficult to overcome.

[39] H. Corbet, 'Importance of Being Earnest about Further GATT Negotiations', *The World Economy*, vol. 2 (1979), p. 330.

after all, will never be completely eliminated, and is a force which can at best be channelled.

8. *Graduation of developing countries*

While it is the industrial nations which stand accused in the discussion over the safeguard clause, there is no denying that tariff levels are very high in most developing countries and that extensive use is made of NTBs. During the Tokyo Round this meant that the industrial countries were, in effect, able to turn the tables by putting the developing countries' graduation in trade-policy terms on the agenda (i.e. it was proposed that the more advanced LDCs be required to 'graduate' to the commitments made by other GATT signatories, thus losing preferential treatment).[40] It was the developing countries which had first been successful in pressing home their demand for the preferential treatment they receive to be at least legally recognised; previously, as in the case of the General System of Preferences, such treatment had only been provided according to a GATT waiver. The price they had to pay for this success, it seems, was that the principle of graduation was incorporated into the so-called enabling clause:[41] 'Less-developed contracting parties expect that their capacity to make contributions or make negotiated concessions . . . would improve with the progressive development of their economies and improvement in their trade situation and they would accordingly expect to participate more fully in the framework of rights and obligations under the General Agreement.'

How should this demand be assessed? The first point to note is that because (*a*) the GATT rules are not *uniform* but *universal* in nature[42] in that they differ in substance according to different categories of countries (DCs — LDCs), and (*b*) classification in one of these categories is subject to modifications, with transitions occurring as a result of development processes (e.g. Japan), the principle of graduation becomes a *logical* necessity. Certainly it is inconceivable that a country such as South Korea, if it acceded to OECD membership at the end of the 1980s, could retain any preferential

---

[40] For an overall view, cf. I. Frank, 'The "Graduation" Issue for LDCs', *Journal of World Trade Law*, vol. 13 (1979), p. 289 ff.; K.A. Koekkoek, 'On the Case for Graduation', *Intereconomics*, vol. 18 (1983), p. 225 ff.

[41] The exact title reads 'Agreement on Differential and More Favourable Treatment, Reciprocity and Fuller Participation of Developing Countries',

[42] On this distinction, cf. P.P. Streeten, 'What New International Economic Order?' in U.E. Simonis (ed.), *Ordnungspolitische Fragen zum Nord-Süd-Konflikt*, Berlin 1983, p. 86 ff.

status within GATT.[43] However, there is still a total lack of any *operational* criteria for identifying *justified* claims that a fully responsible role should be adopted. The development of suitable criteria as the result of a consensus of the GATT signatories could well prove to be one of the most important tasks in future negotiations. Otherwise there is a great danger that a number of developing countries will 'be graduated' by industrial countries taking unilateral action. It already appears, for instance, that new legislation from the US Congress to allow the extension of the country's GSP which is due to expire shortly is being tied to conditions with regard to the dismantling of trade barriers in developing countries (reciprocity). Here one has to agree with Diaz-Alejandro who describes the graduation principle as an 'extravagant demand'[44] as long as the primary concern of industrial nations is to distract attention from their own trade policy shortcomings.

9. *Conditional most-favoured-nation clause*

It was pointed out at the beginning of this chapter that there is a *de facto* undermining of the MFN principle in the real world of international trade. Since the Tokyo Round,' though, there is now also an ongoing 'official' discussion concerning the transition from *unconditional* to *conditional* MFN treatment. As is well known, a number of detailed trade policy codes were enacted in the course of the Tokyo Round,[45] which in the main were signed only by the industrial countries and by a very small number of more advanced developing countries (for details see Table 2). However, the rights and duties flowing from these codes apply only to those countries which have actually accepted them, with the result that a complex net of *conditional* MFN clauses has now emerged which are valid for a different group of countries in each case.

Given that the legal controversy over the compatibility of the new codes with Article 1 of GATT is still continuing, cases of dispute are likely to arise in increasing numbers. As early as 1981 a quarrel arose between the USA and India over the material injury test within the framework of the Code on Subsidies and Countervailing

---

[43] Even now the average tariff level of 38% (1978) and a share of export subsidies in total export value amounting to 22% (1978) represent an explosive issue in trade policy. For details see Chapter II.A.

[44] C.F. Diaz-Alejandro, 'Comment' in W.R. Cline, *Trade Policy*, op. cit., p. 305; cf. also the critique in UNCTAD, op. cit., p. 32 ff.

[45] On the detailed contents of the codes, cf. B. Balassa, 'The Tokyo Round and the Developing Countries', *Journal of World Trade Law*, vol. 14 (1980), p. 102 ff.

Table 2.   AGREEMENTS IN FRAMEWORK OF TOKYO ROUND: STATUS OF ACCEPTANCE BY DEVELOPING COUNTRIES^a, DEC. 2, 1983

	Technical barriers	Government procurement	Subsidies and countervailing duties	Bovine meat	Dairy products	Customs valuation	Import licences	Civil aviation	Anti-dumping
Argentina	S	O	O	A	A	S*	S	O	O
Brazil	A	O	A	A	A	A*	O	O	A
Chile	A	O	A	-	-	O	A	-	O
Egypt	A	O	A	O	S	O	O	S	A
India	A	O	A	-	O	A*	O	O	A
Korea	A	O	A	O	-	A*	O	-	A
Malawi	-	-	-	-	-	A*	-	-	-
Pakistan	A	-	A	-	-	O	-	-	A
Philippines	A	O	O	-	-	O	A*	-	-
Rwanda	S	-	-	-	-	-	-	O	O
Singapore	A	A	O	-	-	O	O	-	O
Uruguay	-	-	A	A	A	-	-	-	O

A = Accepted.
S = Signed (acceptance pending).
O = Observer.
* = Provision, condition and/or additional declaration.
^a Includes only those developing countries having at least accepted or signed one agreement.

Source: Compiled from GATT Document L/5517/Add. 5, Dec. 5, 1983.

Duties.[46] A complicating aspect in these cases is that some of the codes include individual dispute settlement procedures, and how these relate to GATT's overall dispute settlement procedure is as yet unclarified. The general problem of a conditional MFN clause obviously goes even deeper than this: there is a danger that, just at a time when many developing countries have become increasingly significant for their part in world trade, making it necessary that the resulting problems should be solved within GATT, these very countries might be excluded from the continuing development of GATT's principles. Seen against this background, it may be less surprising that during the Tokyo Round it was the developing countries which pleaded for the 'unity and integrity of the GATT system'.[47]

10. *Conclusions*

GATT's member-countries face fundamental and serious decisions in the problem areas of the safeguard clause, the principle of graduation and the conditional most-favoured-nation clause; if a new round of multilateral trade negotiations takes place as expected, these problems will provide a considerable amount of explosive material. One would hope that the parties arrive at workable solutions to these matters of general significance *before* totally new aspects (e.g. the broadening of GATT to include trade in services) cause a distraction. For the chief threat to GATT's future role is not to be found in the modification of its original principles (which in fact now exist only as ruins), but rather in the dwindling readiness of many member-countries to accept compromises, i.e. a lack of willingness to come to a general consensus in complex negotiations.

The expectation that the multilateral system of GATT will not be able to solve the problems it now faces in due course is no doubt one of the factors contributing to the current prominence of regionally oriented policy approaches including such differing concepts as:

— the recommendation that the countries of the Asia-Pacific region should take the initiative in a *return to liberal world trade*;[48]

---

[46] For a more precise treatment, cf. J.H. Jackson; 'GATT Machinery and the Tokyo Round Agreements' in W.R. Cline, *Trade Policy*, op. cit., p. 174 f.; W.R. Cline, 'Reciprocity', op. cit., p. 19 f.
[47] R. Krishnamurti, 'Multilateral Trade Negotiations and the Developing Countries', *Third World Quarterly*, vol. 2 (1980), p. 263.
[48] Cf. L. Dunn *et al.*, op. cit., p. 116 ff. On this issue Lorenz points out the circular argument involved when renewed liberalisation is expected to solve the problems which were caused to a substantial degree by earlier rounds of liberalisation. Cf.

— the plea for *greater inter-regional policy coordination* as a means of overcoming foreign trade conflicts *ex ante*;[49] and

— efforts to give *institutional reinforcement to existing areas of interdependence*, as have been intensively discussed for some time with regard to the Pacific Basin.[50]

Of course anyone who has studied the matter will be aware that regional policy coordination is treading a hard and rocky road, at the end of which there have so far rarely been any convincing results. This is hardly a problem which applies only to developing countries: witness the EC's most recent summit failures. On the other hand, a realistic point of view requires that the imperfect results of regional policy coordination should not be measured against the theory-derived *ideal* of multilateral liberalism, but against the *reality* of increasing bilateralism.

D. Lorenz; 'International Division of Labour versus Closer Cooperation? With Special Regard to ASEAN-EC Economic Relations' (Paper Presented at the Third Conference on ASEAN-EEC Economic Relations, Oct. 26-28, 1983, Bangkok), revised version, Jan. 1984, p. 33 f.
[49] Cf. ibid.
[50] See the detailed analysis of the relevant proposals and their preconditions and implications presented in Chapter III.

II

BASIC TRADE POLICY ISSUES OF THE PACIFIC DEVELOPING COUNTRIES AND JAPAN

A. IMPORT RESTRICTIONS AND EXPORT PROMOTION MEASURES IN SOUTHEAST ASIAN COUNTRIES

1. *Empirical background*

The Pacific Basin in general and the Southeast Asian region in particular (which, contrary to conventional terminology, here includes the ASEAN Countries as well as Hong Kong, South Korea and Taiwan) have in recent years attracted particular attention in the USA[1] as well as in the EC countries.[2] Indeed, Southeast Asia has emerged as one of the world's most dynamic growth regions and will continue to play an important role within the foreseeable future. The economically most advanced countries of the region are expected to reach industrial maturity within only a few decades. The traditionally strong position of Japan as the region's trading partner is seen not without feelings of envy, and in the EC countries questions are increasingly asked as to the basic reasons for their own relatively weak position, and as to adequate strategies and instruments in order to intensify interregional economic transactions.

Taking as an indicator the foreign trade intensities, i.e. the ratio of actual trade flows to those which can be expected from the shares in world trade of the respective countries (see Tables 3 and 4), the following facts can be shown:

1. the dominant position of Japan as Southeast Asia's trading partner: export and import intensities of Southeast Asian countries with Japan range between 2 and 3 on an average (the standard value being 1);

---

[1] cf. L.B. Krause, *U.S. Economic Policy Toward the Association of Southeast Asian Nations: Meeting the Japanese Challenge*, Washington DC 1982.
[2] cf. N. Akrasanee and Ch. Rieger (eds), *ASEAN-EEC Economic Relations*, Singapore (Institute of Southeast Asian Studies) 1982.

Import restrictions and export promotion measures in Southeast Asian countries

Table 3.   EXPORT INTENSITIES OF SOUTHEAST ASIAN COUNTRIES WITH JAPAN, U.S.A., E.C. AND ASEAN, 1984

Exporting country i	Importing country j			
	Japan	U.S.A.	E.C.	ASEAN
Indonesia	6.4	1.1	0.1	2.8
Malaysia	3.0	0.7	0.4	6.6
Philippines	2.7	2.1	0.4	2.5
Singapore	1.3	1.1	0.3	7.3
Thailand	1.8	0.9	0.7	3.5
Hongkong	0.6	1.8	0.4	1.2
Korea	2.4	1.9	0.3	1.4
Taiwan	1.4	2.6	0.3	2.3

CALCULATED AS:

$$I_x = \frac{X_{ij}}{X_i} : \frac{M_j}{M_w - M_i}$$

I_x = Intensity of exports of i to j
X_{ij} = Exports of i to j
X_i = Total exports of i
M_j = Total imports of j
M_w = Total world imports
M_i = Total imports of i

Table 4.   IMPORT INTENSITIES OF SOUTHEAST ASIAN COUNTRIES WITH JAPAN, U.S.A., E.C. AND ASEAN, 1984

Importing country i	Exporting country j			
	Japan	U.S.A.	E.C.	ASEAN
Indonesia	2.5	1.5	0.4	3.3
Malaysia	2.7	1.3	0.4	4.9
Philippines	1.4	2.2	0.3	2.7
Singapore	1.4	1.2	0.2	6.0
Thailand	2.8	1.1	0.4	3.3
Hongkong	2.6	0.9	0.4	0.8
Korea	3.0	1.8	0.3	1.8
Taiwan	2.4	1.8	0.3	2.7

CALCULATED AS:

$$I_m = \frac{M_{ij}}{M_i} : \frac{X_j}{X_w - X_i}$$

I_m = Intensity of imports of i to j
M_{ij} = Imports of i to j
M_i = Total imports of i
X_j = Total exports of j
X_w = Total world exports
X_i = Total exports of i

Sources: Authors' calculations from data of IMF, Direction of Trade Statistics, *Yearbook 1985*; Council for Economic Planning and Development, Republic of China, *Taiwan Statistical Data Book*, 1985.

2. the relatively strong position of the USA with intensity values ranging mostly between 1 and 2 (with minor exceptions);
3. the relatively weak position of the EC countries: the highest export intensity is recorded at 0.7 in the case of Thailand, the highest import intensity is at 0.4 (for Indonesia, Malaysia, Thailand and Hong Kong).

Variations in transport costs may be a partial explanation, but they are certainly not a major determinant of these results. A more important explanation could be found in the trade policy measures of the various countries if they were applied in a discriminatory way.

This *possibility* will be taken here as a motive to analyse in some detail the trade policy approaches followed by Southeast Asian countries. After a compact general view of the various countries' industrialisation strategies, we will deal with import protection measures, i.e. tariff as well as non-tariff barriers, before turning to the numerous instruments of export promotion. Recent developments in trade policy (e.g. ASEAN tariff preferences, Indonesia's counterpurchase regulations) will be presented where appropriate. A major part of the chapter will, however, deal with more general trade policy issues like the economic assessment of export subsidies and their conformity with GATT rules.

2. *Trade policy framework of industrialisation in Southeast Asia*

It is a well-known fact that the developing countries of Southeast Asia are among the most successful exporters of manufactured goods within the Third World. To a considerable extent they are responsible for the dynamic evolution of the international division of labour and have contributed to overcoming its traditional complementary structure and its development towards an interdependence of increasingly substitutive character. The share of manufactured exports in total exports is about 25–35% in the case of Malaysia, the Philippines and Thailand, well above 50% in the case of Singapore (including entrepôt-trade), and 85–100% in the case of Hong Kong, South Korea and Taiwan. Indonesia (an OPEC member) must be regarded as an exception with a share as low as 3%. These figures have resulted from an export-oriented development strategy which all these countries (again excluding Indonesia) have turned to, albeit at different points of time and in various intensity:

— Due to unique conditions which from the beginning have excluded a broad import substituting industrialisation, the city-states of *Hong Kong* and *Singapore* decided relatively early to follow a world-market-oriented development path.[3] Hong Kong as a regional centre of finance and trade (the share of services in GNP exceeds 60%) comes close to being a borderline case of a complete *laissez-faire* economy, and has always developed under free port conditions; at no time did the colony aim at import substitution. In contrast to this, the short history of Singapore shows distinct periods in terms of trade policy orientation: between 1960 and 1965 the prospect of a Malaysian common market was a strong argument for the potential merits of building up a domestic market-oriented industry behind tariff walls, but following the political separation from Malaysia, the Economic Expansion Incentives Act (1967) initiated the promotion of foreign investment primarily in manufactured exports. Import quotas were almost completely eliminated and import tariffs drastically reduced. Up to now the liberal trade policy has been maintained. Labour shortages as well as increases in real wages, however, forced the country to shift from labour-intensive to human capital-intensive and technology-intensive exports.

— In *South Korea* and *Taiwan* the transition from import substitution to export promotion occurred even earlier than in Singapore,[4] the relevant point of time being the early 1960s in both cases. The policy measures applied in order to overcome balance of payments problems and slackening growth were in principle identical: abolishing the system of multiple exchange rates, massive devaluation plus various measures to promote manufactured exports, e.g. tax holidays, loans at preferential interest rates, establishment of export processing zones etc. At the same time, import substitution continued and in South Korea, starting in 1972, proceeded to heavy industry sectors, not least for military reasons.[5]

[3] cf. Chia Siow Yue, 'Singapore's Trade and Development Strategy, and ASEAN Economic Cooperation, with Special Reference to the ASEAN Common Approach to Foreign Economic Relations' in R. Garnaut (ed.), *ASEAN in a Changing Pacific and World Economy*, Canberra 1980, p. 241 ff.

[4] Cf. W.T. Hong, 'Export Growth and Transformation of Industrial Structure' (paper presented to the International Forum on Industrial Planning and Trade Policies, Seoul, Korea, June 1–12, 1982); Kuo, Sh.W.Y. Kuo, G. Ranis, J.H.C. Fei, *The Taiwan Success Story: Rapid Growth with Improved Distribution in the Republic of China, 1951–1979*, Boulder, Colo. 1981.

[5] Cf. Yung Chul Park, 'Export-Led Development: The Korean Experience 1960–78' in E. Lee (ed.), *Export-Led Industrialization and Development*, Singapore 1981, p. 79 ff.

— *Malaysia*[6] experienced a relatively short period of import substitution behind relatively low tariff walls (15% on an average in 1963). A stronger orientation of manufacturing industries towards the world market began in 1968 with the Investment Incentives Act. The well-known instruments of export promotion came to be applied with particularly strong emphasis on the establishment of export processing zones (mainly for the electronics industry) and hence on foreign investment on a large scale.

— The *Philippines* were following a highly protective, long-lasting import substitution policy during the 1950s and 1960s,[7] initially supported by quantitative import restrictions, later by imposing extremely high and escalating tariffs on imported goods. Declining growth rates and high unemployment rates led to the Export Incentives Act, the floating of the Peso and the establishment of the first export-processing zone. These measures paved the way to a stronger export orientation; however, they are still accompanied by a distorted structure of incentives biased towards domestic consumer industries. However, in 1981 an ambitious liberalisation programme was set up.

— The trade policy in the case of *Thailand* developed in a similar way [8] with rapid import-substituting industrialisation starting in the early 1960s. About a decade later the growth contribution of industries substituting imports declined considerably, and up to now domestic demand expansion is by far the most important source of growth. After the revision of the Investment Promotion Act and the Export Promotion Act in 1972 an expansion and diversification of manufactured exports began, though without — as in the case of the Philippines as well — giving up the high protection of import substitution sectors. On the contrary, the new Investment Promotion Law of 1977 has improved their priority status by renewing their privilege on reduction of import duties and business taxes on imported materials and components, as is the case for export-oriented production. If we further consider the import restrictive measures of 1978, there can be some doubt as to the real commitment to export orientation.

— The export production of *Indonesia* is strongly dominated by the

[6] Cf. M. Ariff, 'Malaysia's Trade and Industrialization Strategy with Special Reference to ASEAN Industrial Co-operation' in Garnaut, *ASEAN*, op. cit., p. 280 ff.
[7] Cf. R.M. Bautista, 'Trade Strategies and Industrial Development in the Philippines: With Special Reference to Regional Trade Preferences' in Garnaut, *ASEAN*, op. cit., p. 175 ff.
[8] Cf. N. Akrasanee, *Thailand and ASEAN Economic Cooperation*, Singapore (Institute of Southeast Asian Studies) 1980.

oil sector, whereas manufactured exports have always played only a minor role. Indonesia — at a fairly low level of economic development and disposing of a huge domestic market, the potential expansion of which will be heavily dependent on improving the distribution of income — finds itself still in the first phase of import substitution with high tariff protection. Numerous export promotion measures are applied, particularly towards foreign investment[9] but have up to now been of only limited success (e.g. textile exports).

3. *Nature and scope of protective trade policy measures*

The general view given in the preceding chapter on the role of foreign trade in the industrialisation strategy of Southeast Asian countries has demonstrated that in reality we often find a coexistence of import substitution and export promotion or export diversification. This applies particularly to the Philippines and Thailand, but also on a more advanced level of development to South Korea. The following chapters will be dealing in some detail with trade policy measures starting with instruments of import restriction. An examination of the literature on trade and development policy clearly shows that this question has hitherto attracted only little attention. Quite understandably the focus has been on those trade barriers which have hampered manufactured *exports*, particularly by NICs, to markets in the industrialised countries.[10]

Without wishing to justify these measures in any way, we will here turn to the reciprocal question of barriers protecting the markets of Southeast Asia. At least some of the countries in question have after all made economic progress to such an extent (South Korea stands at the threshold of OECD) that they have to accept certain obligations concerning their own trade policy. This implies that some countries can e.g. no longer or only in a very limited sense make recourse to infant industry arguments.

(a) *Regional comparison of tariff policy*. This chapter is aimed at a comparative analysis of the degree of tariff protection accorded to industrial production in the countries in question. It is not possible, however, to present only most recent data in a complete way. Particularly in the case of effective rates of protection which can only be

---

[9] Cf. K. Sihotang, *Private ausländische Direktinvestitionen in Indonesien: 1870–1980*, Stuttgart 1983, p. 210 ff.
[10] Cf. A.S. Yeats, *Trade Barriers Facing Developing Countries*, London 1979; H. Müller-Godeffroy *et al.*, *Der neue Protektionismus*, Bonn 1983.

calculated on the basis of input-output tables, reference to less recent data cannot always be avoided.

In order to exlude misunderstandings in interpreting the data we will first recall shortly the various concepts of measuring the degree of protection. Differentiation is made between:

(i) *nominal tariff protection*, defined as the actual tariff rates;

(ii) *(implicit) nominal protection*, defined as the ratio of the domestic price and the world market price of a product; and

(iii) *effective protection*, taking into consideration also tariffs on inputs. The effective protection increases with the degree of tariff escalation and with a declining share of domestic value added in production.

Considering first *nominal tariff protection*, i.e. legal tariff rates, recourse can be made to a comparative analysis for the ASEAN countries for 1978. Although going back to the late 1970s, these data are presented here because of their high comparability. More recent developments are referred to below.[11] The comparison of unweighted average tariff rates leads to the following conclusions (see Table 5):

The average tariff level for the whole ASEAN region is 26%. There are, however, considerable deviations as to sectors and countries. With an average tariff rate of 44%, the Philippines appears to be the most protective, followed by Indonesia with 33% and Thailand with 30%. Tariffs are substantially lower than the average in Malaysia with 15% and not unexpectedly in Singapore with only 6%.

As regards sectoral distribution we find exceptionally high tariff levels in the case of beverages and tobacco. Their purpose is, however, not mainly protection but raising revenue, which explains, for example, the Singaporean figure of more than 400%. Excluding this sector, the average tariff rate for Singapore would be close to zero.

The use of averages weighted by the respective import values reveals markedly different results (see Table 6): the ASEAN average tariff rate in that case drops from 26% to 21% and the market of Thailand appears to be the most highly protected. However, weighted averages may not adequately reflect the level of protection: particularly high tariff rates will receive only low weights if they manage successfully to restrict imports.

---

[11] Cf. also D.A. DeRosa, 'Trade and Protection in the Asian Developing Region', *Asian Development Review*, vol. 4 (1986), no. 1, p. 27 ff.

*Import restrictions and export promotion measures
in Southeast Asian countries*

Table 5.   ASEAN: AVERAGE UNWEIGHTED TARIFF RATES, 1978[a] (%)

	Indonesia	Malaysia	Philippines	Singapore	Thailand	Regional
Food and live animals chiefly for food	42.9	10.7	67.2	1.3	42.6	33.0
Beverages and tobacco	46.0	346.8	82.5	458.2	62.4	199.2
Crude materials, inedible except fuels	14.2	2.8	27.4	0	18.4	12.6
Mineral fuels, lubricants and related materials	15.2	7.1	14.9	9.0	14.2	12.1
Animal and vegetable oils, fats and waxes	30.0	0.3	43.9	0	24.7	19.8
Chemicals and related products, n.e.s.	26.8	19.2	41.1	37.2	28.1	30.5
Manufactured goods classified chiefly by materials	37.9	14.9	52.0	0.4	32.0	27.4
Machinery and transport equipment	18.0	10.7	23.0	1.4	18.0	14.2
Miscellaneous manufactured articles	49.9	19.0	68.9	3.4	37.8	35.8
Commodities and transaction not classified elsewhere in the PSCC	21.7	7.7	62.5	0	20.8	22.5
Overall	33.0	15.3	44.2	5.6	29.4	25.5

[a] Groupings as per Philippine Standard Commodity Classification (PSCC).

Source: Republic of the Philippines, Tariff Commission, *Tariff Profiles in ASEAN*, Manila, Jan. 1979, vol. I.

Table 6.   ASEAN: AVERAGE WEIGHTED TARIFF RATES, 1978[a] (%)

	Indonesia	Malaysia	Philippines	Singapore	Thailand	Regional
Food and live animals chiefly for food	14.9	9.7	22.5	2.3	34.3	27.8
Beverages and tobacco	36.8	189.9	99.8	318.7	68.9	171.3
Crude materials, inedible except fuels	15.9	2.04	13.8	0	7.2	2.6
Mineral fuels, lubricants and related materials	16.5	6.2	19.7	4.6	1.2	8.4
Animal and vegetable oils, fats and waxes	32.3	1.2	30.0	0	23.0	5.3
Chemicals and related products, n.e.s.	19.2	5.0	20.3	0.4	19.3	10.8
Manufactured goods classified chiefly by materials	13.9	6.9	28.1	0.3	20.1	11.0
Machinery and transport equipment	25.7	7.6	22.8	1.3	32.5	28.4
Miscellaneous manufactured articles	35.4	14.4	28.3	2.2	30.3	14.2
Commodities and transaction not classified elsewhere in the PSCC	14.6	6.3	82.0	0	29.5	16.5
Overall	20.2	6.6	23.0	3.7	30.4	20.9

[a] Groupings according to Philippine Standard Commodity Classification (PSCC).

Source: As Table 5.

Table 7.   ABSOLUTE, RELATIVE AND CUMULATIVE
FREQUENCY DISTRIBUTION OF TARIFF RATES IN ASEAN, 1978

Tariff rate	No.	% distribution	Relative cumulative frequency
Indonesia			
Total	1,707	100.00	
0	85	4.98	4.98
1–10	318	18.63	23.61
11–20	380	22.26	45.87
21–30	185	10.84	56.71
31–50	437	25.60	82.31
51–70	243	14.23	96.54
71–100	43	2.52	99.06
Over 100	16	0.94	100.00

Tariff Rate	No.	% distribution	Relative cumulative frequency
Malaysia			
Total	3,059	100.00	
0	1,479	48.35	48.35
1–10	240	7.85	56.20
11–20	352	11.51	67.71
21–30	551	18.01	85.72
31–50	312	10.20	95.92
51–70	54	1.76	97.68
71–100	17	0.56	98.00
Over 100	54	1.76	100.00

Tariff Rate	No.	% distribution	Relative cumulative frequency
Philippines[a]			
Total	1,379	100.00	
0	3	0.22	0.22
1–10	363	26.32	26.54
11–20	258	18.71	45.25
21–30	202	14.64	59.90
31–50	261	18.93	78.83
51–70	197	14.29	93.11
71–100	93	6.74	99.85
Over 100	2	0.15	100.00

Table 7 (*contd.*)

	Singapore		
Tariff Rate	*No.*	*% distribution*	*Relative cumulative frequency*
Total	2,563	100.00	
0	2,357	91.96	91.96
1–10	20	0.78	92.74
11–20	85	3.32	96.06
21–30	24	0.94	97.00
31–50	17	0.66	97.66
51–70	11	0.43	98.09
71–100	7	0.27	98.36
Over 100	42	1.64	100.00

	Thailand		
Tariff Rate	*No.*	*% distribution*	*Relative cumulative frequency*
Total	1,440	100.00	
0	100	6.94	6.94
1–10	167	11.60	18.54
11–20	197	13.68	32.22
21–30	633	43.96	76.18
31–50	153	10.62	86.80
51–70	129	8.96	95.76
71–100	44	3.06	98.82
Over 100	17	1.18	100.00

[a] As of Jan. 1, 1981.

Source: R. Tumbocon-Haresco, 'Turning an Economy on Taxes', in *ASEAN Business Quarterly*, 2nd Quarter 1981, p. 26.

A further crude method of comparing tariff protection can be found in the frequency distribution of various tariff levels (see Table 7). The respective results conform in principle to those shown above:

— In Singapore and Malaysia, 92% and 48% of tariff items respectively may be imported free of tariffs. Only 3% of all tariffs in Singapore and 14% in Malaysia range above 30%.

— In contrast to this, the share of tariff rates above 30% is 43% for Indonesia, 40% for the Philippines and 24% for Thailand. For the Philippines the figure refers to 1981, thus already partly including the recent liberalisation program (see below).

In the case of South Korea, data on nominal tariff protection are available for 1978 as well[12] showing an average tariff level of 38% which is considerably higher than the ASEAN average. Excluding again the atypical sector 'beverages and tobacco', we find the highest protection for transport equipment (47%) and consumer durables (44%), i.e those sectors which have been the main target of import substitution.

Turning now to nominal and effective[13] rates of protection and examining still the South Korean case (see Table 8), it is noticeable that the implicit nominal protection stands at a much lower level (18% in 1978) than the average tariff rate (38%), which points to a certain degree of tariff redundancy (caused by prohibitive tariffs and/or quantitative import restrictions). The effective rate of protection is 31% on average, but increases to 131% for consumer durables and 135% for transport equipment.

The same results can be obtained in principle in the case of ASEAN countries (excluding Singapore with its extremely low tariff level) so that the following conclusions may be drawn:

(i) The implicit nominal protection (i.e. difference between domestic and world market prices) in many cases turns out to be lower than the average tariff rate, i.e. tariffs are to a certain degree redundant.

(ii) The rate of effective protection, on the other hand, is significantly higher than legal tariff rates, due to escalation effects; aver-

---

[12] Cf. K.Y. Wang 'Export Assistance Regimes in the Pacific Asian Developing Countries — the Cases of South Korea, Taiwan, the Philippines and Thailand' (paper presented at the Pacific Cooperation Task Force Workshop on Trade in Manufactured Goods, Seoul, June 28–30, 1983).

[13] The effective rate of protection may be calculated according to the Balassa method or the Corden method, the difference being the respective treatment of non-traded inputs. The rank correlation coefficient between both calculations is, however, very high.

Table 8.   NOMINAL AND EFFECTIVE RATES OF PROTECTION
IN THAILAND AND SOUTH KOREA, 1978 (%)

	Thailand		*Korea*	
	Nominal	*Effective*	*Nominal*	*Effective (Balassa) (Domestic Sales)*
Processed foods	9.0	78.5	39.8	− 29.4
Beverages and tobacco	69.1	4.0	20.2	28.0
Construction materials	12.2	91.7	− 7.2	− 15.0
Intermediate products I	14.8	16.2	− 2.4	− 37.9
Intermediate products II	19.2	55.3	1.3	7.9
Non-durable consumer goods	64.6	212.4	14.9	31.5
Consumer durables	57.3	495.6	40.2	131.2
Machinery	21.4	58.3	17.8	47.4
Transport equipment	80.5	417.2	30.9	135.4
All Industries	27.3	70.2	17.8	30.6
Non-import-competing	50.8	99.6		
Import-competing	35.7	85.9		
Export	− 13.7	− 40.3		

Sources: N. Akrasanee, *Industrial Sector in the Thai Economy,* Thai University Research Association, Research Report No. 1, Bangkok, November 1980; Y.K., Wang, *Export Assistance*, op. cit.

Table 9.   AVERAGE AND EFFECTIVE RATES OF PROTECTION
IN THE PHILIPPINES, 1980 and 1985 (%)

Sector	*1980*	*1985 (projection)*
Consumption goods	115.0	43.2
Intermediate goods	26.8	14.0
Inputs into construction	31.5	24.7
Capital goods	23.9	19.6
All manufacturing	70.3	31.0

Source: R.M. Bautista, *The 1981–85 Tariff Changes and Effective Protection of Manufacturing Industries*, University of the Philippines, School of Economics, Discussion Paper no. 8213, August 1982.

age effective protection is 70% (1978) in the case of Thailand (see Table 8), 70% (1980) as well for the Philippine manufacturing sector (see Table 9) and 55% (1973) for the manufacturing sector in Malaysia.[14] Effective protection rates reach extremely high levels in consumer industries and transport equipment. The protective effect for consumer durables in Thailand, for example, amounts to almost 500%.

(iii) As can be expected, export production is being discriminated against by the tariff policy just described because in the production of export goods either expensive domestic inputs have to be used or imported goods the prices of which have been raised by a high tariff; furthermore there is in some cases the negative influence of export taxes. Thus the effective rate of protection for export-oriented sectors was – 16% in the Philippines in 1974[15] and – 40% in Thailand in 1978 (see Table 8). Accordingly the need to compensate for this discrimination is one of the main arguments in support of fiscal and financial measures of export promotion which meanwhile are being applied in all the countries under review — (see Chapter II.A4*a*).

After this general comparative review of the level and structure of tariffs we will now turn to some recent developments in tariff policy. Many countries of the region have recognised the need to reduce sectoral overprotection and rationalise the tariff structure. However, only limited progress has been made in actual implementation of policy reforms. A remarkable liberalisation programme is being carried out in the Philippines where an ambitious tariff reform, initiated in 1981, was scheduled to be completed in 1985. After full implementation of the programme, the average tariff rate is expected to decrease from 44% to 28%. Furthermore the variations in tariff rates will be narrowed, thus reducing effective protection from 70% to 31% in 1985 (see Table 9) for the whole manufacturing sector. In early 1981 and 1982 the peak tariff levels were reduced as planned to a maximum of 50% for fourteen priority sectors (see Table 10). It thus seems that the results aimed at for 1985 may well be within reach.[16] Simultaneously there is a liberalisation of import licensing, to which we will return below when dealing with non-tariff barriers to trade.

Tariff reform plans in Thailand are still largely under discussion. Recently tariffs and taxes were reduced for some categories of imports, notably electric and electrical household goods, aiming at increasing the efficiency of domestic production and reducing import smuggling. As tariffs on many components of production were reduced at the same time, these measures however, left the

[14] Cf. Ariff, 'Malaysia's Trade', op. cit., p. 284,
[15] Cf. Bautista, 'Trade Strategies'; op. cit., p. 181.
[16] On the other hand, at the beginning of 1983 the government decided to impose a surtax of 3% on all imported goods. In general terms, the economic policy orientation of the Philippines must be considered as crucially dependent on the development of its foreign debt, which at present has already assumed critical proportions.

Table 10. PHILIPPINES: TARIFF RATES FOR 14 INDUSTRIAL SECTORS, 1980/2 (%)

Sector	Raw materials		Intermediate goods		Finished goods	
	1980	1982	1980	1982	1980	1982
Food processing	5-100	5-50	Free-100	Free-50	10-100	10-50
Textiles and garments	10-50	10-30	50/70	40	30-100	40/50
Leather and footwear	10/50	5/10	50/70	30	100	40
Pulp and paper	10/20/50	10/20	30/50/100	20/30	30-100	20/50
Cement	10	10	100	40	50	50
Iron and steel	10	5	30	30	50	30
Automotive	-	-	10-100	25	30/70/100	40
Wood and wood products						
Products	10	10	35	20	70	35
Motorcycle and bicycles	-	-	35	30	70	45
Glass and ceramics	10	10	30	25	55	35
Furniture	40	30	50	40	100	50
Domestic appliances	25	20	50	30	70	50
Machinery/other capital equipment	-	-	25	20	20	30
Electrical/electronics	-	-	35	25	35	30

Source: R. Tumbocon-Haresco, 'Turning an Economy on Taxes', op. cit., p. 24.

effective protection of the sectors in question essentially unchanged
so that producers offered only little resistance. How fast planned
tariff reductions will proceed in other sectors is at present an open
question. The same applies to the drastic tariff reductions in the
framework of the 1983 tariff reform in South Korea aimed at the
gradual introduction of a 20% unified tariff system by 1988.[17]

(*b*) *Preliminary assessment of ASEAN tariff preferences.* Any
analysis of tariff policy measures in Southeast Asia would be
incomplete without including the ASEAN Preferential Trading
Arrangements which the Foreign Ministers of the five original
member-countries signed in February 1977.[18] The central feature of
this remarkable trade policy approach to integration is the introduction of tariff preferences for intra-ASEAN trade leading to a step-
by-step liberalisation. This concept aims at eventually deepening
specialisation and the division of labour, thus increasing the relative
share of trade flows within ASEAN which at present stands at a
fairly low level of about 17%.[19]

The preferential tariffs bear two *potentially* important consequences in terms of other countries' (e.g. the EEC's) economic
relations with ASEAN. On the one hand, imports from outside the
integration area are discriminated against rendering trade diversion
possible; on the other hand, there may be an additional growth
potential for firms being located in any of the ASEAN countries but
producing for the *whole* ASEAN market. Both effects can of course
only be of major importance if the preferential tariffs are applied to
product lines with significantly high intra-ASEAN flows. What then
is the state of realisation at the time of writing?

Up to now, preferences have largely been negotiated following an
incremental product-by-product approach. Often negotiations are
conducted on a bilateral basis, the results then being offered to the
other ASEAN countries as well. Furthermore, since April 1980 there
are tariff reductions across the board for all items below a certain
minimum import value (referring to 6-digit CCCN classification).
In both areas considerable progress has been made in quantitative

[17] Cf. ESCAP, 'The Case History of Successful Export Policies: The Republic of
Korea', Document E/ESCAP/Trade to PMMT/5, 12 May 1986, p. 12.
[18] Cf. W. Duscha, 'Die Integrationsbestrebungen der ASEAN — Abriss einer
Bestandsaufnahme zu Beginn der 80er Jahre', *Internationales Asienforum*, vol. 13
(1981), p. 340 ff.; Bautista, 'Trade Strategies', op. cit., p. 192 ff.
[19] Cf. W. Lütkenhorst, 'Die ASEAN-Staaten and Konzepte einer pazifischen
Wirtschaftskooperation' in A. Woll, K. Glaubitt, H.–B. Schäfer (eds), *Nationale
Entwicklung und internationale Zusammenarbeit — Herausforderung ökonomischer Forschung*, Berlin 1983, p. 264.

terms: As of March 1, 1983, the number of negotiated preferences was 8,560 and the ceiling for across-the-board preferences has been lifted in several steps from US$ 50,000 initially to US$ 2.5 million. If both developments are taken together, the total figure of preference items may now be around 20,000. Moreover, the preference margin increased from initially 10% in 1980 to a minimum of 20–25% at present. Two important qualifications have, however, to be made:

(i) The product-by-product approach is time-consuming and above all open to pressure group influences. Not surprisingly it has resulted largely in negotiating tariff preferences for items which are either to a limited extent or not at all traded within ASEAN. Strange examples such as snowploughs (Philippines) or nuclear power plants (Indonesia) are too numerous to be listed here.

(ii) The across-the-board approach, disposing of a built-in mechanism independent of troublesome negotiations, is certainly more promising, but it unfortunately suffers from long lists of excluded items. The Task Force set up by the Fifteenth ASEAN Ministerial Meeting in 1981 concluded: "In the across-the-board approach the exclusion lists eliminated virtually all tradable items."

As might have been expected, the first empirical investigations of the ASEAN system of tariff preferences clearly show:

(i) that the tariff preferences are heavily concentrated in only a few sectors (especially machinery), particularly those in which the other ASEAN countries can not be expected to produce efficiently for export in the foreseeable future;[20] and

(ii) that — as was calculated in the case of the Philippines — even a 100% tariff reduction for all items with import values below US$ 500,000 could only result in trade creation in the range of 2% of total imports.[21]

It clearly follows that at present ASEAN tariff preferences are not yet a major factor contributing to regional liberalisation. Their future importance will be crucially dependent on national attitudes towards structural change as a consequence of further specialisation. This chapter does not, however, intend to speculate on that issue.

(c) *Non-tariff barriers to trade.* NTBs, the importance of which has

[20] Cf. G. Tan, *Trade Liberalization in ASEAN*, Singapore 1982
[21] Cf. Ooi Guat Tin, *The ASEAN Preferential Trading Arrangements (PTA): An Analysis of Potential Effects of Intra-ASEAN Trade*, Singapore 1981.

generally increased recently, form to some extent a twilight zone of trade policy measures in which not only legal regulations but particularly the method by which they are executed settle matters. There is ample scope for arbitrary administrative decisions and as a corollary some potential for illegal practices. This is generally true and not particularly characteristic for the Southeast Asian region alone.

We present below some key areas of non-tariff measures and quote some illustrations of their importance without pretending in any way to offer a complete survey.

There are some NTBs involved in the process of customs clearance, customs valuation and customs classification which are of course intimately entwined with tariff policy itself. Following the results of a questionnaire on the experience of Singaporean exporters to other ASEAN countries,[22] customs clearance in Indonesia turns out to be particularly cumbersome. On the one hand the necessary infrastructural facilities are reported to be inadequate and bureaucratic procedures are overly time-consuming, and on the other hand existing rules are apparently not applied in a systematic or reliable way. In the case of Malaysia corresponding complaints have decreased under the present Mahathir administration.

The decisions involved in customs valuation practices are often open to controversy. If the customs value of imported goods is fixed at a level above its real price, the effect is nothing less than a hidden tariff increase.[23] Particularly in this regard, however, customs authorities can act largely at their own discretion. In the questionnaire quoted above, once again Indonesia and Malaysia are referred to as negative examples, whereas customs valuations procedures in Thailand received relatively good reports. In Indonesia, a special measure — a so-called 'check-price' for imported goods — is taken as the basis of customs valuation whenever the declared import price would actually be lower. This procedure has been introduced to prevent underinvoicing, but unjustified tariff increases are often the actual result. Above all the check-price system is reported to be too rigid in the case of necessary adjustment to cost-oriented reductions in import prices.[24]

Manipulation of the basis for customs valuation is also made use

[22] Here reference is made to an ongoing research project of the Institute of Southeast Asian Studies, Singapore.
[23] It is thus questionable whether this should be regarded as a non-tariff barrier at all.
[24] Cf. on the role of the check-price as an instrument of export promotion (by underinvoicing of exports) in the 1960s: M.M. Pitt, 'Alternative Trade Strategies and Employment in Indonesia' in Krueger *et al., Trade and Employment in Developing Countries*, vol. 1: Individual Studies, Chicago/London 1979, p.195 ff.

of in Taiwan and the Philippines. In Taiwan the declared price may be replaced by the wholesale price at the port of entry; moreover, a mark-up of 20% is in certain cases added to the declared price before calculating customs duties. In the Philippines customs valuation operates on the basis of the price for standard wholesale quantities in the exporting country (plus 10% for insurance and freight).

As regards customs classification there is no uniform practice in ASEAN countries. Some countries refer to CCCN (Customs Cooperation Council Nomenclature), others to SITC (Standard International Trade Classification). Reportedly there is also a tendency to classify imported goods according to the principle of maximising tariff rates in either one or the other sytem. No judgement can yet be made as to the possible contribution in that respect of the customs code agreed upon by the national customs authorities of ASEAN countries.

Import licensing is applied in several countries to varying degrees. It is of minor importance in Malaysia, Thailand and Taiwan,[25] where less than 10% of import items are subject to special controls. In contrast to this, import licensing is regarded as a major trade barrier in South Korea, particularly when seen in connection with quantitative restrictions. Critical remarks concentrate above all on the fact that the quota system is modified every half-year, thus impeding long-term sales planning, and that in regard to the licensing itself it is not clear what are the criteria of distribution and of the involvement of the many and diverse decision-making bodies. In 1978 35% of all imported goods still fell under licensing controls. Meanwhile a liberalisation program was set up, aiming at increasing the competitiveness of the South Korean industry; in the short run it also serves the purpose of preparing South Korea's accession to OECD in terms of an adequate trade policy. Since 1978 the liberalisation ratio has increased to 80% in 1983 and is supposed to reach 95% by 1988. This may be interpreted as a considerable progress, yet some reservations have to be made:

(i) Only a certain proportion of liberalised items can be imported free of any control. Others are still subject to import surveillance, the respective official term being 'elastic import liberalisation'.[26]

[25] Cf. R.J. Langhammer, 'Sectorial Profiles of Import Licensing in Selected Developing Countries and Their Impact on North-South and South-South Trade Flows', *Konjunkturpolitik*, vol. 29 (1980), p. 22 ff.; GATT, *Accession of Thailand, Supplementary Memorandum on Foreign Trade Regime*, Geneva, March 15, 1982, (Doc.L/5291).
[26] Cf. M. Eli, *Wirtschaftliche Entwicklungsperspektiven der Republik Korea*, Hamburg 1979, p. 116 ff.

(ii) The import liberalisation is strongly biased in terms of its sectoral distribution. More than 40% of import items in consumer durables and machinery and more than 60% in transport equipment were still subject to licensing in 1981 (see Table 11). The same applied to 49% of all items of electrical machinery in 1983. Many observers have thus come to the conclusion that the main purpose of the liberalisation programme was to mollify external critics.

(iii) Potential import increases due to progressive liberalisation are restricted because for a certain part of liberalised import items 'emergency tariffs' are applied amounting to 70–85%.[27]

In the Philippines a programme to reduce import controls is also being carried out as a complement to the tariff reductions discussed above. Of all import items subject to licensing (about 1,300), 260 in early 1981 and a further 600 in early 1982 were liberalised, implying that for almost 300 items at the same time a previously established import ban was lifted.[28] All remaining tariff items were scheduled to be liberalised in 1983. In March 1982, however, there was a setback and some consumer durables (TV sets, refrigerators, air-conditioners, washing machines etc.) were returned by the Philippine Central Bank to the list of imports covered by licensing. On the other hand, import restrictions for industrial machinery, equipment and spare parts have been removed, taking effect on January 1, 1984. In this regard, firms producing for the domestic market now enjoy the same rights as those producing for export.[29]

Indonesian trade policy has recently moved clearly towards increasing import restrictions. By the end of 1982 import controls for seven manufacturing sectors,[30] including more than 400 tariff items, were tightened up. In these seven sectors only a few selected authorised importers registered at the Trade Ministry are allowed to import goods. In many cases this goes along with quantitative import restrictions, and in some cases import bans can be expected to emerge in the near future.[31] All these measures are part of a programme of export encouragement and import reduction containing also more restrictive local content regulations, as well as counterpurchase regulations which will be the subject of the next chapter.

It is quite difficult at present to draw any clear conclusions concerning a general trend for Southeast Asia in the field of NTBs.

---

[27] Cf. *The Korea Herald*, July 19, 1983
[28] Cf. *Nachrichten für Aussenhandel* (Cologne), April 19, 1982.
[29] Cf. *Business Day* (Manila), June 9, 1983.
[30] Electrical and electronic goods, chemical goods, automobile spare parts, metal industries, machinery, textiles and heavy equipment.
[31] Cf. *Nachrichten für Aussenhandel*, Dec. 15, 1982

Table 11.   SOUTH KOREA: SECTORAL DISTRIBUTION OF
IMPORT LIBERALISATION, DEC. 31, 1981

Sector	*Ratio of liberalization (CCCN 8-digit, %)*
Agriculture and fishery	72.1
Mining and energy	93.6
Food processing	45.4
Beverages and tobacco	25.5
Construction materials	98.4
Primary intermediate input	83.9
Secondary intermediate input	91.8
Non-durable consumer goods	72.9
Durable consumer goods	56.1
Machinery	59.5
Transport equipment	39.8
Total	74.7

Source: Korea Development Institute, 'Tariff Policy: Present Status and Reform Plan', Seoul, July 1982, p. 32 (mimeo, in Korean).

Apparently there is no clear tendency for the whole region. On the one hand we can witness some progress in liberalisation, yet on the other hand this is overlapped by the introduction of new restrictions. Particularly in the steel sector, import restrictive measures are currently advancing, including Malaysia's import ban for steel bars.[32] In general, however, it is possible to perceive a broad tendency to practise short-term modifications of trade policy measures in response to actual balance of payments needs, thus providing an insecure basis for any long-term planning of foreign trade transactions.

(*d*) *Recent trends in the field of countertrade.* Accepting the UNCTAD definition of non-tariff barriers as those trade policy measures (excluding tariffs) which exercise influence on the price, volume and direction of foreign trade, counterpurchase regulations also fall under this heading. They may follow from different motivations (securing of certain import sources, particularly for raw materials; saving up foreign exchange) and take various forms (see Walsh, 1983; de Miramon, 1982). In the past they have been applied primarily in foreign trading with Eastern socialist countries. Recently, however, countertrade has advanced and broadened considerably, and this is also true of the Southeast Asian region where declining raw material prices and the resulting balance of payments problems were among the contributing factors. Without any doubt

[32] Cf. *Japan Economic Journal*, April 12, 1983.

the most prominent example is the controversial counterpurchase policy of Indonesia which took effect on January 1, 1982, with the aim of promoting non-traditional exports. The increasing importance of countertrade is, however, not restricted to the Indonesian case.[33]

— Although *Malaysia* has traditionally taken a negative attitude towards countertrade, a committee was appointed by the government in June 1982 to explore potential markets, eligible products and adequate procedures in order to increase countertrade. Only a little later, preliminary discussions took place in South Korea about bartering Malaysian rubber and petroleum for South Korean naval vessels. The first actual barter deal was accomplished between a Malaysian general trading corporation (Sime Darby Pernas Trading Corporation) and Mexican tyre companies, which exchanged rubber for cocoa beans, which the Malaysian trading corporation in turn resold to US confectionery manufacturers.

— In *Thailand* and the *Philippines* there is less official support for barter trade but even so there are signs of growing interest. In Manila there is talk of exchanging military transport equipment for textiles involving a Belgian firm. Thailand has already exchanged tapioca for fertilisers with South Korea since 1981. The scale of these deals, however, is very small.

— The current discussions on countertrade are not so much influenced by the marginal examples just described as by the strict counterpurchase policy that *Indonesia* has pursued since the beginning of 1982. All government overseas purchases exceeding 500 million rupiah (about US$ 735,000) are now linked to counterpurchase commitments with the following characteristics:

(i) Indonesia has insisted on a 100% counterpurchase (East European countries normally demand 20–30%);

(ii) Counterpurchases are restricted to "non-traditional" exports (excluding oil and gas) and must be "additional";

(iii) Counterpurchases have to be made on a bilateral basis, i.e. be directed to the country from which the Indonesian government agency made the original purchase.

(iv) Unfulfilled obligations are subject to a cash penalty of 50%.

After an initial period of strong resistance, particularly from Japan, a first contract was signed in August 1982. Quite unexpectedly the largest Japanese trading house, Mitsubishi, accepted the

[33] Cf. *Far Eastern Economic Review*, Jan. 27, 1983.

Indonesian rules of the game in order to participate in a fertiliser purchase.[34] A further contract with the participation of more Japanese trading corporations reveals an increasing degree of flexibility on the Indonesian side: agreement could be reached on a period of ten years for counterpurchase, and the cash penalty was reduced from 50% to 20% of unfulfilled obligations.[35] There is only scattered and controversial evidence on the total amount involved in counterpurchase contracts up to now: Indonesian sources presented a figure of US$ 560 million in the spring of 1983,[36] which would be equal to about 10% of the country's non-traditional exports.

An evaluation of the increasing counterpurchase practices has to be negative in terms of economic efficiency. The Indonesian case shows that there are not sufficient marketable products of the necessary quality available (otherwise the counterpurchase policy would of course be superfluous), and that consequently foreign trading partners have to bear with additional marketing costs and risks. Thus a country prescribing counterpurchase will either have to reduce its export prices or pay a risk premium to the foreign partner allowing him to cover his marketing costs. In any case the result will be a deterioration of the terms of trade and the conservation of export productions which would be inefficient without counterpurchase interventions. Furthermore, the most questionable effect in the long run could be that the attempt at balancing foreign trade values bilaterally will jeopardise the variability and thus the growth potential of the international division of labour. On the other hand it is fairly understandable that these arguments, referring as they do to an optimal international division of labour, are not very attractive to developing Southeast Asian countries. Their justification for countertrade measures follows, at least in part, from the need to compensate for protectionist measures applied by industrialised countries. This particular argument has been emphasised recently by the Malaysian Premier Mahathir,[37] and he can indeed point further to the fact that countertrade measures do not violate existing GATT rules. The responsiblity of the industrialised countries must therefore not be overlooked: it is their trade policy which will at least partly determine whether increasing countertrade will only be a short-term episode or a long-term trend in international trade relations. In the latter event, in the view of many observers, Japan with

---

34 Cf. *Japan Economic Journal*, July 13, 1982.
35 Cf. *Japan Economic Journal*, Nov. 30, 1982.
36 Cf. *Business Day* (Manila), May 6, 1983.
37 Cf. *Far Eastern Economic Review*, March 17, 1983.

her large trading corporations would possibly gain most, at least in relation to her competitors.

4. *Analysis and assessment of export promotion measures*

In the preceding chapters we have concentrated mainly on those trade policy measures which try to improve the competitiveness of domestic producers by means of tariff and non-tariff protection.[38] We will now turn to those measures aiming at increasing export production. There is, however, a link between both categories of policy measures in terms of their justification, as will be demonstrated below when we discuss the issue of the GATT conformity of export subsidies.

(*a*) *Regional comparison of export promotion measures.* As export-oriented development strategies have been adopted by more and more Southeast Asian countries during the 1960s, the various instruments of export promotion have taken on a largely uniform look. Although the instruments are very similar in principle, they exhibit many diverse forms. All in all, a 'patchwork' of export incentives has emerged which in some cases lacks transparency. Systematically, differentiation can be made between financial incentives, fiscal incentives and factor incentives (see Table 12 and Tables A.1 and A.2 following Chapter II.A).

(i) Financial incentives include on the one hand long-term loans and short-term refinancing of export credits at preferential rates of interest, and on the other hand various forms of export credit guarantee and insurance. These measures are to be found in all countries with only very few exceptions: there are no preferential export credits in Hong Kong and no export credit guarantees in Thailand. The interest rate difference between export credits and normal credits varies considerably: in 1980 it amounted to 2% in Taiwan, almost 3% in Singapore and as much as 10% in South Korea.[39]

(ii) By far the most important incentives are fiscal. Above all they include tax holidays and tax reductions. The exemption from corporate income tax is generally applied for up to ten years, the only exception being Hong Kong where the tax rate is as low as 17%

---

[38] With the exception of the last chapter, since counterpurchase measures are aimed at export promotion — although in a non-market regulatory framework.

[39] In June 1982, however, preferential rates for export credits were abolished in South Korea.

Table 12. CLASSIFICATION OF EXPORT INCENTIVES

	Indonesia	Malaysia	Philippines	Singapore	Thailand	Hong Kong	Korea	Taiwan
1. FINANCIAL INCENTIVES								
(a) Loans/Interest reductions	x	x	x	x	x	–	x	x
(b) Guarantees	x	x	x	x	–	x	x	x
2. FISCAL INCENTIVES								
(a) Tax exemptions and relief	x	x	x	x	x	x	x	x
(b) Depreciation allowances	x	x	x	x	–	x	x	x
(c) Exemption/Remittance of customs duties and taxes on imports	x	x	x	–ᵃ	x	–ᵃ	x	x
3. FACTOR INCENTIVES								
(a) Training	–	–	–	x	–	–	–	–
(b) Research and development	–	x	–	x	–	–	–	x
(c) Sites, buildings, facilities	x	x	x	x	x	x	x	x

ᵃ Irrelevant because of almost complete free trade regime.

Sources: Investment Incentive Programs of the Pacific Basin, ed. by International Business Education Program, Graduate School of Business Administration, University of Southern California, Los Angeles 1983; *The ASEAN, Hong Kong, South Korea and Taiwan Economies: Their Structure and Outlook into the 1980s*, Economist Intelligence Unit, London 1980.

anyway. Moreover, firms are allowed to carry over losses in Indonesia, the Philippines and Thailand, and all countries offer various tax deduction schemes, e.g. concerning the costs of export promotion, organisational costs and pre-operating expenses, training costs or reserves for exchange rate fluctuations and losses from export sales. Furthermore, depreciation allowances have to be mentioned which are offered in all countries except Thailand. Exemption from or drawbacks of customs duties and excise tax on imports being used for export production is now a general feature. These measures are in some cases supplemented by the establishment of bonded factories, which in 1981 took in 6% of all imports in South Korea and 10% in Taiwan.

(iii) A last category of export promotion measures may be termed factor-incentives including, for example, the subsidisation of training programmes in Singapore[40] or the official promotion of research and development activities in Singapore and Taiwan. In the first place, however, factor incentives refer to export processing zones, which meanwhile are to be found in all the countries in question. These zones offer a whole package of incentives including the above-mentioned financial and fiscal measures plus specially favoured sites, appropriate buildings, electricity and water supply, preferential administrative treatment etc.[41]

What are the quantitative effects of all these incentives listed above? In answering this question reference is made here only to the case of South Korea, from which of course generalisations must not be made without further qualifications: it has been calculated that in 1978 the quantifiable export incentives amounted to 22% of the total value of exports (see Table 13), 50% thereof falling to the share of internal tax reductions, 38% to tariff reductions and 12% to interest subsidies.

The aggregate effects of all the single incentives are obviously anything but small. This leads to the issue of evaluating export incentives in economic terms.

(*b*) *Economic assessment I: On the GATT conformity of export subsidies.* As has been demonstrated, export incentives are applied in various forms and can be regarded as government interventions

---

[40] Within the framework of the following programmes: Industrial Training Grant Scheme, Government-Industry Training Centers, Overseas Training Scheme, Industrial Development Scholarship Scheme.
[41] For a well-balanced assessment, cf. UNIDO, *Export Processing Zones in Developing Countries* (UNIDO Working Papers on Structural Changes, No. 19), Vienna, August 1980, Doc. ICIS 176.

Table 13.   SOUTH KOREA: SCOPE AND STRUCTURE OF EXPORT PROMOTION MEASURES, 1962–78

	Official exchange rate (won/$) (A)	Export premium (won/$) (B)	Direct subsidy (million won)	Reduction of internal tax (million won)	Tariff reduction[a] (million won)	Tariff rebate (million won)	Interest subsidy by postponing tariff collection[b] (million won)	Total export subsidy (million won)	Interest subsidy[c] (million won)	Export subsidy per $ (won) (C)	Export subsidy and premium D=B+C (won)	Exports (million $)	subsidy/ exchange rate (D/A, %)
1962	130.0	–	566	310	255	–	–	1.165	34	21.3	21.3	54.8	16.4
1963	130.0	39.8	354	527	571	–	–	1.599	147	18.4	58.2	86.8	44.8
1964	213.7	39.7	350	992	1.197	–	–	2.700	161	22.7	62.4	119.1	29.2
1965	266.7	–	–	2.398	2.692	–	–	5.603	513	32.0	32.0	175.1	12.0
1966	271.0	–	–	5.021	5.333	–	–	11.434	1.080	45.7	45.7	250.3	16.9
1967	269.5	–	–	7.724	8.224	–	–	19.584	3.636	61.2	61.2	320.2	22.7
1968	276.9	–	–	11.127	19.261	–	–	36.678	6.290	80.6	80.6	455.2	29.1
1969	288.7	–	–	17.207	22.551	–	–	49.732	9.974	79.9	79.9	622.5	27.7
1970	311.1	–	–	26.827	35.613	–	–	77.604	15.164	92.9	92.9	835.2	29.9
1971	350.8	–	–	41.852	54.333	–	–	119.526	23.341	112.0	112.0	1.067.6	31.9
1972	394.0	–	–	47.453	111.208	–	–	179.568	20.907	110.6	110.6	1.624.1	28.1
1973	398.3	–	–	64.845	210.788	–	–	308.993	33.360	95.8	95.8	3.225.0	24.1
1974	406.0	–	–	101.763	248.998	–	–	390.959	40.198	87.7	87.7	4.460.4	21.6
1975	484.0	–	–	169.129	171.565	35.600	3.778	380.070	59.562	74.8	74.8	5.081.0	15.5
1976	484.0	–	–	259.268	125.586	258.000	10.933	731.637	77.850	94.8	94.8	7.715.1	19.6
1977	484.0	–	–	479.893	116.30	308.600	14.114	1019.399	100.491	101.46	101.46	10.046.5	21.0
1978	484.0	–	–	691.460	140.75	355.800	20.490	1369.997	161.489	107.78	107.78	12.710.6	22.3

[a] Includes exemption or reduction of tariffs by Tariff Law 28, 29 and 32 (equipments of major industries, reexports and raw materials for exports) and by regulations for foreign capital introduction.

[b] Postponed tariff collection × annual rate of discount rate on tills × 0.25 (divided by four since the average grace period is three months).

[c] Outstanding export loans × (discount rate on bills for prime firms – lending rate for exports).

Source: Y.K. Wang, *Export Assistance Regimes . . .*, op. cit., p. 12.

with a strong influence on competition in the world market. It is thus
not at all surprising that they constitute one of the main trade policy
issues touched upon by GATT rules. The relevant articles are Article
XVI and VI, the former dealing with subsidies, the latter with
countervailing duties.[42] Article XVI generally allows *production*
subsidies as well as *export* subsidies on *primary* products but at the
same time prohibits *export* subsidies on *manufactured* goods.
Developing countries have, however, always been exempted from
this restriction. This practice has recently been reaffirmed by the
Agreement on Subsidies and Countervailing Duties which was
accepted during the Tokyo Round in 1979. This Agreement states
that 'subsidies are an integral part of economic development programmes of developing countries' (para. 1), particularly for
promoting *manufactured* exports. Reference is made, however, to
the graduation principle when saying that 'a developing country
signatory should agree or enter into a commitment to reduce or
eliminate export subsidies when the use of such export subsidies is
inconsistent with its competitive needs' (para. 5).[43] Accordingly,
developing countries should be interested in a narrow interpretation
of subsidies, whereas industrialised countries will favour a broad
definition.

Problems with GATT rules on export subsidies emerge, however,
just when it comes to their operationalisation. No accepted legal
definition of export subsidies is available, which implies the need to
decide case by case whether a certain export incentive may be justified or whether it will lead to unjustified distortions of competition.
There is unanimity only to the extent that the exemption of import
duties and indirect taxes will *not* be regarded as subsidy if applied to
imported goods which are physically incorported in export production.[44] This follows directly from the destination principle of taxation. But even further export subsidies can be justified on the
grounds of their economic rationality. Consider the following
argument:[45]

[42] Cf. P. Low, "The Definition of 'Export Subsidies' in GATT", *Journal of World
Trade Law*, vol. 16 (1982), p. 375 ff.; B. Stecher, *Zum Stand der internationalen
Handelspolitik nach der Tokio-Runde*, (Kieler Diskussionsbeiträge 69), Kiel, August
1980

[43] This commitment may be interpreted as the price to be paid by the developing
country signatories for the USA's willingness to apply the material injury test before
levying countervailing duties. Until now the USA was exempted from this obligation
by the so-called "grandfather clause" (cf. Frank, 'Graduation', op. cit., p. 299).

[44] In order not to complicate the matter here the shifting assumptions and the problem of the so-called *taxe occulte* will not be dealt with.

[45] Cf. B. Balassa and M. Sharpston, 'Export Subsidies by Developing Countries:
Issues of Policy', *Commercial Policy Issues*, November 1977, p. 34 ff.

(i) The need for a particular promotion of manufacturing industries in developing countries is generally accepted because of positive external effects generated by manufacturing (e.g. technical progress, human capital formation).

(ii) The optimal policy solution would be the granting of *production* subsidies which correspond to GATT rules. An equal subsidy effect would result for domestic as well as export production without causing distortions.

(iii) For the majority of developing countries this policy approach is, however, not feasible, taking into consideration their low tax-raising capacity.

(iv) The second-best solution combines tariff protection for the manufacturing sector with *export* subsidies which are intended to compensate for the resulting discrimination of export production.

We can thus conclude that combining import tariffs and *export* subsidies (both at the same level) has exactly the same effect (excluding price effects, of course) as applying *production* subsidies. The latter are not prohibited by GATT rules and are used to a considerable degree in industrialised countries.[46] If the need to protect the manufacturing sector in developing countries is accepted in principle, then the discrimination of *export* subsidies under GATT rules can clearly not be justified. This argument cannot, however, be used to justify unreasonably high *levels* of export subsidisation. It is only valid if tariff protection for domestic industries is not excessively high and there is a legitimate expectation that a developing country 'reduces the subsidies to the extent that import controls are lifted'.[47]

This reasoning brings us back to the graduation principle, i.e. to the increasing commitment to liberalising trade in the course of industrialisation. Coming back to the case of South Korea, it is certainly incompatible with this demand that the share of export subsidies in total export value between 1965 and 1978 has not decreased but increased considerably from 12% to 22% (see Table 13). Here again the responsibility of the industrialised countries must not be overlooked. Their trade policy practice increasingly results in putting up quantitative barriers without any link to export subsidies by developing countries. This rising tide of trade barriers

---

[46] Cf. K.H. Jüttemeier and K. Lammers, *Subventionen in the Bundesrepublik Deutschland* (Kieler Diskussionsbeiträge 63/64), Kiel, Nov.· 1979; V.L. Kelkar, 'GATT, Export Subsidies and Developing Countries', *Journal of World Trade Law*, vol. 14 (1980), p. 370.

[47] J.B. Donges, *Aussenwirtschafts- und Entwicklungspolitik*, Berlin 1981, p. 43.

outside the GATT system neither contributes to strengthening the role of GATT, nor does it motivate developing countries to reduce their export subsidies.

(c) *Economic assessment II: On the redundancy of incentives.* Whereas the preceding section concentrated on the *legitimacy* of export incentives, we now turn to their *effectiveness*. It is an altogether open question whether the numerous incentives, particularly fiscal ones, really serve their purpose of inducing export-oriented investment and above all of attracting foreign capital. To the extent that this is not the case, investment incentives would turn out to be redundant, their main effect then being forgone tax revenues.

The simplest approach to an empirical analysis of this issue would be a comparison of investment first before and then some time after the introduction of new incentives. However, in most cases this method is bound to fail because the introduction of new incentives is often only a corollary of a principal reorientation in a country's economic strategy. In these cases the investment climate changes radically, and it will not be feasible to isolate the effects of new incentives from those of the new economic constellation in general.

A second method is to interview a representative sample of businessmen in order to clarify the relative importance of incentive within the whole set of investment motives. Such interviews have been conducted for several countries and sectors.[48] In most cases they lead to the conclusion that incentives are only able to *reinforce* primary investment motives (e.g. low labour costs, high capacity of the domestic market), but not to take their place. In many cases the answer is that generous incentives are regarded as an *indicator* for a host-country's positive attitude towards foreign investment, which again points to the secondary importance of incentives. It is, however, true that incentives in the case of export-oriented redeployment investment are relatively more important than in the case of domestic market-oriented investment.

We may thus conclude that at least some of the privileges could be removed, thus increasing the tax revenues of host-countries without reducing the inflow of foreign capital. Since most incentives are capital-oriented, this would furthermore partly remove the discrimination against labour-intensive production, which would

---

[48] Cf., for example, UNIDO, *Industrial Redeployment Tendencies and Opportunities in the Federal Republic of Germany* (UNIDO Working Papers on Structural Changes no. 5), Vienna, Nov. 1978; S. Tambunlertchai and J. Yamazawa, *Manufactured Export Promotion: The Case of Thailand* (paper presented at the Conference on Trade and Industrial Cooperation in East and Southeast Asia at the Institute of Developing Economies, Tokyo, March 8–9, 1983).

conform to the comparative cost advantages of many Southeast Asian countries, notably all ASEAN countries except Singapore. Eliminating 'ballast' from the heterogeneous incentive systems could also be in the interest of foreign investors who should be more concerned with fundamental economic-political determinants of investment than with an imposing façade of diverse incentives which is repainted every few years.

5. Conclusion

Let us return to the question raised at the beginning of this chapter, viz. whether the relatively weak position of EC countries in the Southeast Asian market may partly be explained by trade policy measures, particularly import barriers. Put another way, is there any empirical evidence that, at least in some Southeast Asian countries, trade policy measures are biased against EC countries? The answer is clearly negative.

After all, there would obviously be no reason for such a policy. The majority of the countries in question, above all Hong Kong, South Korean, Taiwan, Malaysia and Thailand, report a foreign trade surplus in relation to the EC. Furthermore, particularly in the dynamic area of manufactured exports from this region, the EEC market is of special importance. About 14% of total ASEAN exports, but more than 20% of ASEAN manufactured exports, are directed towards the EEC market. On the other hand, as much as 27% of total ASEAN exports, but only a low 8% of ASEAN manufactured exports, go to Japan.

There is, however, continuing discussion of the foreign trade deficit with Japan from which most countries of the region suffer. Consequently, if discriminatory trade policy measures were applied at all, they were directed against Japanese exporters. A study of non-tariff barriers in ASEAN exports shows, for example, that in Indonesia certain imports from Hong Kong. Singapore and Japan are stored in special warehouses which, because of their remote location, give rise to high transportation costs. While this may only be a peripheral phenomenon, the same is less true of recent trade policy measures in Taiwan. Taiwan's policy of restricting certain imports to particular regional sources[49] has recently adopted a clearly anti-Japanese stance. The import ban of February 1982 concerning about 1,500 Japanese consumer goods (including video tape recorders, electronic calculators and black and white TV sets)

---

[49] Cf. A. Gälli, *Taiwan: Economic Facts and Trends*, Munich 1980, p. 137

attracted considerable attention. While most of these import bans were lifted during 1982, the import ban on certain Japanese trucks and buses, however, was prolonged for one further year.[50] In South Korea similar measures were discussed at the end of 1982.

These examples must certainly not be over-stressed. They involve only small actual quantities and have to be interpreted as essentially political gestures. On the other hand, they may demonstrate that the countries of Southeast Asia are interested in eliminating one-sided foreign trade structures. An important objective is the regional diversification of foreign trade. So far the EC countries dispose of a 'comparative' advantage over Japanese competitors, which is not based on cost considerations but is the result of a 'preference for diversification' in economic relations.

The political framework of the Southeast Asian growth market is thus basically favourable to EC countries. Whether EC businessmen will be able to profit from the resulting opportunities will essentially depend on their determination to open up the regional market in the same way as the large Japanese trading houses have successfully done in the past.

---

[50] Cf. *Nachrichten für Aussenhandel*, Jan. 27, 1983 and Feb. 25, 1982; *Japan Times*, Nov. 21, 1982.

Table A.1.   FINANCIAL EXPORT INCENTIVES IN
SOUTHEAST ASIAN COUNTRIES

	Loans/Interest reductions	*Guarantees*
Indonesia	– Refinancing of export credits by state-owned banks at preferential rates	– Government export credit guarantee and export insurance covering 85% of potential losses
Malaysia	– Various MIDF loans for the purchase of land, buildings and machines (up to 2 years' grace period after commencement of production) – Refinancing of export credits by BNM at preferential rates	– Export credit insurance scheme from MECIB covering 85% of potential losses
Philippines	– Firms in export processing zones and those with at least 60% Philippine equity receive preference in the granting of government loans	– Government guarantees for commercial loans to firms registered with the BOI or the EPZA – PEFLGL guarantees for loans to exporters
Singapore	– 5 to 10-year EDB loans with preferential interest rates for approved skill-intensive or technologically desirable projects – MAS will rediscount export bills at preferential rates; same for local exporters by DBS	– Various export credit insurance from ECICS
Thailand	– IFCT loans at low interest rates, 3 to 15 years	
Hong Kong		– Export credit insurance from ECIC covering 90% of potential losses
Korea	– Numerous banks specialising in financing for foreign trade transactions (KDB, KEB, MIB, KDFC, Ex-Im-Bank of Korea) – Refinancing of export credits by commercial banks and Bank of Korea at preferential rates	– Government guarantees for loans to selected industrial sectors
Taiwan	– Medium and long-term financing of exports and imports through Ex-Im-Bank) – Modernization credits from Development Bank	– Export guarantees and insurances from Ex-Im-Bank

Table A.1—Key

Key

BNM	Bank Negara Malaysia
BOI	Board of Investments (Philippines)
DBP	Development Bank of the Philippines
DBS	Development Bank of Singapore
ECIC	Export Credit Insurance Corporation (Hong Kong)
ECICS	Export Credit Insurance Corporation of Singapore
EDB	Economic Development Board (Singapore)
EPZA	Export Processing Zone Authority (Philippines)
IFCT	Industrial Finance Corporation of Thailand
KDB	Korea Development Bank
KDFC	Korea Development Finance Corporation
KEB	Korea Exchange Bank
MAS	Monetary Authority of Singapore
MECIB	Malaysian Export Credit Insurance Berhad
MIB	Medium Industry Bank (Korea)
MIDF	Malaysian Industrial Development Finance Berhad
PEFLGL	Philippine Export and Foreign Loan Guarantee Corporation
PNB	Philippine National Bank

Sources: Investment Incentive Programs . . ., loc. cit.; The ASEAN, Hongkong, South Korea and Taiwan Economies . . ., op. cit; Yen Kyun Wang, 'Export Assistance Regimes in the Pacific Asian Developing Countries – the Cases of South Korea, Taiwan, the Philippines and Thailand', Paper presented at the Pacific Cooperation Task Force Workshop on Trade in Manufactured Goods, Seoul, June 28-30, 1983; 'Asean at a Glance', *Far Eastern Economic Review*, 13.8.1982; Republic of Indonesia, Department of Trade and Cooperatives, *Export Policy*, January 1982.

Table A.2   FISCAL EXPORT INCENTIVES IN
SOUTHEAST ASIAN COUNTRIES

	Tax exemptions and relief	Depreciation allowances	Exemptions/ remittances of customs duties and import taxes
Indonesia	– Exemption from corporate income tax and dividend tax (2–6 years) for investments in priority sectors – Losses incurred during the first six years of operation may be carried over without limit, losses incurred later for up to 4 years	– Investment allowance (20% over 4 years) as alternative to tax holidays in the case of original investment; additionally in the case of further investment – in some cases accelerated depreciation on immovable assets and equipment (10–25%)	– Customs duty and tax exemption for imports of machinery equipment and spare parts; raw materials and components exempted for 2 years, unlimited if used for export production

Table A.2 (*contd.*)

Malaysia	– 2–8 years exemption from company tax, development tax and excess profits tax for pioneer companies (incl. 100% export companies) and for companies receiving Labor Utilisation Relief – 5% of the increase in export sales deductible from taxable income – 200% of export promotion costs deductible from taxable income	– Accelerated depreciation allowance on modernising investments of companies exporting at least 20% of production	– Customs duty and tax exemption for all imports of companies located in Free Trade Zones (export obligation of 80–100%) – Outside Free Trade Zones reduction or exemption if imports are not locally available
Philippines	– Exemption from all non-income taxes up to 20 years (50 years 100%, afterwards on a diminishing percentage) – Tax deduction of organisational and pre-operating expenses – Tax deduction of reinvestment of undistributed profits (25–100%) – Loss carry-over, for up to 6 years, of losses during first 10 years – 200% of costs of labour and local raw materials may be deducted from taxes when used for manufactured exports – Registered export traders may deduct 20% of export sales from taxable income for the first 5 years – 50% of labour training expenses deductible from taxable income – Export producers receive credit on taxes and customs duties that would have accrued on the importation of machinery, equipment and spare parts had they not been purchased locally	– Accelerated depreciation allowance on fixed assets	– Customs duty and tax exemption for imports of machinery, equipment and spare parts up to 7 years after registration – Customs duty and tax exemption for imports of raw materials and components if used for export production

Table A.2 (*contd.*)

	Tax exemptions and relief	Depreciation allowances	Exemptions/ remittances of customs duties and import taxes
Singapore	– Exemption from corporate income tax for 5–10 years for pioneer industries – Reductions of corporate income tax for export firms (export quota 20%; minimum export S$100,000) – Tax reduction on new capital expenditures in excess of S$10 million – Exemption from 40% witholding tax on interest payments on foreign loans for productive equipment – Reduction (from 40 to 20%) of withholding tax on royalties or technical assistance fees paid to non-residents – 200% tax deduction of export promotion expenses in the first 2 years – 10–50% of approved expenditure on fixed assets deductible from taxable income	– Accelerated depreciation allowance (up to 33.3%) on capital expenditure on plant and machinery	– Customs duty and tax exemption for all imports and in industrial production

Thailand	– Exemption from corporate income tax for 3–8 years
	
	– Loss carry over for 5 additional years
	
	– Applying to investment promotion zones:
	  – reduction of up to 90% of business tax up to 5 years
	  – reduction of 50% of corporate income tax for 5 additional years
	
	– 200% of cost of transportation, electricity and water supply may be deducted from taxable income
			– Customs duty and tax exemption (or 50% reduction) for imported machinery
			
			– 90% reduction of customs duty and tax on imported raw materials for 1 year; full exemption if used for export production

Hong Kong	– No specific fiscal incentives. Corporate income tax generally at a low level of 17%	– Various depreciation allowances, e.g. 20% on industrial buildings in the first year	– Generally no customs duties (with few exceptions)

Table A.2 (*contd.*)

Korea	– Applying to foreign investors: Exemption from corporate income tax, dividend tax and tax on technology income for 5 years, reduction of 50% of additional 3 years – Exemption from withholding tax on interest payments on foreign loans	– Accelerated depreciation allowances in selected sectors and for export-intensive firms, e.g. extra 30% on fixed assets if 50% of production exported	– Applying for foreign investors: customs duty and tax exemptions of machinery, equipment and spare parts – Drawback of customs duty and taxes on imported raw materials and components if used for export production (in some cases deferral of payment 4 months)
Taiwan	– Exemption from corporate income tax for 5 years – Exemption from witholding tax on interest payments on foreign loans – 10% reduction of corporate income tax for 2 years if merging of firms leads to export increase – Organisation and pre-operating expenses may be deducted from taxable income – Deduction of reserves for losses from exchange rate adjustment and for losses from export sales – Income tax exemption on licensing and technical service fees (case-by-case decisions)	– Accelerated depreciation allowance (50% reduction of service years)	– Customs duty and tax exemption for imported machinery and equipment. In some sectors import duties may be paid in instalments over 30 months, starting up to 5 years after beginning of production – Customs duty and tax free import of raw materials and components in Export Processing Zones

The fiscal incentives included in the table do not exclusively apply to export-oriented production but partly also to priority sectors in general. As a rule export-oriented firms do however benefit most from the privileges.
Sources: As Table A.1.

B. JAPAN'S TRADE POLICY IN CONTROVERSY

1. *Japan's export offensive after the oil crises*

Japan has coped relatively well and relatively quickly with the problems arising from the second oil crisis, in particular by effectively restricting private and public energy consumption.[1] In addition to these measures, Japan reacted to the challenge by initiating an export offensive aimed at specific market gaps — primarily in the production of sophisticated high-technology industrial goods. Japan concentrated all of its export efforts on producing goods demanding a high degree of skilled work and a solid research and development background. Thus, Japan focussed its exports on only a few product groups, and upset the balance of some vital sectors of the economy in Europe and the USA. German industry once led the world in the field of phototechnology, but Japan has now taken over that lead. Switzerland, that classic clockmaking country, had to look on while Japan slowly destroyed its lead on the world's clock and watch market. For years the USA had a leading position as a producer of radio and television sets. Japan has taken over this position. It can furthermore be expected that the leader on the world's machinery market — at present West Germany — will be hard-pressed by Japanese machinery production.

The market share of imports from Japan into West Germany and the other European countries as of 1984 does not, however, reach extraordinary proportions. Only about 3% of the total imports into EEC countries are of Japanese origin, — and in West Germany they amount to about 4% of the total imports. Expressed in absolute terms, West Germany's imports from Japan in 1984 reached a total of US$ 6.4 billion, in contrast to which exports from West Germany to Japan reached only $ 2.4 billion. The German-Japanese trade deficit thus climbed from $ 2.1 billion in 1979 to $ 4.0 billion in 1984; while in its trade with the EC Japan even reached a surplus of $ 9.3 billion in 1984. In bilateral trade with the USA in the same year, Japan acquired a surplus of $ 33.5 billion.[3] To sum up, Japan's trade relations with Europe and the USA have been characterised in

---

[1] Between 1973 and 1979 the energy consumed per unit of GNP decreased by 22%.
Cf. Neues aus Japan, published by the Japanese Embassy and Consulate General in West Germany, no. 269, July/August 1980, p. 5 ff.
[2] Excluding trade within the EC countries.
[3] Cf. IMF, Direction of Trade Statistics, *Yearbook*, 1985.

recent years by increasing structural imbalances.⁴ In addition, Japan's success in exporting to third markets is worth nothing, particularly since this success is even more pronounced than that of its direct exports to West Germany, the EC and the USA.

Particular attention, however, must be given to the fact that Japanese manufacturers of iron and steel, ships, petrochemical products, office machines and electronic data-processing equipment, information and data transfer devices, optical instruments and cameras, clocks, watches and consumer electronic devices, NC machine tools, motorcycles and motor-vehicles have not simply watched the success in exporting to world markets appear overnight — although the strong devaluation of the Yen since the end of 1978 did give the Japanese export trade a strong impetus. The fact that for twenty years Japan had a trade deficit with Europe should also not be overlooked. In German-Japanese trade, the first surplus (amounting to DM 58 million) for the Japanese after many years was noted in 1969, after which it steadily increased, reaching DM 713 million in 1971 and 1,209 million in 1972.

In any case, major efforts had to be made to increase Japan's ability to meet competition in order for it to gain a better foothold in Europe and the USA. Foreign markets were studied on a well-planned, methodical basis, detailed market studies were carried out, training programmes developed, service nets set up etc. — all this followed long-term advance planning and programmes of export marketing prepared and carried out with great perseverance. The Japan External Trade Research Organisation (JETRO) has set up a virtually perfect system of export promotion with representatives organised in a 'small-grid net' all over the world. Thus it is in a position to relay all relevant market information back to Tokyo without delay.

The prerequisite for all these activities was high-quality, technologically advanced and cost-efficient production. Thus Japanese industry never ceased in its efforts to raise the quality standard of its products by making use of specialised technology, including automation, as well as by introducing forms of organisation suitable for comprehensive quality control by creating Quality Circles and Zero-Defect Campaigns. Since their conception, more than 1 million Quality Circles with more than 8 million members have come into existence. Today there are no more doubts about the exceptionally high standards of Japanese goods. An additional factor to be

---

⁴ The Japanese have frequently emphasised that because of their extraordinary dependence on the import of raw material, linked as it is to current account deficits, it will not be possible to attain a bilateral trade balance.

considered is the Japanese advantage in price competition. Generally the domestic market is first opened up and then Japanese manufacturers frequently try to gain a foothold in East and Southeast Asian markets before subsequently attempting to enter Western markets. This sequence leads to the realisation of scale economies thanks to the application of highly sophisticated modern technology, which in turn gives Japan considerable cost advantages in tough international price competition. From all points of view — cost, quality and technology — Japan's competitive position has consistently improved. Furthermore, Japan's exports have been restructured step by step to concentrate on those sectors of the economy known to be dealing with products traditionally in the hands of the major exporting countries. This has also resulted in extremely high export shares in the favoured fields of production. In 1980 Japan's export share[5] reached 57% in automobiles, 61% in motorcycles, 67% in clocks and watches, 37% in steel, 40% in color televisions, 70% in consumer electronics, 78% in video equipment, 75% in cameras and 64.1% in machinery.[6] In many cases, an increase in market shares was given priority over profitability. Twenty years ago, Japan's share of world automobile production was less than 0.5%. Today one out of every four cars manufactured worldwide is Japanese — the result of its systematic method of opening foreign markets. The percentage of automobile exports in total Japanese exports has risen steadily from 4.4% in 1965 to more than 20% in the early 1980s.

In 1984 the major customers for Japanese exports were the USA (about 35.6%), the EC countries (about 10.9%), the Asian-Pacific developing countries — ASEAN, PR China, Hong Kong, South Korea, Taiwan (about 24.4%) — and the member-states of OPEC (about 9.5%). These figures could easily give the impression that Japan is heavily export-oriented, but this is not the case. In 1983 only approximately 15% of Japan's gross domestic product was exported. As a comparison, the percentage of the GDP exported by West Germany was above 30%. In the face of its heavy dependence on imports, Japan's export ratio must even be considered astonishingly low; however, it has been steadily expanded. In addition, increasing import prices will force Japan to intensify its export efforts. As domestic expansionary forces taper off, Japan can in the future be expected to expand its exports further in order to maintain its domestic economic stability. There is no doubt that Japan fulfils

[5] Cf. *Japan Economic Yearbook 1981/82; The Oriental Economist.*
[6] Export share in 1978 for machines (Ministry of International Trade and Industry).
[7] Cf. OECD, Statistics of Foreign Trade, Series A.

the prerequisite for such an export offensive in its ability effectively to meet competition in international markets.[8]

Japan's export efforts present so great a threat to nations at present facing low growth rates, decreased utilisation of capacity and high unemployment as well as a high balance of payments deficit, that Western industrial nations may find protectionism to be the only choice open to them. This would indeed not be in the best interests of an open world economy, a vital interest for both West Germany and Japan. The bilateral agreements already in effect can certainly be considered protectionist misdevelopments, e.g. the request of Brussels for the Japanese government to limit the export of 'sensitive' products (automobiles, colour television sets and tubes, certain machine tools) to Europe, or the so-called 'voluntary restraint' of Japanese automobile exports to the USA as a reaction to pressure exerted by the US government. If as a result of these and similar measures Japan increases its exports to those countries which still keep their borders open — seemingly as compensation for the cutbacks caused by voluntary restraint — resistance to protectionism may collapse there too. In addition, no matter how great the protectionist pressure brought to bear on external economic relations with Japan, it will remain virtually without effect in third markets — precisely where Japan is causing exports from its competitors such as West Germany the most trouble.

2. *The reproach of social dumping*

Japan is frequently accused of 'social dumping'. Voices can be heard calling it the land of low wages and salaries, with relatively low social welfare expenditure, long working hours, short vacations and a social security system which is not geared to protect the interests of the individual worker.

As a rule, Japan's wage increases are linked to production growth, although the principle of lifelong employment does strongly influence wages policy. But the fact that since 1968 the rate of wage increases in manufacturing industry has regularly exceeded that of productivity increases deserves special attention.[9] The sometimes considerable difference between wage and productivity

---

[8] A report compiled by the European Management Forum in Geneva, Switzerland, in 1981 on international competitiveness refers to Japan as the absolute leader of the field of twenty-one countries.
[9] Cf. *Labour and the Economy Illustrated* (Japanese Industrial Relations Series, Japan Institute of Labour), Tokyo 1980, p. 17.

increases levelled out after 1975; nevertheless, in 1975–80 the average annual productivity increase was 7.4%, while wages increased by 8.5%. Comparison with other countries shows that between 1970 and 1977 the average annual wage increase was 16.8% in Japan, 7.5% in the USA, 9.7% in West Germany, 15.9% in Britain, and 15.4% in France (1972–7). Thus it was Japan that had the greatest growth rate for the period in question.[10] By the mid-1970s, Japan had succeeded in reaching the wage level of the UK, and by the end of the decade it had also eliminated the lead of the French wage-level. In contrast, the absolute difference between labour costs in Japan and in West Germany is still considerable — due less to the level of hourly wages than to incidental labour costs (i.e. employers' share of social insurance, voluntary social security benefits etc.). A study by the Institut der deutschen Wirtschaft[11] shows that in 1979 the average hourly wage of a worker in manufacturing industry in West Germany was DM 12.46, while that of a worker in Japan was DM 9.69. Incidental labour costs in West Germany were DM 8.68, while in Japan, they were only DM 2.08. Thus total labour costs in West Germany amounted to DM 21.14 and in Japan to DM 11.77. However, between 1970 and 1979 hourly labour costs in West Germany rose by 124.4%, while in Japan they rose by nearly 200%.[12]

While most statements about labour costs in West Germany refer to actually paid man-hours, labour costs in Japan are based on actual hours worked. Thus the comparison of labour costs in Japan with those in West Germany is further complicated by the great length of paid annual leave and holidays and by the greater incidence of sick leave in West Germany.

The Japanese Ministry of Labour has prepared a comparative study of international labour costs in which statistical data from other countries is adapted to the Japanese system by conversion to a paid man-hour basis. According to the results of this study, the cost of labour in West Germany for an actual hour worked was 51.8% above the average Japanese level.[13] At any rate, up till now Japan has been in a position — thanks to its wage policy — to maintain cost advantages over West Germany — even if it is no longer pos-

---

[10] Cf. *Wages and Hours of work* (Japanese Industrial Relations Series, Japan Institute of Labour), Series 3, 1979, p. 6.
[11] Cf. 'IWD' Information Service of the German Business Institute, Cologne, no. 26, June 26, 1980, p. 5.
[12] The German Business Institute (Institut der deutschen Wirtschaft) in Cologne has calculated an increase for the same period of 262.3% based on the national currencies. Percentages given in the body of the text refer to the increase of labour costs per hour based on the West German Mark. Cf. *IW-Trends*, 3/80, July 18, 1980, p. 52.
[13] Cf. *Wages in Japan*, Ministry of Foreign Affairs, Japan, June 1979.

sible to talk of a 'low-wage country'. Today we note that Japan's countinuing process of adjusting to the European-American wage level is still proceeding rapidly. And — as Helmut Laumer has noted — the Japanese wage system, strongly attuned as it is to the seniority of employees, will further emphasise this tendency in the future. The demographic structure indicates that in the coming decade the percentage of older workers will increase considerably in number and thus contribute to a disproportionate wage increase.[14] Meanwhile, in East and Southeast Asia, Japan is known as a high-wage country.

Thanks to the prevailing regulations concerning hours of work, time off and vacations, Japan has a further competitive advantage. According to statistics presented by the Japanese Minstry of Labour, Japanese wage-earners worked an average of 2,132 hours in 1980, while the average German wage-earner put in only 1,746 hours.[15] However, also in this area, changes are becoming more and more noticeable. The data published by the Ministry of Labour clearly show that from 1969 the number of actual hours worked per week, month and year, as well as the number of workdays, has dropped steadily. In 1969 the average number of days worked per year was 273.6; by 1979 it had dropped to 255.6.[16] The vast majority of large enterprises has switched to the 5-day working week, followed in part by small and medium-sized firms. The Japanese Institute of Labour reports that as early as 1978 44.7% of all firms had introduced the 5-day week. It is standard in some cases, while others have introduced it more slowly, sometimes limiting it to one 5-day week per month. Nevertheless, 72.3% of all wage-earners benefit from the introduction of this form of shorter working hours.[17]

Standard practice concerning paid annual leave in Japan is still very different from present regulations in Europe and the USA, although certain aspects have become similar to those in West Germany. In Japan, however, the accrued paid annual leave is frequently not taken — or only taken in part. Toyota, for example, offers its employees annual leave of between 12 and 20 days according to length

[14] Cf. W. Laumer, 'Japans Wirtschaft in den achtziger Jahren — Perspektiven, Chancen, Risiken' in *Ifo-Dokumentation*, Munich 1981, p. 91.
[15] The order of magnitude and tendency of these figures is confirmed by those for 1978 published by the Sohyo labour organisation for 1978. Cf. *Sohyo News*, no. 364, 15 March, 1981, p. 84.
[16] Cf. *Economic Survey of Japan 1980/81*, Economic Planning Agency, Japanese Government, Tokyo 1981, p. 259. On the question of the reduction of working hours in Japan cf. also S. Nishikawa and H. Shimada, 'Employment and Unemployment: 1970 to 1975', *Keio Business Review*, no. 13, 1974, p. 43 ff.
[17] Cf. *Labour and The Economy Illustrated*, p. 19.

of employment with the firm. However, only 65% of all paid leave accrued is actually used. But here too a change is in sight; Toyota is now encouraging its employees not to take single days off but to take longer periods — as in other industrial nations.[18]

If Japan were to adapt its practices with regard to working hours, paid annual leave and holidays (International Harmonisation of Work and Leave Conditions),[19] this would in reality mean: lowering permissible overtime, extending annual leave and requiring that it be taken in full, abolishing wage differences between men and women, making the five-day week standard practice, and standardising wages in all industries — small, medium and large. To demand that all these changes should be implemented immediately would, of course, be unrealistic, and not even in Europe could a similar programme be expected to find general acceptance. Moreover, the justification for such a programme would be debatable — for who possesses the objectively correct and internationally acceptable norms for social benefits? On the contrary, should it not be thought of as arrogant to declare one's own opinion of the suitable extent and form of social benefits valid and binding on other nations — regardless of differences in culture and tradition? Furthermore, it should not be overlooked that many Japanese firms — at least those within the framework of the "lifelong employment" system — offer numerous voluntary social benefits.

The fact that the Japanese social security system is less sophisticated than that of most European nations contributes further to competitive advantages. Statistical surveys of member-countries made by the OECD show that in 1978 the percentage of the GNP borne by employers' contributions to social insurance was 11.8% in France, 6.84% in West Germany, 9.43% in Italy, 7.9% in the Netherlands, and 13.16% in Sweden. The corresponding percentage of Japan's GNP was only 3.71%.[20]

Japan will certainly not be able to avoid giving more serious attention to the problems of social security in the future than hitherto. The Japanese public is becoming increasingly concerned with the problem of the aged — in particular, securing their support, accommodation, and medical treatment. Kazuo Okochi, in partic-

---

[18] Cf. *Jetro-Informationen*, March 1981.
[19] Cf. ibid. Here it is stated, for example: 'In December of last year a meeting of senior management of Japanese and European automobile companies took place, in the course of which strong criticisms were expressed from the side of the Europeans concerning the long Japanese working week and the high rate of overtime worked by the average Japanese labourer.'
[20] Cf. *Revenues Statistics of OECD Member Countries 1965–1980*, OECD, Paris 1981, p. 84. Cf. also H. Laumer, 'Japans Wirtschaft . . . .', op. cit., p. 23.

ular, has for years been actively supporting programmes to improve the living and employment conditions of senior citizens in Japan. Incomes drop drastically after retirement age — usually 55. Temporary employment for the retired is frequently accepted, and usually underpaid; but it is becoming more difficult to find. Thus a social descent generally begins at retirement age.[21]

A satisfactory solution to the problem of pension schemes is thus of immediate urgency — no matter whether the system of severance pay on leaving employment is retained, modified or abandoned.[22] The age pyramid of the Japanese population is also rapidly changing, and with this change both the social insurance expenditures from the various pension funds and government subsidies — so-called transfer payments — will have to be increased.[23] In 1978 the percentage of the entire Japanese population aged 65 and over was 8.6% (in West Germany, 15.2%). Thus it is not surprising that expenditure on pension schemes — an important item of transfer payments — differs greatly between the two countries. While the transfer quota (= the share of transfer expenditures in the national income) reached 21.9% in West Germany in 1978, Japan's transfer quota for the same year reached only 12.3% — primarily due to the more favourable. age pyramid.[24] However, because of increasing life expectancy while at the same time birth rates are falling, the age pyramid of Japanese society is becoming more and more top-heavy. Statistics indicate that in twenty years pensioners will account for approximately 15% of the population.[25]

In 1979 provision for a raise in the transfer quota so as to adjust to increasing social insurance needs in face of the changing population structure was made in the New Economic and Social 7-Year-Plan of the Japanese government. By 1985 the transfer quota will be

---

[21] Cf. K. Okochi, 'Lebensumstände und Beschäftigungsverhältnisse älterer Leute in Japan' in W. Kraus (ed.), *Humanisierung der Arbeitswelt. Gestaltungsmöglichkeiten in Japan und in der Bundesrepublik Deutschland*, Tübingen 1979, p. 285 ff. The trend gradually to raise retirement age to 60 was intensified by an initiative in that direction taken by the large steel companies and private banks.

[22] About 90% of those businesses employing more than 30 employees offer severance pay. According to official Japanese data the average sum paid on retirement is 3,288 million yen (*Neues aus Japan*, no. 267, March/April 1980, p. 5). According to a publication of the Ministry of Foreign Affairs, however, severance pay reached a sum between 6 and 13 million yen. Cf. *Löhne in Japan*, p. 13

[23] Cf. S. Lörcher, 'Sozialversicherung, Altersversorgung, Rentensystem' in M. Pohl (ed.), *Japan 1979/80. Politik und Wirtschaft*, Institute of Asian Affairs, Hamburg 1980, p. 81 ff.

[24] Cf. New Economic and Social Seven-Year-Plan (Summary), p. 50

[25] Cf. H. Shimada, *The Japanese Employment System* (Japanese Industrial Relations Series, Japan Institute of Labour), 1980, p. 32.

increased to 14.5%.[26] In general, Japan must prepare for heavy social burdens. In the draft budget of 1981 the government committed 8,337 billion yen for social insurance purposes: this sum, equal to US$ 40.2 billion, accounts for 18.9% of the ordinary budget. Circumstances will not allow social security expenses to remain at this level for very long. Furthermore, the relatively low public sector share will rise as measured by the share of government spending of the GDP. In 1979 this share reached 31.5% (in West Germany 46.4%).[27] This goes hand in hand with a relatively low tax quota. In 1980 the share of tax revenues in the GDP amounted to 17.1%, in contrast to 24.4% in West Germany. In the same year the percentage of the GDP taken up by taxes and social security contributions reached 24.6% (in West Germany 38.4%).[28]

The Japanese admit that the necessary expansion of social infrastructure e.g. housing, schools and hospitals — has been neglected in the past decades, but thanks to their thoroughness and speed they will certainly remedy the situation before long. The Japanese Government's New Economic and Social 7-Year-Plan provides for an increase in the taxload ratio (share of tax burden in national income) from 19.9% in 1978 to 26.5 in 1985.[29] Nevertheless, Japan will hardly find it necessary to adopt a 'European' system of social security — and especially not a system that has been overstrained by too little adaptation to changes in basic data — and thus is no longer in a position to meet demand with the limited resources at hand.[30] Japan will have to construct and expand its own system in its own way. The scope of the social security system represents an inherently Japanese domestic problem, closely linked to East Asian culture and Japanese history, and to the objective social security needs of the Japanese nation, as well as to the selected and preferred institutions offering social services. The solidarity of the family unit continues to be firmly anchored in Japanese society, and this solidarity will continue to make an important contribution to ensuring a steady living standard.[31] The Japanese tendency to grasp private initiatives in order to ensure the standard of living is a strong

---

[26] Cf. *New Economic and Social Seven-Year-Plan* (Summary), p. 20.
[27] Cf. *The OECD Economic Outlook*, 1979.
[28] Cf. West German Federal Ministry of Finance, *Information service on financial policies abroad*, no. 1/1982, March 5, 1982, p. 16.
[29] Cf. *New Economic and Social Seven-Year-Plan* (Summary), p. 50.
[30] Cf. R. Vondran, 'Japanische Wirtschaftserfolge — Schicksal oder Motivation für die übrigen Industriestaaten?', *Ifo-Dokumentation Japan*, p. 4.
[31] According to an official Japanese publication, a comparison of the average insurance sum *per capita* of the population in 1977 was for Japan DM 30,962, and for West Germany DM 9,058. Cf. *Neues aus Japan*, no. 267, March/April 1980, p. 5.

one, as is indicated by the extraordinarily high savings-income ratio and the amount of capital deposited with private life insurance companies. The Economic and Social 7-Year-Plan of 1979 called for the creation of a 'New Japanese Style Welfare Society', a society which should make use of the creative strength of the free market system, of the initiative of the individual, and the solidarity of the community. The Plan explicitly mentioned that public and private efforts will have to be combined to create that 'welfare society'.[32]

There are many and varied reasons for Japanese competitive strength. The main reasons, however, are not the relatively low wage-level or even wage and social dumping. The essential factors are rather the intellectual attitudes of the Japanese and their influence on technological development, and on the increase in productivity as well as the continuing improvement of economic performance and efficiency. Already two decades ago, Karl Hax researched the reproach of unfair foreign trade competition by means of social dumping, and emphasised Japan's 'natural cost advantage', which was also to be found 'in other nations in a different form, e.g. easily accessible resources'.[33] In view of the great changes in Japanese society in the 1960's and 1970s the reproach of wage or social dumping seems today to be completely unjustified.

3. *Access to the Japanese market*

The growing export surpluses in trade with Europe and the USA have caused the Japanese to demand that the balance of trade must be considered at the global rather than at the bilateral level, and that 'invisible items' be considered in judging trade surpluses. Thus the Japanese ambassador to West Germany — speaking at an event sponsored by the German-Japanese Society in Bremen on 19 February 1981 — strongly emphasised: 'In trade between Japan and the EC the former was able to register a surplus of US$ 5.1 billion — at the same time, however, coping with a deficit of US$ 3.4 billion from invisibles.' He went on to say that the Japanese government remains firmly of the opinion that 'trade between Japan and the EC can and should be improved by an increase of exports from the EC to Japan'.[34] European and American exporters emphasise time and

---

[32] Cf. *New Economic and Social Seven Year Plan* (Summary), p. 9 ff.

[33] K. Hax, *Japan. Wirtschaftmacht des Fernen Ostens. Ein Beitrag zur Analyse des wirtschaftlichen Wachstums*, Cologne/Opladen 1961, p. 129.

[34] From an address of the Japanese Ambassador Bunroku Yoshino on 19 February 1981 on the occasion of the founding of the German-Japanese Society in Bremen. Published in the series '*Speeches of the Japanese Ambassador to the Federal Republic of Germany Bunroku Yoshino 1979–1981.*'

again that such statements are of little help if Tokyo is not willing at the same time to take drastic measures to open its domestic market. Statistics on Japanese imports leave no doubt that the item 'imported finished products' is greatly underdeveloped for such a highly industrialised nation. Once again, the comparison with Western markets: the share of imported finished products in total imports in 1980 was 54.1% in the USA, 58.3% in West Germany, 67.3% in Britain , 57.9% in France, and 49.7% in Italy but in the same year it stood at only 22.9% in Japan.[35]

In the accusations directed at Japan by the EC during the GATT proceedings initiated according to Article XXIII on April 7, 1982, the European Commission was able to base its case on the fact — among others — that in 1980 the *per capita* import of manufactures reached $547 in the USA, $ 796 in the EC, and only $233 in Japan. As was to be expected, the trade deficits of West Germany and the EC have increased from one year to the next. In 1984, EC exports to Japan did not even cover 50% of the EC imports from Japan. The Japanese government has from time to time implemented emergency import programmes as a reaction to pressure from abroad. However, this form of import expansion is hardly suited to help alleviate the present situation, since Japan has used this practice either to expand its own stores of raw materials or to import finished products which it is incapable of producing itself (e.g. passenger jets for international flights), with no change of its one-sided import structure whatsoever.

Japan has since removed most of its tariff barriers to European finished products in the framework of GATT. As early as 1976, Japanese import tariffs were on average lower than those of the EC and the USA. On April 1, 1980, Japan of its own free will anticipated the agreements of the Tokyo Round by lowering import tariffs by as much as 25%. A further anticipatory reduction of tariffs, covering some 1,650 items , followed on April 1, 1982. In late May 1982, 215 tariff reductions including the elimination of individual tariffs, to come into effect on April 1, 1983, were made known. Japan can be justly proud of its place among those industrialised nations with the lowest tariff rates — and this today and not in 1987 when all the tariff reductions agreed upon in the Tokyo Round will have become effective. Japan can further defend its trade policy by

---

[35] Cf. OECD, Statistics of Foreign Trade, Series A, March 1982. To what extent the low Japanese rate of import of manufactures has been induced by economic policy measures (hidden protectionism) or can be explained by Japan's specific resource endowment, is a subject of controversy. G.R. Saxonhouse takes the latter viewpoint in his article 'The Micro- and Macroeconomics of Foreign Sales to Japan' in Cline, *Trade Policy*, p. 259 ff.

referring to its quantitative import restrictions on fewer items than the restrictions introduced by the EC countries. In early 1982 Japan had 27 import restrictions, 22 import quotas for agricultural products, and 5 import quotas for non-agricultural products. On the other hand, the trade policy of individual EC member-countries — some of which show great generosity in setting their own quotas — does not at present set a particularly good example of free market access. France and Italy still refuse to abolish their import restrictions — most specifically those on Japanese automobiles; France has set down that the number of imported automobiles from Japan is not to exceed 3% of the total number of car registrations in any given year, but it is a known fact that some Japanese freighters transporting cars to France were not unloaded at their port of destination. Italy's import restrictions have succeeded in limiting the annual import to 2,000 automobiles. France has set import quotas for 46 products, 27 of which are from the industrial sector. In addition, a total of nine EC countries have set up discriminatory import restrictions specifically aimed at a limitation of imports from Japan, and not of a general nature.[36] The USA demands that Japan abolish its import quota for agricultural products, while the USA itself uses the quota system to protect domestic agricultural commodities — indeed to protect some of the same products as the Japanese protect. Fair play would seem to demand that only then should Japan be expected gradually to abolish its protection of agricultural commodities when it finds it can expect similar readiness from other nations. As a whole, this applies to the trade policy of the three largest and most important world trade partners — which instead of blaming each other, should make every effort to maintain and reinforce the basis of multilateral trade. Reciprocity considerations — for example those that have emerged in the USA *vis-à-vis* Japan — undermine GATT's Most-Favoured-Nation principle, and endanger the trade system built up with so much effort and at present in such a precarious position (see Chapter I).

In this context reference should be made to one of the basic principles of Japanese trade policy. In the USA and in Europe, it is common practice to place increasingly uncompetitive sectors of domestic industry threatened by imports under the protection of a strong tariff policy or of market regulations, which are already virtually a permanent matter of course for the textile industry, and more recently for the steel, ship building and automobile industries as well. Japan on the other hand does not offer its fully expanded

36 Cf. on this subject *Japanwirtschaft*, no. 3/82, May 1982, published by the Deutsch-Japanisches Wirtschaftsförderungsbüro, p. 11 ff.

industries this kind of protection, whereas it does take steps to protect emerging industries such as the computer and information industries. The extent of this protection, however, reaches its limit when, as a result of state support, private initiative for further technological development can be expected to taper off.[37]

Now that the *de jure* liberalisation of foreign trade has taken place, mention must rightly be made of those non-tariff barriers to trade which still handicap exports to Japan. The following three areas are frequent causes of objections:

(*a*). Import testing procedures with their standards, ordinances, export regulations, tests, details of customs clearance and licensing procedures;

(*b*) The Japanese distribution system; and

(*c*) The public procurement policy.[38]

In 1980 Japan accepted the Standardisation Agreement set up by the Tokyo Round and revised the Law of Industrial Standardisation. However, it has been maintained that Japan has not complied sufficiently with those obligations. In accordance with the Amendment to the Japanese Law of Foreign Exchange and Trade Control, which went into effect on December 1, 1980, there is in principle a free flow of capital. In addition, this new Japanese Foreign Trade Law has greatly simplified the formalities necessary for financial transactions based on the merchandise and service trade. However, the Law contains a considerable number of safeguard clauses, and only time will tell how they will be applied. Despite the progress being made, Japan's import testing and licensing procedures are still open to widespread criticism, especially since they are sometimes more restrictive than tariff barriers and import quotas. For example, import authorisation is often made dependent not only on presentation of production descriptions and operating instructions but also on exact construction drawings, diagrams of switches, data concerning the origin of supplied inputs (as for example in the case of medical apparatus), and — last but not least — the description of production processes; in the face of all this, it is understandable that many firms find exporting to Japan too dangerous to their own competitive positions and too great a risk to their own technological

---

[37] Cf. J. Abbeglen and A. Etori, 'Japans Technologie heute', *Spektrum der Wissenschaft*, no. 4/1981, p.12.
[38] Cf. *Administrative Importbeschränkungen in Japan. Zur Wirkung tarifärer und nichttarifärer Handelshemmnisse*, published by the Bundesverband der Deutschen Industrie e.V., March 1982, p. 10.

advantage.[39] And complaints are still heard concerning Japan's technical testing procedures — not only do they severely limit imports, but some of these tests are considered unique in the industrialised world, and, even worse, individual prefectures vary in their interpretation and application of these testing procedures.[40] Examination and licensing procedures which have been set up and agreed upon internationally are frequently not accepted as valid. Irritation is caused by difficult legal texts and export regulations, as well as too little knowledge and circulation of the legal bases for these regulations. And this is further compounded by the extremely complicated, lengthy and costly logistics of the customs procedure. In the BDI (Bundesverband Deutscher Industrie) document "Administrative Import Restrictions in Japan", attention is drawn to the documents necessary for recognition of the CIF-Value per product catgory: invoiced purchases, calculation of the acquisition price as shown by freight invoices, insurance documents etc., sales invoices, and cost components of the profit and loss statement per product group. The conclusion is correctly drawn that "due to these regulations foreign firms [are] forced to present a virtually 'crystal-clear' picture of their sequence of operations, including the structure of operating results. Since as a rule the licenses have to be renewed every two years, interested Japanese circles are permanently provided with the most up-to-date information about their competitors.'[41] Furthermore, by linking import licenses for individual imported goods to a Japanese importer, manufacturers from abroad are not only dependent on a Japanese partner but must also avoid any change — since in the latter case the import licensing processes have to be repeated.

To be fair, discussion of non-tariff barriers to trade should take account of the fact that Japanese health awareness makes highly specific demands of domestic production as well as of imported goods — demands which are simply non-existent in many exporting countries. In Japan traditional medicines and herbal medicines are becoming increasingly popular, and food preservatives are forbidden in principle. Japanese regulations on the permissible level of emission of exhaust fumes make the importation of cars from those

---

[39] Cf. ibid., p. 18 ff. The report refers to the clinical testing of all medical equipment, which takes from 3 months up to 2 years. Only after the test report is completed is a decision made concerning the import licensing.
[40] Cf. ibid., p. 6 ff.
[41] Cf. ibid., p. 11 ff. In the documentation given by the Bundesverband der deutschen Industrie (BDI) it is further stated: 'This is a procedure which, within the industrialised countries, may be considered unique' (p. 12).

countries with less stringent emission norms difficult.[42] In the mean time, the regulations concerning emission control of imported auto-mobiles are being relaxed somewhat. Generally, however, these regulations are no more discriminatory as trade barriers than the German Pure Beer Regulation (*Reinheitsgebot*), linked as it is to the ban on foreign beer containing artificial preservatives and stabilising additives. But since the EC Commission does not con-sider the Pure Beer Regulation to be consumer-protective but rather an inadmissible restriction on the import of foreign beer and thus a violation of Article 30 of the Rome Treaty, and has even opened legal proceedings at the European Court of Law, it remains to be seen if the bureaucrats in Brussels will take a similar stance against consumer habits, laws relating to food processing and distribution and environmental protection in Japan as an importing country. There is no reason why so-called 'harmonisation' of food hygiene and consumer protection laws should always have to mean adapta-tion to the lowest common denominator, — nor why this dubious procedure should be considered as the 'abolition of trade barriers'.

The Japanese system of distribution of goods is certainly another major trade barrier. More than 350,000 wholesale firms occupy an extraordinarily strong position in all aspects of the Japanese market due to the important roles they play in financial, employment, transport and advisory capacities, and Europeans and Americans find it difficult to grasp the complicated channels of distribution and trade practices. In addition, trade is concentrated on relatively few major firms: a large portion of the Japanese foreign trade is handled by Sogo Shosha — nine giant world trading firms (Mitsu-bishi Corporation; Mitsui & Co. Ltd.; C. Itoh & Co., Ltd.; Marubeni Corporation; Sumitomo Corporation; Nissho-Iwai, Co. Ltd.; Toyo Menka Kaisha, Ltd.; Kanumatsu-Gosho Ltd.; Nichimen Co., Ltd.). They identify and create markets, finance deliveries, find new sources of raw materials and organise international investment projects and imports.[43] In the fiscal year 1979 these turn-over giants were responsible for 42% of total exports and 56.5% of total imports.[44] Presumably they give preference to orders from

---

[42] To be sure, we find the methods of the 'Type Designation Test' (which includes an entire series of individual tests) as well as the 'Type Notification Test' discriminatory — regardless of any proof of the fulfillment of Japanese regulations on exhaust gases.

[43] Cf. 'Schaltstellen der Wirtschaft und des Welthandels' in *Wirtschaftspartner Japan*, published by the Institute of Asian Affairs, Hamburg, and the German Chamber of Industry and Commerce in Japan, Hamburg, 1980.

[44] Cf. H. Laumer, 'Sogo shosha: Japans multinationale Handelsunternehmen — weltweit ohne Pendant', *Ifo-Studien*, no. 3/4, 1981, p. 155.

domestic producers, particularly when these producers are members of the same industrial group as themselves; the chance that they will put a product on the domestic market against the will of Japanese firms with which they have a business relationship is virtually nil. Furthermore, foreign importers find the system of Japanese distribution complicated and time-consuming, and in the case of textiles and processed foods extremely lengthy as well. However, when measuring the complicated and over-staffed Japanese distribution system against the traditional European system, one must not overlook that this very same system also has to play a role in securing social welfare. It has evolved over decades, and was no more created as a barrier to trade than was the Japanese language, which is still by far the most effective non-tariff barrier to trade of all. It is indeed understandable that Japan for reasons of social policy, has no desire for abrupt changes in this field, as Japanese experts themselves have often and clearly stated. The well-functioning interplay of state and economy in Japan has also evolved over decades: in West Germany it is either praised for its efficiency or branded with the slogan 'Protectionism of the Third Dimension'.[45] Critics tend to overlook the history of this traditionally close cooperation in which the government in former times exerted even greater influence: it had already been in existence long before Japan began to emerge from its complete isolation and participate in the international division of labour.

As regards the awarding of public contracts to foreign exporters, Japan ratified the GATT Agreement on Government Procurement even before 1981. But let there be no illusions about the actual reduction of import restrictive measures in this sector. The same is true of all other industrial nations as well as Japan; the great deeds of the Japanese are missing — but so also are the great and noble examples set by those who enjoy the role of accuser. For example, in March 1982 AT&T's most recent request for bids for fibreglass cabling between Washington and New York led to the following result: the leading Japanese computer firm Fujitsu presented the lowest bid (US$ 56.5 million), yet the contract was awarded to the lowest American bidder, Western Electric, whose offer was US$ 75 million.[46]

---

[45] In contrast to Count Lambsdorff, Klaus von Dohnanyi is full of admiration for the openminded cooperation of government and business. Cf. K.von Dohnanyi, *Japanische Strategien und das deutsche Führungsdefizit*, Munich 1969, p. 36, pp. 89 and 90.
[46] Cf. *Japaninfo*, no. 6, 'Aktualität in Japan: Deutscher Dienst für Politik, Wirtschaft und Gesellschaft', March 22, 1982, p. 2 ff.

In late January 1982 the Japanese government agreed on a programme of 67 separate measures for the reduction of non-tariff
barriers to trade, which were taken from a list of altogether 99
complaints from the EC and the USA.[47] There is still much to be
done, however, concerning non-tariff barriers to trade if foreign
goods are to be given the same chances on the Japanese market that
Japanese goods enjoy on foreign markets. On the other hand, there
is no denying that Japan's trade barriers often serve as an excuse for
other nations. The West German and US Chambers of Commerce in
Tokyo have been of the opinion that non-tariff barriers often serve
only to justify the inactivity of their own national industry.[48]
Bernhard Grossmann of the Deutsche Industrie- and Handelskammer (German Chamber of Industry and Commerce) in Japan
has stated that the major non-tariff barrier to trade for German
exporters to Japan was their own misplaced attitude that the Japanese would adapt their market to German expectations.[49] In any
case, European and US firms have not gone to the same efforts to
gain a foothold on the Japanese market that we have come to expect
from Japanese firms exporting to Europe and the USA. Our exporters
have occupied themselves for too long predominantly with European
and North American markets while neglecting Japan, the second
largest market in the non-communist world, and overlooking market
niches. This of course was largely due to the long-term protectionist
import policy of the Japanese. Furthermore, the great distances to
East Asia, language and communication barriers, previously
unknown product and marketing problems, and setbacks in gaining
access to the Japanese market, all contributed to this lack of enthu-
siasm. The Japanese government has now found it advisable to create
an interministerial court of arbitration for complaints by foreign
exporters on the difficulty of access to the Japanese market. A pro-
visional response to any complaint has to be made within 10 days of
receipt, and the definitive response is to be given without delay.
Only time will tell if and how this institution will be able to settle
differences of opinion and especially whether it will answer satisfac-
torily accusations of the 'splendid isolation' of the Japanese market.

The Japanese government seems to be constantly facing the
expectation that it should present an extensive package of new liberalisation measures to open its market further. But even if the

---

[47] In nine cases the Japanese government did not feel it was in a position to implement
changes at that time. Fifteen cases were found to be the result of misunderstandings,
and in eight cases the Japanese government refused to undertake any changes.
[48] Cf. *Süddeutsche Zeitung*, Aug. 18, 1981.
[49] Cf. *Handelsblatt*, July 9, 1980.

Japanese should make tremendous concessions, e.g. by prohibiting those agreements between Japanese firms which would have a detrimental effect on imports (as, for example, in the case of Thyssen Nippon), the EC countries and the USA cannot expect to be presented with export successes 'on a plate'. Lasting success in Japanese markets can only be expected when foreign exporters make an effort to understand the realities of Japanese economic life, as well as the Japanese language, culture, thought patterns and living standards. Many export commitments to Japan have been doomed to failure because of arrogance as well as the absence of effort to utilise all available methods and possibilities of information in order to gain insight into the Japanese ways of decision-making, their distribution channels and their traditional trade practices. Little access can be gained to the demanding Japanese market in the future without careful attention being paid to the needs and preferences of the Japanese. Since the Japanese market is willing to accept only highly specialised goods of excellent quality, high demands are placed on the packaging and presentation of consumer goods, whereas in the case of industrial goods, e.g. machinery, first-class service is expected.[50] In many cases there has been a lack of presence in Japan, as well as a lack of careful planning, of suitable product and marketing concepts, and of a longer-term corporate strategy. However, there are sufficient examples of Europeans and Americans — with the help of business acumen and experience in Asia — succeeding in thrusting through to the basic problems of Japan's 'insider society' and become virtually insiders themselves. With this background they have also found a Japan that is as astonishingly open as it is easy to grasp, a Japan that will and can hide nothing. In addition, discussion concerning increasing imports by Japan must focus more explicitly than previously on the fact that increases in imports are as a matter of principle only possible via a healthy Japanese domestic market.

The situation between Japan and the EC would probably also improve, and tensions would subside if Japan could decide to extend its own production in Europe. First rudimentary efforts have been made in the form of joint ventures, but these are by no means sufficient to relieve the countries in Europe noticeably of Japanese export pressure. Japanese investment in West Germany today is

---

[50] In order to facilitate the access of small- and medium-scale German firms to the Japanese market, the Institute of Market Advisory Studies was opened in the German Chamber of Industry and Commerce in Japan in September 1979 with the specific task of advising German firms on questions of access to the market, setting up business contacts, and identifying concrete sales opportunities.

already 3½ times that of the German investment in Japan. However, its purpose is to be found less in production than in distribution, service activities and the opening of new markets. Only 17% of direct Japanese investment in the EC falls in the field of production itself, and in West Germany the percentage is even below this average.

4. *The Yen exchange rate and current account balance*

In the course of the second oil crisis Japan had to cope with an extraordinary move into deficit of its current account balance which in 1979 reached US$ 8.7 billion and in the next year climbed as high as $ 10.8 billion. From the end of October 1978 until April 1980, the yen lost about 33% of its value against the US dollar, although the Japanese Central Bank strongly intervened against too heavy a devaluation by inputting large amounts of foreign exchange reserves.[51] However, the Central Bank did not resist the pressure to devaluate the yen, by means of which Japanese products could strongly reinforce their competitive position on the world market. Producers saw themselves more or less forced to increase their export efforts by the devaluation of the yen and the restrictive financial policy, while the real import of goods and services quickly diminished in the face of rising import prices.[52] Thus one of the basic prerequisites for a reinforcement of the yen was created. As early as mid-1980 the trade and current account balance moved strongly into surplus — which was also expressed in the reverse development of the yen exchange rate. The rise of the dollar in 1981, however, did not spare the yen, which was once again devalued against the dollar.

In face of the strong expansion in Japanese exports, there seemed justification in the question whether there was not a fundamental undervaluation of the yen beyond all the short- and medium-term exchange rate fluctuations. This could at least have partly explained the tremendous Japanese trade surplus *vis-à-vis* Europe and the USA. In particular, Japan has been accused of excessive exchange-rate manipulation in an effort to keep the yen rate artifically low to increase exports, limit imports, and produce current account surpluses at the expense of other countries.

Putting the question into a historical perspective, it is noteworthy that when Japan resumed foreign trade in 1947, the yen/dollar

[51] Cf. on the same subject W. Rieke, 'Vergleich Japan-Bundesrepublik. Die grössere Dynamik führte zum Erfolg', *Handelsblatt*, 20 Aug. 1981.
[52] Cf. *Wochenbericht des Deutschen Instituts für Wirtschaftsforschung 30/81*, July 16, 1981, p. 352.

exchange rate was set at 360 yen, remaining unchanged for nearly 25 years. But from 1965 Japan has had uninterrupted trade surpluses and since 1968 has also had a considerable current account surplus. There is no doubt that within the system of fixed exchange rates at that time, the yen had slipped into a 'fundamental undervaluation' which of necessity had to lead to a revaluation. The currency realignment according to the Smithsonian Agreement caused the yen in December 1971 to appreciate for the first time against the US dollar. The new exchange rate of 308 yen implied an appreciation of 16.9%, and meant at that time that Japan had to accept the greatest appreciation rate of all countries of the Conference of Ten.[53]

Following the switch to the system of flexible exchange rates on 14 February 1973, the yen's value continued to rise in the course of that year to about 260 per US dollar. This was primarily due to the current account surpluses which Japan had accrued between 1971 and 1973. As a result of the first oil crisis at the end of 1973 Japan in the following year had a current account deficit of US$ 4.7 billion, which the Japanese succeeded in reducing to $ 0.7 billion by 1975. In the course of strong export growth, Japan once again reached considerable trade surpluses, and was able to combine them with a constantly rising current account surplus which in 1976 reached $ 3.7 billion, in 1977 $ l0.8 billion, and in 1978 $ 16.5 billion. Apart from the aggregate figures of Japan's balance of payments, it was not overlooked that Japan's overall positive trade and current account balance was the result of its deficits *vis-à-vis* oil-producing countries and other countries producing raw materials, and of its pronounced surpluses *vis-à-vis* individual regions such as the USA and the EC. Predictable reactions were not long in coming. From 1976 on the yen was once again gaining strength and in 1978 it reached its absolute peak rate of 176 yen to the US dollar. Between 1976 and 1978 the yen had appreciated by about 40%.

However, in the following phase of depreciation caused by the second oil crisis, the yen exchange rate sank steadily and in 1979 reached a rate of 220 yen to the US dollar which in early 1980 dropped to nearly 250 yen. After some further fluctuation, the yen rate once again became firm — the result of a consistently restrictive financial policy up to 1981 supported by stabilising wage agreements. In contrast to the heavy deficits in the current account balance in 1979 and 1980, which reached $ 8.7 and 10.8 billion

[53] Cf. H. Schmiegelow, *Japans Aussenwirtschaftpolitik. Merkantilistisch, liberal oder funktionell?, Mitteilungen* of the Institute of Asian Affairs, Hamburg 1981, p. 79 f.

respectively, 1981 brought a considerable surplus of nearly $ 5 billion.

The question under discussion here can only be answered by referring to the free floating Japanese currency. Under these conditions, the exchange rate is an expression of domestic cost and price developments, at least for a longer period of time. As for the frequently expressed opinion that the yen is largely manipulated by the Japanese Central Bank nothing seems to indicate that any intervention by the Japanese Central Bank has exceeded the margin laid down by the International Monetary Fund and the Economic Summit of Rambouillet. The Declaration of Rambouillet in 1975 explicitly permits the financial authorities to work against unusual market conditions and erratic fluctuations in the exchange rate in order to ensure or to reinforce the stability of monetary policy. Particularly after both recent oil crises, Japan found it essential to set a limit to all price increases from the import side and to introduce countermeasures to balance the decreasing yen rate. In particular, the Japanese monetary authorities intervened with large amounts of US dollars when the yen exchange rate reached a level of 230 (this became known in October 1983).[54]

Japan's interventions in the foreign exchange market have not occasioned complaints from the International Monetary Fund since the oil crises, nor have they led to consultations with the Japanese government. In this connection we must also note that between 1973 and 1980 the exchange rate fluctuations of the yen were far more pronounced than those of, say, the German Mark.[55] From 1977 to the second half of 1978 the yen rate increased against the currencies of Japan's foreign trade partners by nearly 40%. At the end of 1978 there was a pronounced depreciation, which continued until 1980, to be followed by an appreciation of nearly 24%, which turned again into a depreciation in 1981.[56]

It is frequently predicted that the yen is on the way to becoming the world's strongest currency, the result of persistent current account surpluses as well as Japan's domestic, political and financial stability.[57] The German Mark is at present far more intensively

[54] Cf. Saburo Matsukawa, 'The Yen', *Financial Times*, Oct. 26, 1981.
[55] Cf. on the same subject Schmiegelow, *Japans Aussenwirtschaftspolitik*, op. cit., p. 51 ff. However, it could also have been argued that the strong fluctuations were essentially caused by the monetary authorities' interventions. Cf. *World Financial Markets*, Morgan Guaranty Trust Company of New York, March 1981, p. 9.
[56] Cf. also the discussion in the 1981/2 Annual Report of the Council of Economic Advisers ('*Sachverständigenrat*') on the assessment of economic development.
[57] Cf. H. Brestel, '*Der Yen auf dem Weg zur "festen Währung der Welt"?*', *Frankfurter Allgemeine Zeitung*, Jan. 2, 1982.

used as an international investment currency than the yen, but this path seems very likely indeed for the yen as well. This is also true of the additional responsibilities within the so-called multi-reserve currency system which the yen will have to bear together with the US dollar, the German Mark, the Swiss Franc, and the Pound Sterling. Up till now, the yen has been used as a reserve currency only in East and Southeast Asia: either the Japanese government has caused its foreign trade partners there to maintain part of their currency reserves in yen securities, or those partners find it of immediate interest to use the yen, — the currency of their largest trade partner and lender — to some extent for their own reserve purposes as well. Altogether it may be said that in 1980 about 3% of the foreign currency reserves of foreign Central Banks were held in Japanese currency, but measured against the share of other currencies which are kept as foreign reserves, e.g. the German Mark (11.5%), this is by no means proportional to Japan's competitive and economic strength.[58]

In view of the status in world trade which Japan has achieved, as well as its political and economic importance, possessing the second largest economic potential in the non-communist world, the further internationalisation of the yen and the Japanese capital market cannot be halted. Japan's economic importance means that it will not be able to remain aloof from its own responsibility for the future of international foreign exchange developments. Above and beyond this, increased internationalisation is in Japan's own interest as well. In consideration of their 'comparatively low capital resources', due to historical reasons, 'Japanese firms are highly dependent on credit and therefore particularly dependent on international financing sources such as the Eurodollar market for short-term foreign trade financing'.[59]

Increased internationalisation was introduced as early as the beginning of the 1970s after Japan abandoned its traditional restraint in foreign exchange policy and the first foreign yen bonds ('Samurai bonds') appeared on the Japanese capital market. The Asian Development Bank took the next step in the same direction when it negotiated the issue of Yen Bonds. It was soon followed by the World Bank, further international organisations, and foreign countries. Although Japanese investors were soon offered the possibility of subscribing to foreign currency bond issues, such as the dollar bond of the European Investment Bank, it still took nearly

---

[58] Data from the International Monetary Fund, *Annual Report 1981*.
[59] P. Baron, 'Der Yen wird international zahlungsfähig', *Süddeutsche Zeitung*, March 28, 1978.

ten years longer to relieve the Japanese financial markets of the *dirigiste* administrative regulations, i.e. reduce the extensive system of foreign exchange, money and capital market controls.

On 1 December 1980, the Amendment to the Japanese Foreign Currency and Trade Control Law came into effect. Despite its elastic, all-purpose clauses and its special provisions for intervention, it succeeded in pushing the yen further towards internationalisation.[60] Trade with Japanese shares in Japan and abroad was liberalised. According to previous regulations, only 25% of the common shares of a Japanese corporation could be owned by foreigners. The regulations concerning the registration and/or approval of capital transfers from and into Japan was abolished, and even private persons were offered the possibility of having unlimited deposits abroad in yen or in foreign currency.[61] To be sure, interim measures to prevent capital drains were however taken.

Furthermore, Tokyo's importance as an international financial centre increased considerably after both Houses of the Japanese parliament passed an amendment to the Japanese bank law in May 1981 which entered into effect on 1 April 1982. This amendment caused Tokyo's financial institutions to proclaim 'an international year of the yen as early as 1982, reflecting their confidence that the Japanese currency would in future have a similar importance to that of the Petrodollar today on international financial markets'.[62] Certainly a precondition for this is that the share of foreign trade transactions on the basis of the yen must in future be increased, and that the yen must become more common as a foreign trade currency.[63] In the light of most recent progress towards internationalisation of the yen, and of the latent need of the yen for investment and reserve purposes, there is no longer any occasion to point out the so-called 'fundamental undervaluation of the yen'.

The regularity of current account surpluses up to 1979 has repeatedly caused great unease, even in Japan. Already at that time authorities found themselves in the position of having to consider concrete countermeasures. The second oil shock and the worldwide

[60] This refers to Law no. 65, which modified major aspects of the 'Foreign Exchange and Foreign Trade Control Law'.
[61] Cf. H. Becker, 'Die Internationalisierung des japanischen Yen' in *Geld in Japan* (OAG series on modern Japan, vol. 2), Berlin 1981, p. 203
[62] Cf. H. Becker, op. cit., p. 216.
[63] In 1980 28.9% of Japanese exports were based on the yen, in contrast to 2% at the beginning of the 1970s. The share of Japanese imports carried out on the basis on the yen has remained unchanged and amounts to about 3%. Cf. *White Paper on International Trade 1981* (Ministry of International Trade and Industry), Tokyo 1981, p. 71.

crisis which followed it temporarily created new conditions for the further development of the Japanese current account balance. Meanwhile, Japan has also had to accept heavy deficits, but on the other hand Japan's foreign trade policy has more than ever found critical observers the world over. Thus Japan has also become aware that a well-balanced current account position is indeed the best means of averting protectionism on the part of the rest of the world which would be highly threatening to Japan itself.

5. *Japan's place in a world of economic blocs*

Since the EC countries have established a joint responsibility for major trade policy issues, Japan feels that it faces an economic bloc in Europe similar to the North American bloc (USA-Canada). The economic potential of 120 million Japanese is confronted with that of 500 million people, i.e. the total population of the European and North American blocs. From the Japanese point of view, the individual EC member-states enjoy the protection of a supra-national trade policy which seems to be on a rapidly accelerating collision course with Japanese interests. However, Japan also feels itself isolated and surrounded by neighbours which are either developing countries[64] or which belong to different political alliances. Action initiated by the EC against Japan in the framework of GATT has made drastically clear to the Japanese how great is their actual isolation as an individual trade partner from the EC bloc. Such conflicts within GATT will probably only further contribute to an additional alienation between Japan and Europe after bilateral talks which have been going on for more than eight years.

In Japanese political and academic discussions, the EC plays an extremely important but also an ambivalent role. On the one hand the Japanese see themselves as victims of the diversion of trade flows caused by the founding and subsequent enlargement of the EC. On the other hand, the EC has also set an example: thus the considerable intra-European trade expansion in past decades is traced back largely to the institutional advantages of a well-functioning economic community. In this connection, Kiyoshi Kojima, one of the leading proponents of intensifying Pacific economic cooperation, expressly mentioned that the intra-trade in the EC between 1958 and 1973 rose from 30% to 49% of the total trade volume, while the

[64] These are primarily NICs, so that Japan has in fact become an object of envy for the industrialised countries of Europe because of its geographical proximity to these countries. On this, cf. Chapter II.A(1).

intra-trade for the same period between the five Pacific industrial nations — the USA, Japan, Canada, Australia and New Zealand — expanded only from 33% to 43%. However, an exact study would be necessary to determine to what extent this divergence in the growth of intra-trade shares has in fact been caused by institutional factors. Nevertheless, Kojima determined that 'if there were no European Community, we would have no need to consider Pacific economic integration either'.[65] Although this comment may overestimate the impact of institutional frameworks, there can be no doubt that Britain's entry into the EC was of particular importance to Australia, New Zealand and Canada, and caused these countries to take a more intense interest in the Pacific as an economic region.

Since the 1960s, Asian countries have increasingly contemplated economic cooperation and the prospect and potential of economic integration. They proceeded from the assumption that an expansion of mutual trade relationships, which had been relatively weak up till that time, would contribute to relieving the balance of payments pressure. They also recognised that efficient economic activity in some individual branches of production would hardly be possible owing to the narrow economic markets. Rapidly attained market limits complicated the establishment and utilisation of optimum plant sizes, the exploitation of decreasing unit costs and a reasonable import substitution. It was generally agreed that the prerequisite for large-scale complementary patterns of production with optimum locations should be created as soon as possible, for if this were not the case, more painful and expensive processes of adaptation and readjustment would be necessary in later phases of development, which could lead to extremely complicated problems. Although the advantages of a large-scale economic integration were recognised and the objectives were formulated again and again, numerous obstacles stood in the way of its realisation. Above all, Japan had always feared that its membership of a comprehensive Asian bloc could be detrimental to its elasticity and balance towards the EC, and towards the emerging economic blocs in Africa and South America. For that reason Japan, in 1962, declined to join efforts towards comprehensive economic cooperation by all Asian countries, i.e. to participate in the founding of a Common Market of eighteen Asian countries, one of the goals of the 18th General Assembly of the ECAFE (the UN Economic Commission for Asia and the Far East) in Tokyo. Instead of this, Japan recommended the creation of smaller regional integration zones, which at some later

[65] K. Kojima, *Economic Cooperation in a Pacific Community* (Japan Institute of International Affairs), Tokyo 1980, p. 10.

point could be joined together to form a larger market. At that time it was obvious from the economic point of view that Japan, South Korea and Taiwan would be envisaged as the nucleus group. At the same time Japan was trying to avoid anything which could possibly endanger potential markets in the People's Republic of China and in North Korea.

In the meantime, the concept 'Pacific Basin Cooperation' has become the subject of intense consideration and discussions. On 6 March 1979 the government created an advisory group to the late Prime Minister Ohira, which was chaired by Saburo Okita. The official task of this advisory group was to prepare a study on how regional cooperation and harmonious relationships between the countries of the Pacific could be intensified and how a regional community could be created within the Pacific Basin Area. Prime Minister Ohira envisioned an 'Age of the Pacific' and was able to point to the fact that nearly half of humanity lives on this large ocean and that the Pacific area has an impressive potential of raw materials. Thus, in considering possible members for an economic community consisting of countries bordering on the Pacific Basin, he took not only parts of Asia into consideration but also Australia and New Zealand as well as Canada and the USA. These considerations also accommodate the fact that the centre of economic influence in the USA is moving steadily westwards towards the Pacific coast region, and furthermore that the Pacific interests of US foreign policy seem to be increasingly at variance with the US position within the Atlantic alignment, not least thanks to the Europeans themselves. The final report of the Pacific Basin Cooperation Study Group, presented to the Prime Minister on 19 May 1980, stated:

This concept of forming a community in a region so replete with potential and diversity is without historical precedent, a fact which bears witness both to the task's great attraction and to its difficulty. Pacific basin co-operation should not be promoted hastily, but carefully and steadily through the gradual congealing of broad international consensus . . . . The next step might be to examine the possibility of establishing an international organization for Pacific basin cooperation among the governments of the countries concerned.[66]

The various concepts of economic cooperation in the Pacific at present under discussion, as well as their empirical bases and their political implications, will be studied more thoroughly in the following chapter.

[66] Pacific Basin Cooperation Study Group, *Report on the Pacific Basin Cooperation Concept*, Tokyo, May 19, 1980, p. 10 ff.

III
CONCEPTS OF INSTITUTIONALISED ECONOMIC COOPERATION IN THE PACIFIC BASIN

1. *Introduction*

Japan's rapid economic rise, the no less impressive economic development of some Southeast Asian Newly Industrialising Countries (NICs), and the tremendous wealth of mineral resources in the Pacific Basin, mean that in the recent past the development in the Pacific region has been a subject of particular interest to observers, in both the political and academic fields. The questions that are frequently given priority, namely those concerning the determinants of the progress in development which has already been made, as well as concerning its uniqueness or transferability — will not be discussed here. What is intended, however, is an analysis of goals, chances of actual realisation and limitations of plans concerning institutionalised economic cooperation in this region which have been in existence since the mid-1960s and have been increasing in number and importance in recent years. The essential problems of these plans are, *inter alia*, related to the fact that they are aimed at the economic cooperation of industrialised nations (Japan, Australia, the United States, Canada, New Zealand) and developing countries (in particular ASEAN), i.e. between countries at varying levels and with varying structures of economic activity. Thus they could assume a pilot function for the creation of cooperative North-South relationships on a regional basis.

Some general reflections concerning international economic relations within the tensions caused by global ambitions, the creation of regional blocs and bilateral agreements (Chapter 2) offer a good starting-point. This enables us to assess systematically the concepts of economic cooperation in the Pacific against a background of actual tendencies in international economic policy. These will be discussed and analysed more closely in Chapter 3 in the framework of a systematic survey of those cooperation plans which have been of particular importance up till now. The empirical analysis of actual economic interdependences in the Pacific Region will be the subject of Chapter 4, and Chapter 5 will offer an evaluation of the possibilities, limitations and impact of any potential economic cooperation in the Pacific.

2. *World economy, an international framework of rules and the New International Economic Order*

(a) *Erosion of International Rules and Increasing Bilateralism.* After the Second World War an historically unique increase in world economic interdependences (in the form of flows of goods and services and capital flows) was based decisively on two institutional pillars: first, the Bretton Woods Agreement for the regulation of foreign exchange problems (with its constituent elements of fixed exchange rates, a gold foreign exchange standard, and the convertibility of the US dollar into gold) and secondly, GATT for the regulation of trade relationships (with its constituent elements of the most-favoured-nation clause and reciprocity, as well as non-discrimination and the general prohibition of quantitative trade barriers). Thus — at least until the end of the 1960s — there was an international framework of rules which was able to provide a widely accepted basis for the process of growing specialisation and division of labour.

After the collapse of the Gold Pool in 1968 (in other words, a splitting of the gold market and a weakening of gold as a reserve medium); after the suspension of convertibility of the US dollar into gold in the Smithsonian Agreement in 1971; and after the fixed exchange rates gradually changed to a system of isolated or bloc-floating of currencies in 1973, the Bretton Woods Agreement — although it was never officially wound up — was robbed of its constituent principles. And despite a certain time-lag, GATT too is obviously not being spared the same fate: whereas the violation of the most-favoured-nation principle due to the granting of general tariff preferences *vis-à-vis* developing countries can be considered as relatively unproblematical, the same cannot be said for the area of non-tariff barriers to trade (NTBs). Even if the general prohibition of NTBs had not already been made dependent on the balance of payments situation (GATT Art. XII),[1] it must be said at the moment that the practice of multiple forms of NTBs has indeed become the rule rather than the exception, and that these measures

---

[1] 'Any contracting party, in order to safeguard its external financial position and balance of payments, may restrict the quantity or value of merchandise permitted to be imported . . .' (GATT, Art.XII).

are increasingly applied outside the GATT framework, thus leading to an economic policy which must be recognised as a neo-mercantilistic relapse into bilateralism. The causes and the consequences of this development have already been discussed in detail (see Chapter I), so that the argument here will be relatively short and will only touch on some of the most vital aspects.

The quintessence of the renewed world trade crisis at present under observation is as follows: rising structural adjustment burdens meeting decreased adjustment capacities (substitution processes in the energy sector due to widely fluctuating oil prices; growing and sectorally concentrated import competition of the NICs). Low growth and high unemployment in most Western industrial nations give the predominant role to national economic policy objectives (primarily full employment), so that the temptation to block off any international economic influences which might be considered negative becomes more and more attractive.[2]

Of course it is perfectly understandable and legitimate to place special emphasis on national economic policy goals, and these must certainly be taken into consideration when setting up rules for international economic relations if they are not to be doomed from the start.[3] As for the present status of the basic rules governing world trade we arrive at the thesis that possible mechanisms for coping with structural changes resulting from an increasingly intense international division of labour are of pivotal importance.[4] In the GATT framework of rules, such mechanisms are however simply regarded as undesirable and exceptional cases detrimental to the functioning of an ideal free trade system, and have therefore been placed at the very edge of all coordinating efforts. However, insofar as the earlier predominantly monocentric world trade system, (with the United States as the dominant economy) has been transformed to a polycentric system (the United States, the EC, Japan, the NICs), and at

[2] 'While the need for adjustment increased considerably in the last decade, the capacity and willingness of national economies to adjust . . . have been visibly reduced by various social forces, making for increased rigidities and uncertainties' (Kitamura, *International Division of Labour*, op. cit., p. 379). For general information cf. M.E. Streit, 'Anpassungsverhalten ökonomischer Systeme', *Wirtschaftsdienst*, vol. 61 (1981) p. 15 ff.

[3] Indeed it was a major shortcoming in the construction of the Bretton Woods agreement to demand monetary discipline of one country (the United States) in order to secure an adequate international liquidity supply.

[4] Particularly regarding the aspect that production efficiency represents only one of the elements of national systems of goals, so that trade-offs may arise with, for example, other distribution-oriented goals. Cf. T.N. Behrman, 'International Sectoral Integration: An Alternative Approach to Free Trade', *Journal of World Trade Law*, vol. 6 (1972), p. 269 ff.

the same time the decades of high growth in world trade seem to be ending, a transition is required from a negative liberalisation policy (reduction of trade barriers) to a positive one (active design of adjustment processes by mutually accepted rules).[5] In particular this would take into account the fact that only a very superficial analysis can reduce the so-called new protectionism to an exclusively foreign trade-related problem. In reality, a close link must be found between the use of specific foreign trade instruments on the one hand and the general orientation of economic systems of trade partners on the other. Thus it cannot realistically be expected that the political authorities should refrain from action in the framework of international economic relations while they are responsible at the same time on a national basis for achieving central goals, particularly full employment. It is this interrelationship that Lorenz quite rightly refers to as the "impact of foreign trade and foreign trade policy on economic systems".[6]

The import competition from NICs demands particular attention in this connection.[7] This import competition has triggered off intense discussion on the conceptualisation of a trade adjustment policy.[8] Even if the argument for trade adjustment policy is still the subject of serious debate due to the demands it places on forecast potential (as concerns the structural changes caused by foreign trade) and on the mobility of the working forces (affected by the structural changes), it can be assumed that any trade adjustment policy only makes sense within the framework of an international coordination of policy: attempts by individual industrialised nations to solve these problems on their own would create the

[5] Cf. Minx, *Von der Liberalisierungs- zur Wettbewerbspolitik*, op. cit. p. 12 ff., 249 ff. K.W. Rothschild (in 'Aussenhandelstheorie, Aussenhandelspolitik und Anpassungsdruck', *Kyklos*, vol. 32 [1979], p. 47 ff.) also emphasises the necessity of complementing the dichotomy of free-trade *vs.* protectionism with concepts of efficient steering of adjustment processes. Noteworthy, but not to be discussed here in depth, is Bhagwati's proposal to link the trade barriers of industrialised countries with compensation payments to be made to the developing countries affected in order to balance out their welfare losses. Cf. J.N. Bhagwati, 'Compensation for Trade Protectionism', in K. Haq (ed.), *Dialogue for a New Order*, New York 1980, p. 75 ff.
[6] Lorenz, *Neomerkantilismus*, op. cit., p. 14.
[7] For more information, cf. OECD, *The Impact of the Newly Industrializing Countries on Production and Trade in Manufactures*, Paris 1979; S. Schultz *et al., Wirtschaftliche Verflechtung der Bundersrepublik Deutschland mit den Entwicklungsländern*, Baden-Baden 1980; ILO, *Employment, Trade and North-South Cooperation* (ed. G. Renshaw), Geneva 1981; S. Borner (ed.), *Produktionsverlagerung und internationaler Strukturwandel*, Berne 1980.
[8] Cf. Glaubitt/Lütkenhorst, op. cit., p. 128 ff.; H. Körner *et al., Industrielle Arbeitsteilung zwischen Industrie- und Entwicklungsländern und Strukturanpassung*, Munich 1981.

danger of trade diversion when anticipatory production decreases of individual branches create short-term market gaps which could be closed by increasing imports from other industrialised nations — the latter enjoying the role of "free riders" at the expense of the developing nations. If, however, the attempt to create a foreign trade policy coordinated by means of rules internationally agreed upon and going beyond mere tariff variations were to fail completely, then what Sautter perceptively diagnosed as the international 'deficit of a framework of rules'[9] would prevail in the future.

After considering all these factors, we have to draw the interim conclusion that the modern polycentric world economy seems to have outgrown its old institutional framework without having found new guiding principles. This may lead us to a more positive assessment of regionally limited concepts of integration, which in the past have often been regarded with caution due to their suboptimality when compared with the ideal of global free trade. If, however, a rapid increase in 'voluntary' self-restraint agreements and other bilateral arrangements are to be characteristics of reality, and their application is to be concentrated on and applied at the expense of new competitors (NICs), then regionally limited attempts at economic integration appear in a different light: under these conditions a 'medium-range' foreign trade policy can be a reasonable alternative — as a kind of second-best solution to bilateralism, which would only increase protectionist pressures.[10] The decisive question is to what extent a greater degree of common interests can be created in any given area of potential regional economic integration than is at present the case within the framework of global economic interrelationships.[11] However, a general *a priori* judgement on this question is not possible since geographic proximity

---

[9] H. Sautter, ' "Soziale Marktwirtschaft" als Ordnungsprinzip für die Wirtschaftsbeziehungen zwischen Entwicklungs- und Industrieländern' in O. Issing (ed.), *Zukunftsprobleme der sozialen Marktwirtschaft*, Berlin 1981, p. 634.

[10] Behind this opinion we find the hope that many trade conflicts could be solved at a regional level and thus not escalate to the dimension of global 'trade wars'. Cf. H.R. Krämer, 'Probleme der Regionalisierung des internationalen Handels' in H. Giersch H.-D. Haas (eds), *Probleme der weltwirtschaftlichen Arbeitsteilung*, Berlin 1974, p. 567. Gilpin sceptically characterises this position as 'benign mercantilism, one qualification of which is its belief that 'regional blocs would stabilize world economic relations' (R. Gilpin, 'Three Models for the Future', *International Organisation*, vol. 29 [1975] p. 47).

[11] This hypothesis is also found in Minx, *Von der Liberalisierungs- zur Wettbewerbspolitik*, op. cit., p 266 ff., as well as in K. Kojima, 'A New Capitalism for a New International Economic Order', *Hitotsubashi J. of Economics*, June 1984, p. 14.

alone can hardly be a reliable indicator for the accord of economic interests.

(b) *The New International Economic Order: From global dialogue to regionalisation?* The advantages and disadvantages of increasingly regionalised international economic relationships can also be approached from another perspective, i.e. by taking the North-South dialogue on the establishment of a new international economic order as the starting-point. The demand by the developing countries for a new international economic order (NIEO) voiced since the early 1970s was motivated by a variety of factors,[12] such as by the developing countries' disappointment at the increase of the absolute 'income gap' as well as the persistence of the relative one at the end of the first two development decades,[13] and the original process of solidarisation within the Third World — a result of the effects of the OPEC cartel on the world's oil markets. Perhaps the most important prerequisite, however, was the vacuum caused by the disintegration of the Bretton Woods Agreement and the erosion of GATT, leaving behind it a gap the developing countries hoped to fill to their advantage with the conceptualization of a NIEO.

The international conferences held within the framework of the UN System met at first with a certain degree of success and progress to the extent that industrialised and developing countries at least formally agreed to common declarations.[14] In the course of further negotiations, however, the marginal rate of return of such conferences dropped considerably. Increasingly often, global negotiations would reach their limits when the actual putting into operation of compromises which had been formally agreed on was under discussion, i.e. where these compromises were to be turned into concrete action. The last partial success worthy of mention[15] took place during preparations for UNCTAD V when general agreement was reached on the scope and modalities of the Common Raw Material Fund. Following this, however, there has been a chronological series of conference failures — from UNCTAD V (1979 in Manila), to

---

[12] Cf. W. Ochel, *Die Entwicklungsländer in der Weltwirtschaft*, Cologne 1982, p. 255 ff.

[13] Cf. W. Lütkenhorst, *Zielbegründung und Entwicklungspolitik. Das Grundbedürfnisziel in methodologisch-theoretischer Perspektive*, Tübingen 1982, p. 191 ff.

[14] During the Sixth Special General Assembly of the United Nations the Declaration and Plan of Action on the Establishment of a New International Economic Order was passed. The Seventh Special General Assembly further passed a common resolution with no dissenting votes by industrialised countries.

[15] This term in no way offers an evaluation of the actual result. It should simply be emphasised that a compromise was reached at all.

UNIDO III (1980) in New Delhi), and the summit meeting at Cancun (1981) to UNCTAD VI (1983 in Belgrade).

There are varying levels of diagnosis — and accordingly various 'therapeutic' approaches — concerning the reasons why the global North-South dialogue has obviously come to a dead end[16]:

(i) At first glance the problem can be reduced to the fact that there is a lack of readiness for compromise on both sides — the developing and the industrial nations. Indeed, fruitless interplay of unrealistic demands and non-binding promises went on for years, from which it could be inferred that serious efforts at negotiation were lacking. According to this explanation, future efforts should be directed towards motivating the developing countries to giving up some totally unrealistic elements of their catalogue of demands (e.g. the redeployment of certain branches of industry — something the industrial nations may encourage but which they cannot guarantee within the framework of their own economic order), while the industrial nations in their turn should be expected to make increased concessions in other fields (e.g. increased market access).

(ii) The reason why the North-South dialogue has run on to the rocks may go far beyond the simple conclusion that there is a lack of readiness for compromise: it may also be found in the structural deficits of the negotiation process itself.[17] There is a strong assumption that one of the causes of the structural deficits is the simple but weighty fact that the delegations involved find appropriate preparation for any given conference extremely difficult, in particular because a number of global conferences sometimes take place simultaneously. This is particularly true of the 'Group of 77' which is obviously overworked and overtasked in the fields of administration and organisation.[18] The two-stage nature of the processes of coordination and decision making have also had an effect: internal group relations are easily overlooked, but these create a distinct tendency towards radical positions. The Group of 77, for example, has tried to maintain a sense of unity among its members by issuing an extensive catalogue of demands, including all the special interests

---

[16] 'The North-South negotiations have deteriorated to a ritual and a skillful exercise in *non*-dialogue' (M. ul Haq, 'North-South Dialogue — Is There a Future?' in Haq, *Dialogue*, op. cit., p. 271).

[17] For a more detailed discussion of the following paragraphs see H. Mayrzedt *et al., Perspektiven des Nord-Süd Dialoges und internationale Verhandlungsmechanismen*, Cologne 1981, pp. 137 ff and 165 ff.

[18] Cf. K.O. Hall, 'Strengthening Third World Negotiating Capacity' in Haq, *Dialogue*, op. cit., p. 45 ff.

of its members,[19] while in Group B (western industrial nations) the restrictive attitudes of economically powerful group members (the United States, West Germany, Japan) often prevailed in the past, thereby reducing almost to nil the readiness of other industrial nations to make more extensive concessions. Obviously it is the very group structure within the framework of global negotiations which in many cases has led to a narrowing of the initial scope for compromise.

(iii) The foregoing shows clearly that the weaknesses of the negotiating process are closely related to the diversity of interests within the groups of countries involved. Finally, the question thus emerges whether the global negotiating approach is not in principle inadequate in the face of increasing processes of differentiation in the world economy. When one is reviewing the past, the clear evidence of empirical data is on the one hand that a period of US domination was superseded by a multipolarity of the world economy, and on the other hand that the unity of the Third World — if indeed it ever existed — had to give way to a variety of partly overlapping sub-groups (for example OPEC, LLDC, MSAC, NIC). From this point of view the question as to what extent a regionalisation of the North/South negotiations could be a reaction to these developments becomes considerably more important.[20] Efforts towards regionalisation do not necessarily have to be seen as the equivalent of giving up the global dialogue; they can rather be seen as the complementary intensification of that dialogue and could contribute considerably to actual progress in negotiations where common regional interests are at stake. At the same time, this approach is ambivalent because on the one hand it explores the regionally limited potential of common interests and agreements,[21] while on the other hand so-called 'changing majorities' between

---

[19] 'The point is . . . that national interests no longer necessarily coincided . . . with the "general interests" of the Third World, and the possibility of competition and divergent interests within the larger bloc frequently eroded the possibility of meaningful cooperation. As a result the Third World summit meetings could do little more than enunciate "maximum common denominator" positions' (R.L. Rothstein, *The Weak in the World of the Strong: The Developing Countries in the International System*, New York 1977, p. 49).

[20] Cf. H. Mayrzedt, 'Einige Perspektiven der Regionalisierung des Nord-Süd Dialogs', *Aussenwirtschaft*, vol. 36 (1981), p. 143 ff.; Kojima, *New Capitalism*, op. cit., p. 14 f.

[21] In this connection, observers of the North-South dialogue find the only chance for its continuation in the reconsideration of common interests. Cf. Ch. Uhlig, 'Die neue Weltwirtschaftsordnung aus ordnungstheoretischer und ordnungspolitischer Sicht (Korreferat)' in Simonis, *Ordnungspolitische Fragen*, op. cit., p. 43 ff.; Haq, 'North-South Dialogue', op. cit., p. 278.

industrialised and developing countries could be created which might lead to a process of de-solidarisation, particularly within the Group of 77.[22]

We will return later to a political evaluation of regionalised North-South relationships. The next section focusses on plans for economic co-operation in the Pacific region which have been the subject of intense discussion in recent years. These plans are frequently presented by their proponents as a possible model for cooperative interrelationships between countries at varying levels of development.

3. *Concepts and Goals of Economic Cooperation in the Pacific*[23]

(*a*) *'Pacific Visions'*. Many of the publications on economic cooperation in the Pacific (which we shall consider individually below) begin their discussions with those aspects which have already

[22] As early as 1977 Rothstein assumed that 'the rich countries are unlikely to persist in support for regional groups that will then cooperate against the rich countries. The major exception to this would occur if the rich countries began to create a bloc system, dividing up the world among themselves, but this would hardly be the regional "cooperation" that the poor countries advocate' (Rothstein, *The Weak*, op. cit., p. 325).

[23] At this point we feel that a brief discussion of the terminology of the concepts 'integration' and 'cooperation' would help the reader. Without offering a detailed discussion of the heterogeneous definitions used in the literature (Cf. H.R. Krämer, *Formen und Methoden der internationalen wirtschaftlichen Integration. Versuch einer Systematik*, Tübingen 1969; K. Glaubitt/B. Lageman, *Arabische Integrationsexperimente*, Tübingen/Basel 1980), the terms to be used in the above text can be explained as follows: 'Cooperation' will be defined as 'conscious action of economic units (natural and legal entities) for a common purpose' (E. Böttcher, *Kooperation und Demokratie in der Wirtschaft*, Tübingen 1974, p. 22). This implies that cooperation efforts require purposefulness of action on the one hand and agreement on common goals on the other. It is of secondary importance if and to what extent the coordination of action is institutionalised or based on *ad hoc* arrangements.

Thus economic integration — interpreted as a process of increasing interdependences of economic units (and of entire economies) — can (but does not necessarily have to) be a specific element of cooperative efforts. If, for example, two trading partners agree on reciprocal trade concessions in order to come closer to their mutual goal of deepening the division of labour, this would be a case of economic cooperation in the form of trade liberalisation. In contrast, a mere trade relationship between two companies located within different countries would not be classified as cooperation due to the lack of a mutual goal — whereas their forming a 'joint venture' would be judged in a different light. This market-related intensification of trade relations — with no pursuit of common goals — will be termed 'factual integration' in the following text.

been dealt with at greater length in previous chapters. Thus, for example, the Japanese Pacific Basin Cooperation Study Group, as well as referring indirectly to the disintegration of the rules governing international trade, emphasises that 'Pacific Basin Cooperation can . . . be expected to help usher in new relations between advanced and developing countries' and that 'the chance is great that the region as a whole will be a model for developing a new pattern in North-South relations.'[24]

Kojima, who has long been the chief intellectual protagonist for the idea of cooperation in the Pacific, paints a gloomy picture of the present world economic position, but then presents the Pacific region as a new dynamic centre of development and as the saviour of a desolate world economy. 'The 1970s have been a decade of continued confusion and uncertainty. To overcome such a deadlock it is believed essential to create a new development centre for the world economy. The most promising development centre, in this regard, can be found in the economic development of the young Asian and Pacific countries gifted with unlimited potential for development. . . . High expectations are placed on the 'Century of the Pacific' in terms of a new development base for the world economy.'[25]

Japanese economists are certainly not alone in their opinion that once again we are witnessing secular changes in the structure of the world economy in general, and in the share of production held by different regions in particular. The obvious discrepancy in the growth rates of 'old' European and the 'young' Asian industrial countries in this sense is not another rapidly passing episode but rather the expression of a long-term regional structural change encompassing the entire globe. It could well prefigure the collapse of the economic hegemony of Europe and the United States.[26] The OECD project 'Interfutures' also hints at this in its final report — although the terms used to formulate it are cautious: 'With the rise of *Japan*, the development of South East Asia . . . and the new

[24] Pacific Basin Cooperation Study Group, Report, op. cit., p. 21.

[25] Kojima, *Economic Cooperation*, op. cit., p. 2.

[26] The Leontief report on the future of the world economy also arrives in its medium scenario 'X' at the projection that the share of the US GDP in the global GDP will decrease from 32.9% in 1970 to 21% in the year 2000, while Western Europe's share will decline for the same period from 22.6% to 16.7% Cf. W. Leontief *et al.*, *Die Zukunft der Weltwirtschaft*, Stuttgart 1977, p. 52. It is not an uncommon phenomenon, however, for prophecies to be self-destroying. Should the United States succeed in strengthening its economic interrelatonships in the Pacific at the expense of traditional European-Atlantic links, additional growth potential might be opened up.

policy of *China*, an area is taking shape in the Far East which might, in the second quarter of the 21st century, become a centre of the world economy.'[27]

In one of his last great publications on the development of the world economy, Herman Kahn devoted an entire chapter to the creation of a Pacific Trade and Investment Zone, and believed that 'the centre of dynamism that used to be the Mediterranean, at least for Western culture, and which then moved to north-west Europe and to the North Atlantic, is now moving (and has already partly moved) to the Pacific Basin . . . . In effect, the Pacific Ocean, which was once a great barrier, now becomes the world's greatest connector . . . . We believe that a Pacific Trading Investment Area will come into being in the early 1980s among countries that border or focus attention on the Pacific Basin.'[28]

In addition to not unrealistic forecasts based on given economic prerequisites (resources, economic strategy, previous growth rates etc.), a variety of visions of the coming of an 'Age of the Pacific' or 'Century of the Pacific' have already begun to crop up, most of them based on Arnold Toynbee's predictions to this effect. We shall not be seeking to test the legitimacy and validity of these visions here; however, the strategic and potentially explosive arrangement of power in the Pacific must cause us to cast some doubt on these optimistic expectations which imply that a long-term stable centre of global development has been found in this region.[29]

(*b*) *Defining a Pacific Economic Area*. Until now the Pacific economic area has been the subject of discussion, but which are the countries involved has not been exactly defined. The problem is of course caused by the fact that the varying concepts of Pacific economic cooperation or the even vaguer concept of a Pacific Basin Community are based on different perceptions of the relevant region: the criteria of membership in a Pacific cooperation organisation which has yet to be founded are still the subject of difficult discussions among the proponents of this approach.[30] This in itself is

[27] OECD, *Interfutures: Facing the Future*, Paris 1979, p. 399.
[28] H. Kahn, *World Economic Development: 1979 and Beyond*, New York 1979, p. 252 ff.
[29] Cf. also A.H. Zakaria, 'The Pacific Basin and ASEAN: Problems and Prospects', *Contemporary Southeast Asia*, vol. 2 (1981), p. 333 ff.; W. Höpker, 'Die Pazifische Herausforderung. Kooperation und Konfrontation um das Meer der Zukunft', *Beiträge zur Konfliktforschung*, vol. 9 (1979), p. 341 ff.
[30] Cf. also L.P. Ping, 'Reflection on the Pacific Community Concept', *Asia Pacific Community*, no. 8/1980, p. 35 ff.; J.D.B. Miller, 'A Pacific Economic Community: Problems and Possibilities', *Asia Pacific Community*, no. 9/1980, p. 10 ff.;

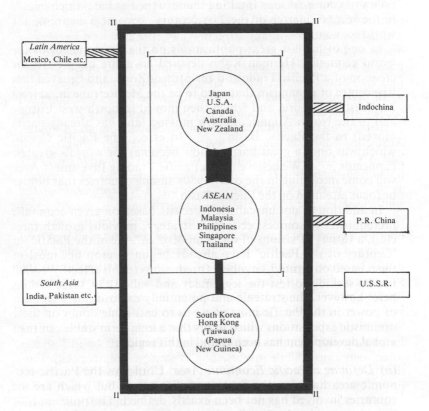

Fig. 1. DELINEATION OF THE PACIFIC BASIN

not surprising: not only does the Pacific region, thanks to its size as well as to the tremendous extent of its economic disparities and cultural heterogeneity, confront all efforts toward co-operation with particular difficulties. The major question remains as to the sense of the word (except for the geographical sense) in which it is legitimate to speak of the Pacific region as a well-defined entity: 'The Pacific is a notional construct except in its capacity as a body of water. The fact that a country faces on the Pacific does not, in itself, provide any common interest with others which do the same.'[31]

M. Nakajima, 'Pacific Basin Cooperation Concept and Japan's Options', *Asia Pacific Community*, no. 9/1980, p. 1 ff.
[31] Miller, 'Pacific Economic Community', op. cit., p. 14.

We shall not be discussing the individual economic and political problem fields which could result from varying membership options within a cooperative organisation in the Pacific area. It is merely our intention to make clear which groups of countries belong to the nucleus and which are located on the periphery of co-operation (see Fig. 1). Those countries whose co-operation is considered essential in all present plans and which thus form the nucleus of potential cooperative efforts are found in Group I, consisting of the five Pacific industrial nations (the United States, Japan, Canada, Australia, New Zealand) as well as the member countries of ASEAN. If this group of countries is extended to include the newly industrialising countries — South Korea, Hong Kong, and Taiwan, as well as possibly Papua New Guinea as a representative of the south west Pacific island states — we arrive at a larger group of countries, Group II, which forms the basis chosen by most co-operation concepts. However, participation at an institutional level or solely in conferences with official representatives is problematical in the cases of Taiwan, because of its special relationship to the People's Republic of China, and of Hong Kong, with its status as a British Crown Colony. This has to be understood from the point of view of most of the Pacific nations which consider the eventual inclusion of China as both desirable and necessary. The need for the Latin American countries bordering the Pacific to be included is often mentioned (Chile in particular is said to be interested). Furthermore it has been the specific interest of the ASEAN countries not to block some form of cooperation with the countries of Indochina later — despite their radically different economic and political systems.

The inclusion of all these countries would of course go beyond the limit of economically sound and reasonable efforts towards cooperation. This is especially true of the inclusion of the Soviet Union — very much a Pacific power — and the countries of South Asia which is sometimes demanded.[32] Considerations of this kind clearly show that the idea of cooperation in the Pacific is still rather vague. This vagueness is also reflected by the varying ideas on the politically relevant time horizon: while some proponents of Pacific cooperation recognise an immediate and urgent need for action even in the 1980s, others consider that realisation can only come about at

[32] Regional cooperative efforts have been initiated in South Asia as well. They will be briefly discussed at the end of Chapter 3. Cf. for more information D. Braun, *Südasien zwischen Konflikten und Zusammenarbeit. Der Ansatz der South Asian Regional Cooperation* (SARC), Ebenhausen, December 1983.

the beginning of the next century.[33]

Following this discussion of the broad spectrum of delimitations and conceptions, we will now turn to those concepts of cooperation which predominate in present discussions, including specific plans of action.

(c) Steps towards cooperation in the Pacific

(ca) "Precocious Thoughts": The Plan for a Pacific Free Trade Area (PAFTA). Kojima's essay 'A Pacific Economic Community and Asian Developing Countries',[34] published in 1966, was the starting point of what has turned out to be two decades of discussions of economic cooperation in the Pacific.[35] In this essay, which was heavily influenced by the relatively strong expansion of intra-European trade that followed the founding of the EEC, he proposes the founding of a free trade area with the five Pacific industrial countries (the United States, Japan, Canada, Australia, New Zealand) as its members. Although from the very outset no claim was made to create an economic community with supranational economic authority, Kojima from the beginning saw only slight chances of realisation for his PAFTA concept, not least due to the predominantly global economic interests of the United States as well as the subordinate importance of foreign trade in the US economy. This is certainly true; however, the actual reason why the PAFTA proposal lacked political resonance is to be found elsewhere — namely, in the predictably asymmetrical distribution of increased foreign trade. Kojima himself offers the corresponding calculations, a synopsis of which we present below.

In the event of a PAFTA being created, the question would then be how the static trade effects (resulting from an intensification of the intra-regional division of labour), as a function of the initial

[33] Cf. K. Sandhu, 'The Pacific Basin Concept: A View from ASEAN' in J. Crawford and G. Seow (eds), *Pacific Economic Co-operation*, London 1981, p. 179.
[34] Published in *Hitotsubashi J. of Economics*, June 1966, p. 17 ff. Kojima remains up to the present, one of the principal proponents of the idea of economic cooperation in the Pacific. However, he has modified his individual proposals, as will be shown later. on PAFTA cf. K. Kojima, 'Asian Developing Countries and PAFTA: Development, Aid and Trade Preferences', *Hitotsubashi J. of Economics*, June 1969, p. 1 ff.; K. Kojima, *Japan and a Pacific Free Trade Area*, London 1971, as well as in retrospect K. Kojima, 'Economic Cooperation', op. cit., p. 4 ff.
[35] Short surveys are given in: W. Lütkenhorst, 'Pacific Basin Interdependencies — A Case for Large-Scale Economic Cooperation?', *Intereconomics*, vol. 18 (1983), p. 28 ff.; S. Okita, 'The Future of Pacific Basin Cooperation', *Asien*, no. 1/1981, p. 53 ff.; T. Morris-Suzuki, 'Japan and the Pacific Basin Community', *The World Today*, vol. 37 (1981), p. 454 ff.; D.G. Timberman, 'In Search of a Pacific Basin Community', *Asian Survey*, 'vol. 21 (1981), p. 579 ff.

level and structure of tariffs and of the elasticities of imports would be distributed. Kojima's model calculation (see Table 14) indicates that there would be a hypothetical aggregate increase in the trade volume of approximately $ 5 billion, which amounts to an increase of 28% against the actually realised value of 1965. The regional structure of these additional trade flows would, however, be asymmetrical to such a great extent that the negative attitude of all potential member states with the exception of Japan becomes understandable: while Japan alone would be able to realize an induced merchandise trade surplus of approximately US $ 1.3 billion, i.e. a sum of over 25% of the total additional trade volume, the United States would notice only a slight positive effect on its merchandise trade balance, while Canada and Australia in particular, and New Zealand to a less extent, would experience a tendency toward an unfavourable net effect. This calculation also shows that those trade flows induced by the reduction of tariffs would concentrate primarily on an intensification of the horizontal exchange of industrial goods with an increase of approximately 40%, while on the other hand the raw materials trade would expand by only 2%. Kojima himself believes that 'the smaller rate of increase in exports than in imports for Canada, Australia and New Zealand should be remedied through dynamic effects of free trade area'[36] which, however, seems a highly speculative assumption for the future.[37]

Although the PAFTA proposal was presented as essentially an integration effort for the Pacific industrialised nations, it was also intended to include some specific measures in the interests of the Asian developing countries, since it would be these very countries which would have to bear a considerable share of the resulting trade diversion. Kojima therefore proposed:

1. to grant the most-favoured-nation clause to the Asian developing nations, thus allowing them to enjoy the benefits of tariff reduction;

2. to import agricultural goods to as great an extent as possible only from other developing countries in Asia and not from industrial countries, as well as limiting agricultural production of any given member-country to the minimum necessary for self-sufficiency;

[36] Kojima, 'A Pacific Economic Community', op. cit., p. 24. In a later publication he himself sees the necessity that 'before its establishment, concerted action by the PAFTA countries to promote export-oriented industrialisation in Canada, Australia and New Zealand would be necessary' (Kojima, 'Pacific Free Trade Area', op. cit., p. 93).
[37] At the commonsense level there seems to be more indication of the opposite, i.e. that the distribution of static and dynamic integration effects would follow the same pattern — e.g. as regards scale effects or the utilisation of new investment opportunities.

Table 14. POTENTIAL ABSOLUTE AND RELATIVE CHANGES
IN INTRAREGIONAL TRADE FLOWS CAUSED BY
FOUNDATION OF PAFTA

(*a*) ABSOLUTE INCREASE (*US$ millions; base year 1965*)

		USA	Canada	Japan	Australia	New Zealand	PAFTA
U.S.A.	X	–	1,405	404	426	66	2,302
	M	–	792	1,457	24	10	2,283
	(X–M)	–	613	– 1,053	402	56	19
Canada	X	792	–	17	39	7	855
	M	1,405	–	76	0	0	1,481
	(X–M)	– 613	–	– 59	39	7	– 626
Japan	X	1,457	76	–	177	33	1,743
	M	404	17	–	8	3	431
	(X–M)	1,053	59	–	169	30	1,312
Australia	X	24	0	8	–	33	65
	M	426	39	216	–	8	651
	(X–M)	– 402	– 39	– 208	–	25	– 586
New Zealand	X	10	0	3	8	–	22
	M	66	7	33	33	–	140
	(X–M)	– 56	– 7	– 30	– 25	–	– 118
PAFTA	X	–	–	–	–	–	4,987

(*b*) RELATIVE INCREASE (*%; base year 1965*)

		USA	Canada	Japan	Australia	New Zealand	PAFTA
U.S.A.	X	–	26	20	61	53	28
	M	–	17	59	7	9	30
Canada	X	17	–	6	30	21	17
	M	26	–	35	0	1	26
Japan	X	59	35	–	50	54	56
	M	20	6	–	1	7	15
Australia	X	7	0	1	–	17	6
	M	61	30	61	–	19	53
New Zealand	X	9	1	7	19	–	10
	M	53	21	54	17	–	34
PAFTA	X	–	–	–	–	–	28

Source: Kojima, *Pacific Free Trade Area*, op. cit., p. 91.

3. to intensify measures for financial and technical development assistance — specifically to increase the productivity of the agricultural sector in the developing countries; and

4. to increase the export chances of these developing countries,

particularly in labour-intensive branches of industry through active structural policies.

However, the broadening of the PAFTA concept to include a concerted development policy on this basis remained purely a statement of intention. In particular, the developing countries of the Pacific were not originally thought of as active, responsible partners in economic cooperation. They saw themselves rather in a passive role as countries whose interests would be protected by suitable side measures. It is thus not surprising that they interpreted PAFTA as 'another rich man's club',[38] and seemed to expect economic disadvantages instead of any positive effects. Also the limited echo from the industrialised nations (with the exception of Japan) was certainly predictable in the face of the basic characteristics of the PAFTA proposal, which were all too obviously made-to-order for Japan's economic interests.[39] Aside from the asymmetrical distribution of trade benefits, the demand for a reduction of agricultural production to a self-sufficiency level would have to appear to the United States, as well as to Canada and Australia, a drastic measure which, furthermore, would certainly not have remained without consequences for the world food situation in the long run.

(cb) Realistic re-orientation: The concept of an Organisation for Pacific Trade and Development (OPTAD). At an early date — particularly after the first Pacific Trade and Development Conference in early 1968 in Tokyo — it became obvious that the option of *institutional* cooperation in the form of a Pacific Free Trade Area had little chance of actual realisation. Thus towards the end of the 1960s a process of reorientation set in, which brought with it a turn to the concept of a *functional* cooperation variant, i.e. cooperation limited to selected problem areas. Hopes for the formation of an integration area in the Pacific which would be able to follow the model of the European Communities — at least on a long-term basis — were abandoned: the OECD frequently replaced the EC as a system of reference, resulting in demands for a corresponding Organisation for Pacific Trade and Development (OPTAD). Thus there was a basic reorientation from the approach 'cooperation as integration' to the approach 'cooperation as coordination'.

However, the first of these proposals aiming at the founding of

---

[38] Kojima, 'Economic Cooperation', op. cit., p. 5.
[39] For a critical opinion cf. also A. Hernadi, 'Pacific Region as a Growth Sub-Center and Japan's Role', *Asia Pacific Community*, no. 5/1979, p. 123 ff.

OPTAD[40] still limited membership to the five Pacific industrial nations. Within the given framework, these five countries were to create committees for the coordination and harmonisation of their trade, investment, and development aid policies, thus taking the first steps on the way to the eventual goal, which still remained the formation of PAFTA.

The increasing economic importance of the Pacific developing countries since the mid-1970s has, however, brought with it major changes in the prerequisites and determinants for efforts towards cooperation. If we stop to consider that in 1984, for example, 21% of Japan's imports were from the developing countries of the Pacific and 20% of its exports were to them,[41] then these figures certainly explain why those countries must be an integral part of any approach to cooperation in the future. If the specific characteristic of Pacific economic cooperation is thus to be found in cooperation between industrialised and developing countries, then the free trade concept (PAFTA) is neither convincing nor satisfactory, whereas rules for the management of structural adjustment processes and the economic conflicts arising out of them, acquire increased importance.[42]

Of decisive influence for the present discussions on the concept of OPTAD is the proposal presented in 1979 by Drysdale (of the Australian National University in Canberra) and Patrick (of Yale University).[43] This proposal was commissioned by the US Senate Committee on Foreign Affairs and was discussed in detail at a hearing of the Subcommittee on Asian and Pacific Affairs of the US House of Representatives in the same year.[44]

Because of the economic hegemony of Japan, the rapid growth of

[40] Cf. on this K. Kojima, 'Japan's Interest in the Pacific Trade Expansion: PAFTA Re-Considered', *Hitotsubashi J. of Economics*, June 1968, p. 25 f.; P. Drysdale, 'Pacific Economic Integration: An Australian View', in K. Kojima (ed.), *Pacific Trade and Development*, Tokyo 1968.

[41] Unless otherwise stated, these include here the ASEAN countries as well as South Korea, Taiwan, Hong Kong and Papua-New Guinea.

[42] It may be recalled that the mutually agreed management of adjustment processes was identified as the main task of trade policy which led us to the rejection of the purist free trade ideal. This is particularly valid in relations to countries whose division of labour is largely interindustrial (in contrast to intra-industrial), as is the case between the industrial and the developing countries (inasmuch as their trade relations are still not complementary).

[43] Cf. P. Drysdale and H. Patrick, *An Asian-Pacific Regional Economic Organisation: An Exploratory Concept Paper*, Washington DC 1979. This proposal is also supported by L. Krause/S. Sekiguchi (eds), *Economic Interaction in the Pacific Basin*, Washington DC 1980, p. 259 ff.

[44] Cf. The Pacific Community Idea, *Hearings Before the Subcommittee on Asian and Pacific Affairs of the Committee on Foreign Affairs* (House of Representatives, 96th Congress, First Session), Washington DC 1979.

domestic production and foreign trade of the developing countries of Northeast and Southeast Asia, and the declining growth rates of West European countries, Drysdale and Patrick suggest that the Pacific economic area can be regarded as a new centre or nucleus of world economic activities. At the same time they diagnose a growing discrepancy between the high degree of economic interdependence on the one hand and a lack of suitable institutional mechanisms of cooperation on the other.[45]

With regard to the membership issue, the already existing organisations in the Pacific are regarded as being either too extensive (e.g. ESCAP) or too limited (e.g. ASEAN or the South Pacific Bureau for Economic Cooperation), or their functional orientation is considered much too one-dimensional (e.g. the Asian Development Bank, which only handles development financing).[46] Therefore a new organisation should be founded, its membership structure oriented to the realities of economic interdependence, and primarily offering a forum˙ for the discussion and the harmonisation of all major policy fields. In this connection Drysdale and Patrick give priority to the consultative function: OPTAD is considered a short-term safety valve for the management of interdependence conflicts, while at the same time being an instrument of longer-term indicative planning of economic structural change in the Pacific region. There is also a third goal: the creation of a stable framework based on rules mutually agreed for the increase of trade, investment and development aid flows between the industrial and the developing countries involved. Although Drysdale and Patrick regard membership of OPTAD as being possible for all countries bordering on the Pacific, in principle they are realistic enough to make the conditions of membership dependent on the criteria of an economic order that is based on the working of market

[45] This is one of Krause's main arguments. He believes that a number of unilateral trade and exchange rate policy measures of the past might have been avoided by improved regional policy coordination. In this connection he explicitly mentions: the US soybean export embargo vis-à-vis Japan (1973), Japan's import restrictions on silk textiles vis-à-vis South Korea and China (1974/5), Australia's import restrictions on a number of labour-intensive manufactured goods vis-à-vis the ASEAN countries (1975–6), Thailand's rice export embargo vis-à-vis the Philippines and Indonesia (1973–4), as well as South Korea's massive currency devaluation without consulting its trade partners (1974). (Cf. 'The Pacific Community Idea', op. cit., p. 24). However, not all these examples are totally convincing. Japan and the United States have the OECD as consultative body at their disposal, while Thailand, Indonesia and the Philippines are all members of ASEAN.
[46] A synopsis of already existing international organisations in the Pacific can be found in M.W. Oborne and N. Fourt, *Pacific Basin Economic Cooperation* (OECD Development Centre Studies), Paris 1983, p. 64 ff.

forces.[47] Since the possible inclusion of South American and South Asian countries bordering on the Pacific will also have to be deferred to a more distant future, immediate interest focusses on the fourteen countries included in country group II (see Fig. 1).

The proposed general guiding principles for the founding of OPTAD are: (i) that the individual member-states should be represented by their governments, (ii) that the United States and Japan may assume a role of leadership, (iii) that the administrative apparatus be kept to a minimum so as to avoid over-bureaucratization, and (iv) that task forces be created to handle specific problem areas, thus playing the role of policy-advising and decision-preparation.

The proposed task forces can be established either as a permanent fixture of the organisational structure or as *ad hoc* committees when needed. Drysdale and Patrick focus particularly on the following policy areas and issues:

— *Trade*. One of the major issues here would be the formulation of a code of business conduct within the framework of which a definition of unfair competition and business practices would be possible. A further major issue would be to propose and implement measures necessary to cope with foreign trade-induced structural changes. In this regard, it is the developing countries' interest in rapid expansion of market access which — as is well known — collides with the industrialised nations' objective of securing socially acceptable, smooth adjustment processes.

— *Development financing*. Two major issues are the easing of access of the developing countries to large regional capital markets as well as a reduction of the share of tied development aid. The problems associated with tied aid are particularly worthy of attention, especially if consideration is given to the fact that Japan and the United States and, above all, Canada tend strongly towards engaging in this type of aid.

— *Foreign direct investment*. Joint preparation of a code of conduct for foreign investors, a code which would not only represent the interests of the host-countries but would also offer a stable basis and framework for private investment decisions.

— *Securing of raw material and energy supplies*. Joint efforts for the intensification of energy research and exploration are proposed, as well as consultations concerning the orientation of national raw material and energy policies. Further, the implementation of a

[47] The term 'market economies' is deliberately avoided here, since the Southeast Asian developing countries (although often referred to as market economies) do not stand up to the strict criteria applied in this connection in academic discussion.

system for the stabilisation of earnings from the export of raw materials in the interest of the developing countries of the Pacific is to be examined.

— *Trade with Communist countries.* To be considered only as a discussion forum.

When the Drysdale/Patrick report was published, the concept of cooperation in the Pacific underwent a sudden burst of activity after having been seemingly shelved for much of the 1970s.[48] The number of study groups, reports and seminars on the individual problem areas associated with economic cooperation rapidly increased.[49] In complete disproportion to this, we still find that little attention is paid to this topic in Europe.

One of the major studies and proposals which followed the Drysdale/Patrick report is the final report presented in May 1980 by the Pacific Basin Cooperation Study Group. This study group had been set up in March 1979 by the then Prime Minister Ohira of Japan as a research advisory committee. The report obviously does not share the expectations concerning the short-term realisation of extensive cooperation plans and in contrast emphasises that 'realisation of Pacific Basin cooperation and construction of a prosperous and stable Pacific regional community are long-range tasks with a purview stretching well into the twenty-first century.'[50] This extremely long-term orientation must be considered the result of a 'cooperation philosophy' very different from that of Drysdale and Patrick; while the former concentrated almost exclusively on economic policy cooperation from a perspective greatly influenced by purely economic considerations, the Study Group has chosen instead a fundamental and much broader starting approach which builds on cultural, social and political processes of convergence and agreement as the necessary foundations of the ensuing economic cooperation. This also explains why the following heterogeneous measures and projects have been considered of urgent and immediate importance:

— the expansion of cooperation and exchange programmes organized by government-financed institutions, e.g. the Japan Foundation and the Japan Society for the Promotion of Science;

[48] An important exception is the joint research project of the mid-1970s by the Australian National University and the Japan Economic Research Center, 'Australia, Japan and Western Pacific Economic Relations'. Cf. the final report: J. Crawford and S. Okita (eds), *Raw Materials and Pacific Economic Integration*, London 1978.
[49] A synopsis is offered in Oborne/Fourt, *Pacific Basin*, op. cit., p. 73 ff.
[50] Pacific Basin Cooperation Study Group, *Report*, op. cit., p. 77.

— the founding of a Pacific Basin Cultural Fund as an umbrella organisation for intra regional cultural activities;

— the promotion of city partnerships ('twinned cities') and joint exhibitions (Pacific Basin Expo);

— intensified student exchanges at high school and college level as well as the founding of a joint university (the University of the Seas);

— more intensive internationalisation of the staff of education and research institutions,[51] as well as initiation of joint research programmes concentrating on regional problems; and

— the expansion of regional tourism, and in particular the design of new forms of tourism to increase the understanding of foreign cultures.

Only after cooperation at the intercultural level has been reached does the Report envisage steps towards economic cooperation — which, however, are kept in a general form. The apparent reluctance to make specific substantive proposals in this regard is 'compensated' for by the number of recommendations for the creation of specialised organisations and committees.[52] However, a very cautious attitude on the more important question of an umbrella organisation for regional cooperative efforts has been assumed. Here the study group recommends founding a small committee for the preparation of further regional seminars and conferences. It is symptomatic of the vague character of the study group's final report that no kind of attempt is made to deal with the issue of membership. Instead a non-committal formula is offered: 'A regionalism that is open to the world, not one that is exclusive and closed, is the first characteristic of our concept.'[53]

In contrast to the Drysdale/Patrick report, the study group thus emphasises the importance of a Pacific cultural identity as the basic premise of economic cooperation. The logical consequence of this basic attitude is the long time-span which it envisages, as well as its lack of concrete plans for cooperation. Thus a development already

[51] 'In this regard the present practices in Japan are undeniably behind the times' (Pacific Basin Cooperation Study Group, *Report*, op. cit., p. 31).
[52] For example, a Pacific Basin Industrial Policy Consultative Forum as a forum of discussion for foreign trade-induced problems of industrial adjustment, or a Pacific Basin Economic Information Centre as a general information pool. Furthermore, a Pacific Basin Declaration on Trade and International Investment is proposed, while at the same time it is found necessary to institutionalise the Pacific Basin Finance Conferences for the discussion of questions concerning the transfer of financial resources. Moreover, joint research projects on marine resources and the improvement of transport and communications systems are recommended.
[53] Pacific Basin Cooperation Study Group, *Report*, op. cit., p. 18.

obvious in the transition from PAFTA to OPTAD continues: the concept of cooperation in the Pacific is, on the one hand, becoming more and more extensive (not only in terms of its objectives but also in terms of its regional scope), while on the other hand — and here an obvious link exists — it is also becoming less operational regarding precise policy and organisational recommendations.

Once again it was Kojima who in 1980 presented relatively far-reaching policy-oriented proposals and thus set a counterpoint to the non-committal results of the Pacific Basin Cooperation Study Group.[54] His argumentation has been particularly strongly influenced by the unsatisfactory state of the *global* North-South dialogue (see Chapter III.2*b*), to which his own case for *regional* cooperation between industrialised and developing countries is intended to offer a contrast.[55] At the same time the obvious failure of his earlier PAFTA proposal influenced him in choosing a more strongly selective, step-by-step approach with the goal 'to foster functional integration in the region employing a problem-by-problem approach towards economic development and trade growth among the constituent economies'.[56]

Concrete proposals aimed especially at a coherent development aid and trade policy of the Pacific industrialised nations form the nucleus of the Kojima Plan:

DEVELOPMENT AID POLICY

Apart from pointing to the need to increase the financial resources made available for development aid, Kojima, like Drysdale and Patrick before him, sees an important policy field in the extent to which development aid is actually given in the form of tied financial assistance. He encourages the founding of a 'Revolving Aid Fund' which would essentially be aimed at decreasing the share of tied aid,[57] while at the same time making this approach an instrument of

---

[54] The most comprehensive presentation can be found in Kojima, 'Economic Cooperation', op. cit.

[55] 'The top priority task of OPTAD is to set a good example by successfully settling the North-South problem in the Pacific region (Kojima, 'Economic Cooperation', op. cit., p. 18). This contrasts, however, with his statement that 'if there were no European Community, we would have no need to consider Pacific economic integration either' (op. cit., p. 10). The founding and enlargement of the EC has undoubtedly had trade-diverting effects, in particular for Australia, New Zealand and Canada due to their earlier close ties to Britain but the EC as such certainly cannot be made responsible for the existence of a North-South problem.

[56] Kojima, 'Economic Cooperation', op. cit., p. 7.

[57] Cf. for a general assessment in economic terms: H.-R. Hemmer, *Wirtschaftsprobleme der Entwicklungsländer*, Munich 1978, p. 471 ff.

regional cooperation (thus avoiding, however, the most efficient solution for the developing countries, i.e. doing without tied aid altogether). The planned fund, which in its initial phase is to be applied to the ASEAN countries and located with the Asian Development Bank, is to have the following characteristics:

— The fund is to function as a regional pool for development aid, into which the industrial nations of the Pacific pay a certain amount of their financial aid. Recipient-countries (initially the ASEAN countries) will be allowed to spend the sums placed at their disposal in all member-countries (also by implication in other developing countries) so that tied aid, although not completely abandoned, would allow a larger choice concerning potential suppliers. This would clearly result in increased efficiency in the use of the funds available.

— If we exclude the unlikely case that the recipient-countries spend the funds in the donor-countries in exact proportion to the ratio in which they were paid in, then a disequilibrium between the latter's corresponding shares of the fund and the induced trade flows would necessarily be the result. In case of a surplus, when the exports of a donor-country are greater than would accord with its initial allocation to the fund, a credit relationship to the fund is entered into meaning that the development aid committment increases automatically by the excess sum for the next time-period.[58]

— If the debit or credit positions of the donor-countries involved do not automatically balance out in the short term but rather assume the character of a 'fundamental disequilibrium', accommodating transactions will be necessary from time to time, in which the accumulated surpluses of any given member-country would be paid off by additional allocations to the fund. In the long-term this only means that the sum of development aid payments is made dependent on the relative competitive strength of any given economy (based on the assumption that this competitive strength is reflected by the differing export demands of the fund's recipient-countries).

— Since there would normally be a considerable difference between the availability of funds and their actual disbursements, the fund

[58] 'Suppose that donor country A provides $500 million worth of aid but only $400 is spent, while donor country B provides $500 million but exports goods and service to the value of $600 million to the recipient countries. Country B would accumulate a $100 credit with the fund, raising its total to $600 million, while country A's total would decline commensurately. Thus country B would have automatically increased its aid commitments to $100 million in the second year' (K. Kojima, 'Economic cooperation in a Pacific Community', *Asia Pacific Community*, no. 12/1981, p. 7).

would have at its disposal a deposit base of unused capital, for which Kojima has proposed a number of spending options: mention is made of a system for the stabilisation of export earnings, particularly concerning ASEAN raw materials[59] (corresponding to the STABEX system of the EC); regionally limited buffer stocks for certain raw materials (rice, timber), as well as measures for the advancement of intra-ASEAN trade (credits for the purpose of short-term settlement of balances, financing of export credit).

In addition to his proposal for the creation of a 'Revolving Aid Fund', Kojima further emphasises the need to increase the volume of development aid, e.g. geared towards the expansion of marine transport systems.

FOREIGN TRADE POLICY

Here Kojima emphasises the central role of dynamic structural changes in the Pacific industrialised countries as the prerequisite for any further market opening. He sees precisely in this a great need for cooperation in order to ensure a balanced distribution of adjustment burdens. In this connection, and corresponding to the 0.7% goal (share of official development assistance in GNP) he proposes the formulation of a similar benchmark figure for the financing of structural adjustment processes: 'A certain percentage, say 0.5% of GNP, could be collected through taxation for this purpose.'[60]

Kojima is indeed correct in drawing attention to the close relationship between development aid and necessary structural changes, particularly to the extent that development aid projects are often geared to expanding export-oriented production. At the same time, it should be clear that any new determination of a quantitative target value is less important than an in-substance discussion of the possibilities and limitations of an acceleration of industrial structural change to the advantage of the developing countries. (The 0.7% goal has, after all, been chosen arbitrarily as well.) As long as there are no operational criteria available, Kojima's 0.5% goal can be fulfilled simply by means of terminological cosmetics i.e. by re-labelling subsidies to ailing industries which have been present all along.

In comparison with the thoroughness of Kojima's discussion of aspects of development aid policy and foreign trade policy, his

---

[59] Cf. also G. Boyd, 'ASEAN Regional Policies' in G. Boyd (ed.), *Region Building in the Pacific*, New York 1982, p. 97.
[60] Kojima, 'Economic Cooperation' (1980), op. cit.; p. 30.

comments on the raw materials safeguards policy remain relatively vague, although it is in this field that Japan's particular motivation for increasing cooperation among the Pacific countries is to be found: 'The need for cooperation in the development of potential resources in the Pacific developing countries together with the need for an assured supply are the primary concerns of nations in the pacific region. We cannot but hope that resource security will be guaranteed by the establishment of an organisation such as OPTAD . . . . This is one of the reasons why the establishment of an organisation such as OPTAD is long-awaited.'[61]

We can thus legitimately simplify the plans for economic cooperation in the Pacific — at least from the Japanese point of view — to the formula that a regional 'deal' is to be made in which the industrial countries of the Pacific would offer an increase and qualitative improvement of their financial resource transfers, as well as a further opening of their markets for industrial goods, in return for a long-term assured supply of certain raw materials. At the same time, this indicates that interest in economic cooperation is by no means evenly distributed, but finds its roots in Japan's extreme lack of raw materials.

As a result of the functional and problem-oriented approach to cooperation, Kojima sees the question of organisation as only secondary, thus simply referring to Drysdale and Patrick's OPTAD concept. Kojima tries to keep open the question of adequate limitation or delineation of membership,[62] but recommends for the beginning that efforts should be focussed on a starting group which would have as its members both the ASEAN states and the five Pacific industrial countries ('the ASEAN — five advanced Pacific countries forum').

(*cc*) *The present state of discussions.* Of the vast number of conferences which have taken place on questions of economic cooperation in the Pacific since 1980, the Pacific Economic Cooperation Conferences have proved by far the most important. However, their influence on the progress of efforts toward cooperation is ambivalent: they have destroyed many illusions concerning any kind of rapid formation of a Pacific cooperation organisation, but on the other hand — and this may be due to the mere fact of their existence — they have indeed been able to reinforce the feeling of solidarity among the Pacific nations. The Conferences are organised

---

[61] Ibid., p. 33 ff.
[62] 'All countries in East Asia and Southeast Asia should be welcomed to take part in OPTAD' (Kojima, 'Economic Cooperation' [1980], op. cit., p. 14).

in a tripartite structure consisting of representatives from the' political, business and academic worlds, and they are open in principle to all countries of the Pacific Basin:

— The first Pacific Economic Cooperation Conference (PECC) took place in September 1980 in Canberra. Since this first conference was initiated on the occasion of a meeting between the Japanese and Australian Prime Ministers Ohira and Fraser, i.e. with high-level support from their respective governments, expectations were originally high. However, almost all the participants in the Conferences were sceptical concerning rapid progress at an institutional level, and interpreted the proposed founding of OPTAD as a very long-term goal indeed. As a short-term measure, the founding of a Pacific Cooperation Committee (PCC) as an informal discussion forum was recommended: 'The seminar . . . recommended that a standing committee . . . be established to co-ordinate an expansion of information exchange within the region and to set up task forces to undertake major studies of a number of issues for regional cooperation. The committee . . . will be unofficial, private and informal.'[63] As planned, the PCC was to serve as a coordinating office for the work of problem-oriented task forces and of (National) Pacific Economic Cooperation Committees. Soon after the Canberra conference, national Committees were constituted in a number of countries:[64] — in Japan the Special Committee on Pacific Cooperation, in Canada the Canada-Pacific Cooperation Committee, in Korea the Korean Committee for Pacific Cooperation, and in Thailand the Pacific Cooperation Committee of Thailand.[65] However, no 'umbrella committee' for Pacific cooperation has been founded since official support for this undertaking has been lacking in the countries involved.

— The second PECC which met in Bangkok in June 1982 was under far less pressure in the form of political expectations. The beneficial result of this was that fewer verbose statements were prepared and

---

[63] Summary Report of Proceedings and Main Recommendations, in Crawford/ Seow, *Pacific Economic Cooperation*, op. cit., p. 31.
[64] Cf. H. Soesastro, *Institutional Aspects of ASEAN-Pacific Economic Cooperation* (ESCAP DOCUMENT DP/EGAPEC/11), Bangkok, 2 June 1982, p. 30 ff.
[65] Immediately before the Canberra Conference, the Pan-Pacific Community Association (PPCA) was founded in the United States, with a status similar to that of other national committees. Formation of a US Committee for Pacific Economic Cooperation is at present under discussion (cf. the Pacific Community Newsletter, vol, 4 (1984), no. 1, published by the PPCA). As a further result of the Canberra Conference, an ASEAN Study Group was constituted which has already presented its final report. Cf. N. Akrasanee *et al.*, *ASEAN and the Pacific Community: A Report* (Centre for Strategic and International Studies), Jakarta 1981.

more concrete work programmes were discussed in the various problem areas. Four academic tasks forces were founded: Trade in Manufactures; Trade in Minerals and Energy; Direct Investment and Technology Transfer; and Trade in Agricultural Products, the work of which is coordinated by a standing committee (a kind of PCC replacement) which always has its headquarters in the country organising the next PECC. The various task forces have all presented their first issue papers, which offer a concrete diagnosis of problems. This is in pleasing contrast to the previously dominant political rhetoric of cooperation.

— The third PECC held in November 1983 in Bali,[66] at which the results of the work of the task forces was discussed, showed that for the time being there is less need for models of institutional cooperation than for a specific focus on those problem areas which are caused by the high degree of economic interdependence in the Pacific Basin.[67]

To sum up, the age of the 'Grand Design' of approaches and models towards economic cooperation in the Pacific, be it PAFTA or OPTAD, is a thing of the past. Incremental progress on the way from informal to formal organisation — from academic discussion to political action — is rather the need of the hour. The blueprint of a new large Pacific organisation is obviously not in sight at the moment. A non-governmental forum seems to be the only realistic possibility in the short term: a loosely-connected and unbureaucratic organisation of academics, politicans and business representatives of the Pacific area. The idea of cooperation in the Pacific is still too vague for more extensive initiatives at the moment; there only seems to be a kind of agreement on what it is not supposed to be; namely, it should not be in any way a political or strategic alliance. It should be an organisation serving purely economic purposes and goals. However, the question of exactly how the cooperation is to be arranged, i.e. which specific policy areas and which instruments are to be covered has not yet been decided, and the decisive question of a suitable criterion for the delimitation of membership in an organisation yet to be founded is still unanswered; but there is basic agreement on the great extent of economic interdependence which actually exists in the Pacific Basin, resulting in the economies involved having a high reciprocal vulnerability, as well as on the fact that additional

66 The fourth PECC was held in Seoul in 1985. No results were available, however, at the time of writing.
67 The introductory portion of the final report of the four task forces discussed at the Bali Conference can be found in the Appendix (pp. 151–61).

Table 15.   CONCEPTS OF PACIFIC ECONOMIC COOPERATION: AN OVERVIEW

Cooperation concept	Membership	Main objectives	Organisational form	Specific measures proposed
Kojima, 1966 Kojima, 1969 Kojima, 1971	U.S.A., Japan, Canada, Australia, New Zealand (association option for Asian and Latin American developing countries)	– Acceleration of intraregional trade expansion – Promotion of industrial structural changes – Increase of development assistance – Increase of agricultural production of Asian developing countries.	PAFTA with 'consolidated policy making body' (Kojima 1966, p. 33)	– Gradual elimination of tariffs between member countries – Immediate elimination of tariffs on imports from associated developing countries – Active adjustment policy to increase exports (agricultural goods and labour intensive manufacture) of Asian developing countries
Drysdale/Patrick, 1979	Country group II (see Fig. 1) with future enlargement options	– Creation of a consultation forum to manage interdependence-related conflicts – Agreement on codes of conduct	OPTAD as forum for consultation and policy coordination	– Creation of a number of task forces – Code of business conduct – Code of conduct for foreign investors
Pacific Basin Cooperation Study Group, 1980	No restrictions (all Pacific countries)	– Creation of a Pacific cultural identity – Enhancement of cultural, social and academic understanding and exchange – Institutionalised economic cooperation only as a long-term vision for the 21st century	No official organisation (only informal preparatory committees)	– Pacific Basin Cultural Fund; Pacific Basin Expo; University of the Seas; Promotion of Tourism; exchange of academics – Pacific Basin Industrial Policy Consultative Forum; Pacific Basin Economic Information Center; Pacific Basin Declaration on Trade and International Investment; Pacific Basin Finance Conferences

Pacific Basin Economic Council, 1980	Country group II (see Fig. 1) plus Latin American Pacific countries plus P.R. China	Stabilisation and improvement of the conditions for a free exchange of goods and capital	No official organisation (Pacific Economic Community as long-term goal)	– Improvements in transport and communication systems – Increased efforts in education: Pacific Management Graduate School; vocational training centers – Pacific Cooperation Fund to explore energy resources – Pacific Basin Energy Data Bank
Kojima, 1980	Country group I (see Fig. 1) as initiative group with future enlargement options	Identical with Kojima 1966	OPTAD (see Drysdale/Patrick 1979)	– Revolving Aid Fund as instrument to regionalise tied aid – Stabilisation of export earnings from ASEAN raw materials regional buffer stocks; financial support for export credits – Establishment of fertiliser plants to increase rice production – Improvements in sea transport systems – 0.5% of GDP to be allocated to finance structural adjustment processes – Long-term contracts to secure raw materials supply

means and mechanisms of policy coordination will be necessary in the future.

The next chapter will be devoted to this economic interdependence after offering a final survey of the most important concepts of cooperation set out in Table 15.[68]

4. *Economic interdependence in the Pacific region: taking stock*

(*a*) *General lines of development.* Regionalisation tendencies — in terms of a relative increase of intra-regional economic inter-dependence — can be the result of exogenous political or institutional impulses. On the other hand they may be due to the working of endogenous market forces, leading to an economic integration area which then develops an internal demand for a political cooperation superstructure. The latter seems to be the case for the Pacific economic area. In general, steps or measures of economic integration policy are often of secondary importance and tend to collapse rapidly when working against basic or constitutive endogenous market forces. 'The regionalisation of world trade is therefore primarily the result of relatively constant geographic, cultural and economic determinants and only secondarily the result of more recent regionally limited measures of economic integration policy.'[69]

In his empirical analysis of world economic regionalisation tendencies up to 1970, Sautter was able to conclude that the Pacific region (with the exclusion of Latin America) could be considered the regionalisation centre *par excellence* of the world economy. He added that, by contrast, there is no justification for speaking of a North Atlantic (Western Europe — USA) trade integration area.[70] What has the situation been in the first half of the 1980s? How important is the intra-trade for the Pacific economic area and which development tendencies are becoming evident?

---

[68] In addition to the extensively discussed concepts, the synopsis also contains a brief outline of the long-term views of the Pacific Basin Economic Council (cf. *Asahi Evening News*, 1 May 1981). Approximately 400 firms — most of them from Pacific industrial nations — are members of the PBEC, which was founded in 1967.

[69] H. Sautter, *Regionalisierung und komparative Vorteile im internationalen Handel*, Tübingen 1983, p. 280.

[70] H. Sautter, 'Regionalisierungstendenzen im Welthandel zwischen 1938 und 1970' in Giersch/Haas, *Probleme*, op. cit., p. 596 ff. To avoid misinterpretation it must be mentioned that Sautter does not consider the absolute volume of trade flows. In his approach, regionalisation coefficients are calculated which expresss the ratio between the actual trade interdependences and those which can be expected according to the share of the given countries in world trade.

In 1984 more than half the exports (61%) and imports (58%) of the fourteen Pacific nations under consideration here (compare Table 17[71]) were transacted within the region itself (including, however, bilateral trade between the United States and Canada). This is an astonishingly high share of intra-trade, particularly when compared with the corresponding values — 52% for exports and 50% for imports — of intra-trade in the EC (the EC of the Nine) in 1984.

Because a considerably lower relative trade interdependence was to be noted in 1965 (intra-export 47%, intra-import 52%), the expressed claim of a distinct relative increase of intra-regional trade in the course of time is certainly valid. Furthermore, it should be added that the further increase in the high intra-regional share of trade was reached in a period marked by the structural upheavals following on two oil price increases and thus by the growing significance of the OPEC countries as world trade partners.[72]

If we glance briefly at the figures of the individual countries, we notice a relative decrease in Japan's intra-trade in the Pacific from 1965 to 1976 (a result of the penetration of new markets due to a policy of regional export diversification), while between 1976 and 1984 it increased tremendously.

The case of the United States deserves particular attention. There can be no doubt that the strong Pacific orientation of the US economy has always been strongly influenced by its bilateral trade with Canada.[73] On the other hand, the remaining countries of the Pacific have been able constantly to increase their position as US trading partners and meanwhile participate in US foreign trade at 24% on the export side and 34% on the import side. Thus it seems fair to speak of a distinct tendency of US foreign trade to turn to the Pacific. This aspect will be discussed in more detail below.

Almost all the developing countries of the Pacific show extremely high intra-trade coefficients. However, Indonesia's 88% is exceptional due to its oil exports; the aggregate values for the ASEAN nations are 76% for exports and 68% for imports, and have been decisively influenced by their very intense trading relationships with Japan. An analysis of the changes in the intra-trade coefficients between 1965 and 1984 yields ambivalent results: Malaysia and the

[71] Table 16 presents a survey of some basic economic data showing above all the remarkably high growth-rates of production and foreign trade during the 1970s.
[72] In the case of Japan, the intra-trade coefficients reached 63% for exports and 62% for imports in 1973. As early as 1974, however, intra-imports rapidly dropped from 62 to 54% of total imports. Cf. Crawford/Okita, *Raw Materials*, op. cit., p. 85 ff.
[73] However, to justify the 'Pacific' interests of the United States by its high trade interdependence with Canada would at best be shadow-boxing. The discrepancy in the case of Canada would be even more obvious, (cf. Table 17).

Table 16. BASIC ECONOMIC DATA OF PACIFIC BASIN COUNTRIES

	GNP per capita (US $), 1984	Annual growth rate of GNP (%) 1965-84	Structure of production (GDP shares %) 1984			Annual growth rate of foreign trade (%), 1970-84	
			Agriculture	Industry[b]	Services	Export	Import
Australia	11,740	1.7	5[a]	32(19)[a]	63[a]	3.8[c]	5.2[c]
Japan	10,630	4.7	3	41(30)	56	7.4	1.3
Canada	13,280	2.4	3	24(16)	72	3.6	1.5
New Zealand	7,730	1.4	8	33(23)[a]	59	4.4	0.1
U.S.A.	15,390	1.7	2	32(21)	66	2.8	3.1
Indonesia	540	4.9	26	40(13)	34	1.4	9.8
Malaysia	1,980	4.5	21	35(19)	44	4.9	7.3
Philippines	660	2.6	25	34(25)	41	7.5	1.3
Singapore	7,260	7.8	1	39(25)	60	12.0[c]	9.9[c]
Thailand	860	4.2	20	27(19)	52	9.0	3.3
Hong Kong	6,330	6.2	1	30(22)	69	10.3	12.1
South Korea	2,110	6.6	14	40(28)	47	14.8	7.5
Taiwan	2,500	7.5	9	44(33)	47	18.1	14.1
Papua-New Guinea	710	0.6	34[a]	30(8)[a]	37[a]	19.5[d]	15.0[d]

[a] 1980. [b] Data for manufacturing industry in brackets. [c] 1970–81. [d] 1972–80.

Sources: World Bank, *World Development Report*, various issues; Council for Economic Planning and Development, Republic of China, *Taiwan Statistical Data Book*, 1985; Asian Development Bank.

Table 17. SHARE OF INTRA-PACIFIC TRADE[a] IN TOTAL FOREIGN TRADE OF PACIFIC BASIN COUNTRIES, 1965/1976/1984 (%)

	1965		1976		1984	
	Export	Import	Export	Import	Export	Import
Australia	47.1	45.1	63.9	58.8	63.6	63.0
Japan	57.5	48.3	49.8	43.3	62.1	50.2
Canada	64.1 (6.5)[b]	75.4 (4.6)[b]	72.8 (8.2)[b]	69.4 (7.8)[b]	80.9 (7.5)[b]	80.0 (10.3)[b]
New Zealand	25.4	46.6	50.5	54.4	54.1	67.5
U.S.A.	37.5 (17.0)[b]	41.5 (19.7)[b]	39.5 (18.5)[b]	44.0 (24.0)[b]	45.6 (24.3)[b]	53.3 (33.7)[b]
Indonesia	61.9	52.0	83.5	76.0	87.5	66.5
Malaysia	60.3	48.3	66.2	73.3	71.0	72.1
Philippines	78.5	82.2	71.1	65.6	80.2	64.7
Singapore	–	–	72.2	59.2	73.0	68.1
Thailand	60.0	57.4	64.6	56.5	54.5	63.7
ASEAN	–	–	73.7	65.6	75.5	67.6
Hong Kong	59.8	45.9	58.4	56.3	54.0	56.2
South Korea	76.0	91.6	71.2	66.0	64.1	63.9
Taiwan	73.6	85.1	74.3	63.8	78.1	64.9
Papua-New Guinea	70.5	85.9	63.3	90.4	51.1	89.3
Total	47.3	51.6	53.5	51.6	61.2	58.3

[a] Defined as trade among the 14 countries included in the table.
[b] Excluding trade between the U.S.A. and Canada.

Sources: IMF, Direction of Trade Statistics, *Yearbook 1985*; Council for Economic Planning and Development, Republic of China, *Taiwan Statistical Data Book*, 1985. Drysdale/Patrick, *An Asian-Pacific. . . .*, op. cit., p. 30 ff.; authors' calculations.

Philippines show the most obvious increase on the export side while South Korea and Hong Kong in particular (due to the diversification of their exports towards the Middle East and Europe) seem to be shifting part of their foreign trade away from the Pacific basin, a tendency also to be observed in the case of Thailand's exports.

Table 18.   SHARE OF PACIFIC DEVELOPING COUNTRIES IN
INTRA-PACIFIC FOREIGN TRADE, 1965/1976/1984 (%)

	1965		1976		1984	
	Export	*Import*	*Export*	*Import*	*Export*	*Import*
Australia	21.2	15.2	19.5	19.6	30.9	21.4
Japan	32.6	25.2	39.1	37.0	32.6	41.4
Canada	1.2	1.3	1.6	4.1	2.4	5.1
New Zealand	3.5	6.2	15.9	10.2	16.7	13.4
U.S.A.	12.5	14.1	18.7	23.7	23.9	27.9

Sources: As Table 17.

Table 18 focuses on the aggregated position of the Pacific developing nations as trade partners of the industrialised countries. Empirical findings here indicate a distinct increase in importance. Between 1965 and 1984 the share of the Pacific developing nations in the intra-Pacific foreign trade of the United States doubled to reach 24% (exports) and 28% (imports); in the case of Japan that share further increased from its high original starting position to include now 42% of all imports from the Pacific. On the export side their share has fallen back to the 1965 level of 32% because of the recent phenomenal growth of Japanese exports to the United States. Canada is the sole exception: the extent of its trade with this group of countries — although on the increase — has remained of virtually no importance.

The interim findings of this empirical analysis are, first, that the Pacific economic area is distinguished by a high *level* of intra-trade interdependencies; secondly, that the *development* of intra-trade coefficients in the course of time follows different patterns for individual countries; and, thirdly, that as an unmistakeable line of development, the Pacific developing nations are becoming much more important as trading partners in the Pacific area.

If plans for economic cooperation in the Pacific do indeed aim at sustaining an integration area which *already exists* by economic policy efforts towards coordination and harmonisation, and thus do

Table 19. SHARE OF LATIN AMERICAN PACIFIC COUNTRIES*a*
IN TOTAL FOREIGN TRADE OF PACIFIC BASIN
COUNTRIES, 1984 (%)

	Export share	Import share
Australia	0.3	0.2
Japan	3.3	2.9
Canada	0.8	2.0
New Zealand	1.4	0.0
U.S.A.	8.3	9.9
Indonesia	0.0	0.3
Malaysia	0.1	0.2
Philippines	0.4	0.0
Singapore	1.1	0.2
Thailand	0.5	0.5
Hong Kong	0.8	0.2
South Korea	2.0	3.4
Taiwan	0.5*b*	2.1*b*
Papua-New Guinea	0.0	0.1

a Chile, Costa Rica, Ecuador, El Salvador, Guatemala, Honduras, Colombia, Mexico, Nicaragua, Panama, Peru.
b Calculated as share of total Latin America excluding Argentina and Brazil.

Sources: As Table 17.

not intend to *expand* the area of cooperation,[74] then the demands to include the Pacific nations of Latin America would prove almost pointless. As Table 19 indicates, the trade interrelationships between the developing nations of the Pacific and Latin America can only be called negligible. The same is true also of Japan, though with some minor exceptions. Recently Japan's economic relationships with Latin America have indeed been intensified, but this applies mostly to its trade with countries such as Argentina and particularly Brazil, neither of which has a Pacific coastline. Summing up, we agree with Wionczek's statement: 'While for Australia and the Asian NICs Latin America hardly existed at all, for Japan it had only marginal economical and political importance throughout the time of Japan's rise to the status of a world economic superpower.'[75] This was only to be expected, due partly to

[74] This objective may, of course, be criticised by pointing to its *status quo* orientation, since often one of the essential motives of economic cooperation is to create new patterns of interaction. However, in the case under discussion here, consideration must be given to the fact that the fourteen countries in question already imply an extensive interpretation of the concept of regional cooperation. Further enlargements would merge any clear distinctions into a virtually global approach (cf. Fig. 1 for possible options).
[75] M.S. Wionczek, 'Pacific Trade and Development Cooperation with Latin America', *Asia Pacific Community*, no. 9/1980, p. 34.

cultural and geographic factors, but also to the dominant position of US firms on the Latin American market as well as the traditional strategy of import substituting industrialisation.

The importance of the Pacific countries of Latin America for US foreign trade (8% of exports, 10% of imports) deviates from the described pattern and has been heavily influenced by the dominant position of Mexico; this would cause considerable political problems over the possible role of the United States in the framework of a Pacific economic cooperation organisation which did not include Latin America (see below).

Table 20.   IMPORTANCE OF PACIFIC REGION AS PRODUCER
OF RAW MATERIALS, 1976 (%)

	Pacific region in world total			Pacific region in market economy total		
	Mine output	Refined metal output	Reserves	Mine output	Refined metal output	Reserves
Copper	38	38	32	49	50	37
Lead	37	35	56	54	51	71
Zinc	38	34	46	54	48	53
Bauxite	32	–	19	37	–	20
Aluminium	–	46	–	–	58	–
Silver	38	–	37	47	–	56
Nickel	60	–	41	80	–	47
Tin	69	75	47	69	75	59
Iron ore	27	–	27	60	–	41
Raw steel	–	33	–	–	51	–
Coal A[a]	13	–	–	46	–	–
Coal B[b]	20	–	34	40	–	85
Cobalt	19	–	37	21	–	48

[a] Anthracite.
[b] Bituminous and lignite.
Source: Drysdale/Patrick, op. cit., p. 36.

We will now look briefly at the extent to which the Pacific region is endowed with raw materials. Table 20 offers information on the relative shares of production and reserves of important mineral resources, while Table 21 shows the importance of the region as a supplier of raw materials for the Pacific industrial nations. It can be seen that trade in raw materials is far more heavily concentrated on a regional basis than is the entire foreign trade. As early as 1973 Japan, by importing from countries of the Pacific basin, was able to cover up to 90% of its imports of iron ore, up to 93% of its coal, 97% of its copper ore, 100% of its nickel ore and bauxite, and 98% of its tin. Similarly high percentages are also to be noted for US

Table 21.   GEOGRAPHICAL STRUCTURE OF THE
PACIFIC INDUSTRIALISED COUNTRIES'
RAW MATERIALS IMPORTS, 1973

	Japan	U.S.A.	Canada	Australia	New Zealand
Iron ore					
(1) Imports (1,000 tons)	134,700	44,100	2,700	14,700	–
(2) % from Pacific^a countries	89.4	93.0	98.8	98.7	–
Coal					
(1)	56,900	87.0	15,000	11.0	0.6
(2)	92.5	86.7	100.0	9.6	100.0
Copper ore					
(1)	2,990	39.2	32.0	–	–
(2)	97.1	100.0	91.6	–	–
Copper ingot					
(1)	410.0	325.0	19.0	0.7	1.3
(2)	33.9	81.4	88.4	9.6	87.9
Nickel ore					
(1)	3,570	28.0	7.0	177.0	–
(2)	100.0	99.8	93.7	100.0	–
Nickel ingot					
(1)	15.0	109.0	15.0	2.2	0.2
(2)	37.7	71.6	7.1	95.4	89.4
Bauxite					
(1)	5,615	13,163	3,490	–	0.5
(2)	99.8	98.4	84.0	–	95.2
Aluminium ingot					
(1)	476.0	461.0	45.0	2.4	2.8
(2)	51.7	87.4	73.8	79.4	94.9
Tin ingot					
(1)	36.0	48.0	6.0	0.04	0.03
(2)	98.0	92.2	84.4	97.7	96.8

^a Includes Latin American Pacific countries. .

Source: Kojima, *Economic Cooperation*, op. cit., p. 35.

imports of raw materials which, however, with the exception of
bauxite and nickel bars involve only considerably lower absolute
orders of magnitude.[76]

However, the dividing line between importers and exporters of

[76] However, various prognoses indicate that the dependence of the US economy on
imports of mineral raw materials may increase drastically in the future. Cf. R.J.G.
Wells, 'ASEAN Commodity Trade', *Asia Pacific Community*, no. 9/1980, p. 62.

raw materials does not run exactly parallel to that between the industrial and developing countries. Australia, for example, has assumed an increasingly prominent position as an exporter of raw materials. In 1974 Japan imported .79% of its wool, 55% of its bauxite, 47% of its iron ore, 27% of its nickel and 24% of its coal, as well as 16% of its wheat, from Australia.[77] On the mineral raw materials market the ASEAN countries have a dominant position as exporters of tin (1979: 69% of world export); they also do, to a limited extent, as suppliers of cobalt and copper. There are considerable deposits of petroleum and natural gas (Indonesia, Malaysia) which have not yet been completely opened up, and moreover ASEAN is the world's first-ranking exporter of natural rubber and timber. It is also today the world's second largest exporter of rice.[78]

All in all, the Pacific economic area presents a picture of a region well equipped with those raw materials which are strategically important for the industrialisation process; thus it differs significantly from the position of, for example, the Western European economic area. The only major exception is petroleum ('the only important resource which is difficult to secure in the Pacific area'),[79] but here too we immediately would notice new perspectives if expectations concerning the petroleum deposits off the coast of Southern China can be realised.

(b) *Japan and the Pacific developing nations.* A pivotal aspect of cooperative efforts in the Pacific is Japan's intention to arrive at a closer and more intensive cooperation with the developing nations surrounding it, which can be divided into the ASEAN countries on the one hand, and the NICs in a narrow sense (Hong Kong, South Korea and Taiwan) on the other.[80] These countries are of course

---

[77] Cf. Crawford and Okita, *Raw Materials*, op. cit., p. 54. On the other hand, Australia imports a large proportion of its industrial goods from Japan (in 1976, 46% of transport equipment and 45% of its electric machinery and appliances). Cf. on the development of the bilateral economic relations of these two countries J.V. Martin, Jr., 'Management of Bilaterial Economic Relations by Japan and Australia' in *Asia Pacific Community*, no. 13/1981, p. 113 ff., and M. Shinohara, 'Trade and Industrial Adjustments in the Asia-Pacific Region and Japan', *Asian Economies*, no. 39/1981, p. 14 ff.

[78] For details see K. Reiter, *Regionale wirtschaftliche Zusammenarbeit von Staaten der Dritten Welt. Eine theoretische und empirische Analyse der ASEAN*, Saarbrücken 1983, p. 206 ff.

[79] Kojima, 'Economic Cooperation' op. cit., p. 36.

[80] Japan's diplomatic offensive *vis-à-vis* the ASEAN countries has its origins in the so-called Fukuda Doctrine of 1977, which attracted considerable attention although it was only a non-committal declaration of Japan's peaceful and cooperative attitude, cf. W.W. Haddad, 'Japan, the Fukuda Doctrine, and ASEAN', *Contemporary Southeast Asia*, vol. 2 (1980), p. 10 ff. In 1981 Prime Minister Suzuki visited all

Table 22.   JAPAN'S SHARE IN EXPORTS AND IMPORTS OF
PACIFIC DEVELOPING COUNTRIES, 1978/84 (%)

	1978		1984	
	Japan's export share	Japan's import share	Japan's export share	Japan's import share
Indonesia	39.2	30.1	47.3	23.8
Malaysia	21.7	23.2	22.6	26.2
Philippines	24.4	27.5	19.6	13.4
Singapore	9.7	19.2	9.4	18.4
Thailand	20.3	30.7	13.0	26.8
Hong Kong	7.7	22.9	4.4	23.6
South Korea	20.7	40.0	15.3	25.0
Taiwan	12.4	33.4	10.5	29.3

Source: As Table 17.

highly dependent on the Japanese economy as a kind of regional centre of gravity for their own economic development — which does not imply that, for example, the ASEAN countries would accept Japanese proposals of cooperation without hesitation (see below). We intend now to look more closely at the extent and structure of economic relationships between Japan and the developing countries of the Pacific. In general terms it can be said that Japan has a dominant role as a trading partner for these countries which mostly far exceeds that of the United States. Only for South Korea and Taiwan is the United States the leading export market, while even in these two cases Japan supplies the greater part of their imports (25% and 29% respectively). With the exception of the Philippines, the Japanese import share for the ASEAN countries varies between 18% and 27%, and its export share between 13% and 47% (see Table 22).

If we remember that Japan carries out some 20% of its foreign trade (20% of its exports, 18% of its imports) with the Pacific developing countries as an aggregate, whereas the share of each

ASEAN countries and renewed Japan's offer of cooperation (with particular emphasis on the development of agriculture, energy and education), as well as announcing an increase in Japan's development assistance (cf. J. Fujiwara, 'Japan-Southeast Asia Cooperation in the 1980s', *Asia Pacific Community*, no. 13/1981, p. 6 ff). Apparently at the same time, chances for creating a future economic community with South Korea were being explored via unofficial channels (cf. A. Hernádi, 'The Pacific Region as a growth Sub-Center and Japan's Role', *Asia Pacific Community*, no. 5/1979, p. 123 ff.)

individŭal country only reaches between 1% and a maximum of 3%, then a considerable asymmetry of mutual dependences becomes obvious. Although there are some very strong differences, each of the developing nations of the Pacific shows great sensitivity to fluctuations of the Japanese domestic economic situation, while the opposite is in no way true of Japan.[81]

Let us now proceed from this global view of foreign trade interdependence to a structural analysis of the patterns of specialisation involved.[82] The first thing to be noticed is that the ASEAN countries continue to be of major importance for Japan in their capacity as suppliers of raw materials — in 1979 70% of ASEAN's total exports but as much as 91% of exports to Japan consisted of raw materials.[83] This means that basically a vertical division of labour still is valid. However, this division of labour is becoming increasingly overlaid with tendencies towards a horizontal (inter-industrial) division of labour — at least in relatively labour-intensive branches of industry. The degree of the horizontal division of labour is however far stronger in the relationship of Japan with the Northeast Asian NICs, as the details of Table 23 indicate. The respective index of the horizontal division of labour (cf. Table 23, note *a*) showed an increase from 9% to 27% between 1965 and 1978. The greatest increase was to be found in coal and metal products, electrical and electronic equipment, transport equipment and precision instruments. The index stagnated in textiles and wood products (in addition to printing products and precision instruments), which were precisely the branches in which the horizontal division of labour with the ASEAN countries had the highest growth rates.

In recent years the NICs under consideration here have developed to become strong competitors of Japanese industry. They have been able to expand their market shares particularly in third markets, but also on the Japanese domestic market (despite the subtle barriers to trade created by some of the less obvious peculiarities of the Japanese distribution system). If we identify the main reason for Japan's

---

[81] Cf. also L.C. Yah, 'ASEAN's External Trade: Intra-ASEAN and Extra-ASEAN Co-operation', *ASEAN Business Quarterly*, no. 4/1979, p. 13 ff.
[82] Cf. T. Watanabe, 'An Analysis of Economic Interdependence among the Asian NICs, the ASEAN Nations, and Japan', *The Developing Economies*, vol. 18 (1980), p. 393 ff.; T. Tanaka, 'The Patterns of International Specialisation among Asian Countries and the Future of Japanese Industry', *The Developing Economies*, vol. 18 (1980), p. 412 ff.; M. Shinohara, 'Emerging Industrial Adjustment in Asia-Pacific Area', *Asia Pacific Community*, no. 11/1981, p. 1 ff.
[83] Calculated from data presented in ESCAP, *Foreign Trade Statistics of Asia and the Pacific 1979*, vol. XVIII, Series A, Bangkok/New York 1982.

Table 23.   JAPAN'S HORIZONTAL DIVISION OF
LABOUR INDEX[a] BY TRADE PARTNERS AND BY
CATEGORIES OF GOODS, 1965/1970/1978

	Asian NICs[b]			ASEAN[c]		
	1965	1970	1978	1965	1970	1978
Food	16.7	15.9	24.9	16.6	18.0	16.3
Textile yarn	11.5	39.6	41.9	2.1	0.6	32.8
Textile products	24.1	31.6	25.8	4.8	19.0	30.7
Wooden products	18.2	27.8	21.6	4.5	21.4	21.7
Pulp, paper	6.4	17.5	9.2	1.4	11.2	9.5
Printing, publishing	13.7	14.3	90.2	7.5	1.8	93.5
Rubber products	20.7	37.7	37.8	0.3	0.1	17.6
Chemicals	7.9	14.9	19.1	4.9	4.7	9.4
Petroleum products	10.4	36.7	19.8	27.1	31.5	8.6
Coal products	0.0	47.8	99.5	0.0	0.0	0.0
Non-metallic products	3.7	11.1	19.0	0.0	0.1	0.8
Iron and steel	21.5	23.0	28.0	0.0	0.0	6.0
Primary iron	0.0	7.3	13.0	0.0	0.3	4.6
Primary nonferrous metal	12.7	15.0	20.9	1.0	1.5	3.6
Metal products	0.3	12.2	21.3	0.1	0.2	0.9
General machinery	1.6	1.3	6.0	0.3	0.2	1.6
Electric-electronic equipment	3.8	20.2	22.4	0.0	0.0	6.4
Transport equipment	0.5	6.8	10.6	0.0	0.0	0.4
Precision instruments	2.5	3.3	16.5	0.0	0.0	21.5
Other manufactures	25.5	44.0	51.0	18.0	30.0	38.4
Total manufactures	8.7	16.3	27.4	3.9	5.9	15.2

[a] The index of horizontal division of labour can be calculated as:

$$\frac{1}{n} \sum_{i=1}^{n} \left(\frac{Eij + Mij - (Eij - Mij)}{Fij + Mij} \right) \times 100$$

E, M = Japan's exports (imports)
j = countries
i = categories of goods
n = number of commodity items
 within a category

This index will be zero in case of a complete export or import specialisation *vis-à-vis* country j; if Japan's exports to and imports from a country j are equal in a category, the index number will be 100.

[b] Hong Kong, South Korea, Taiwan *and Singapore*.

[c] Excluding Singapore.

interest in cooperation with the ASEAN countries in its being supplied with raw materials, then the question arises: what motivates
Japan's particular interest in cooperating with the NICs, which are
its keenest competitors? Some help in answering this question can be
gained by casting a glance at the respective structure of the horizontal division of labour. Here we find as a characteristic feature
that the Asian NICs import predominantly intermediate and capital

Table 24.   MERCHANDISE TRADE BALANCE OF PACIFIC
NEWLY INDUSTRIALISING COUNTRIES WITH IMPORTANT
FOREIGN TRADE PARTNERS, 1971/84 (*US$ millions*)

		Japan	U.S.A.	E.C.
Hong Kong	1971	– 627	574	75
	1984	– 5,479	6,284	853
Singapore	1971	– 431	– 153	– 228
	1984	– 3,006	– 644	– 543
South Korea	1971	– 699	– 147	– 179
	1984	– 3,192	3,233	334
Taiwan	1971	– 583	457	14
	1984	– 3,256	9,826	685

Sources: For 1971: Tanaka *Patterns*, op. cit., p. 432; for 1984; IMF, Direction of Trade, *Statistics Yearbook*, 1985.

Table 26.   SHARE OF INDIVIDUAL COUNTRIES IN JAPAN'S
PRIVATE FOREIGN INVESTMENT IN PACIFIC BASIN
DEVELOPING COUNTRIES, 1951–69/1970–5/1976–81 (%)

	1951–69	1970–75	1976–81
Indonesia	40.9	44.1	57.1
Malaysia	7.6	7.4	4.3
Philippines	9.9	8.2	3.9
Singapore	5.1	6.9	10.5
Thailand	16.5	3.6	2.5
ASEAN	80.0	70.2	78.6
Hong Kong	4.2	10.0	11.8
South Korea	3.2	15.9	7.0
Taiwan	12.7	3.8	2.6
Total	100.0	100.0	100.0

Source: H. Laumer, *Die Direktinvestitionen der japanischen Wirtschaft in den Schwellenländern Ost- und Südostasiens*, Munich 1984, p. 23.

goods from Japan, while their industrial exports consist predominantly of consumer goods. In 1977 54% of South Korea's and 46% of Taiwan's exports to Japan consisted of final products, while respectively 44% and 42% of their imports from Japan consisted of machinery alone.[84] This is indicative of a more *inter*-industrial and less *intra*-industrial division of labour. If an intra-industrial special-

[84] Cf. Tanaka, 'Patterns', op. cit., p. 428 ff.

Table 25.   JAPAN'S PRIVATE FOREIGN INVESTMENT IN PACIFIC DEVELOPING COUNTRIES, 1978/1979/1980/1951–80

	1978		1979		1980		1951–80	
	US$ million	(%ᵃ)	US$ million	(%)	US$ million	(%)	US$ million	(%)
Indonesia	610	13.2	150	3.0	529	11.3	4,424	12.1
Malaysia	48	1.0	33	0.7	146	3.1	650	1.8
Philippines	53	1.2	102	2.0	78	1.7	615	1.7
Singapore	174	3.8	255	5.1	140	3.0	936	2.6
Thailand	32	0.7	55	1.1	33	0.7	396	1.1
ASEAN	917	19.9	595	11.9	926	19.7	7,021	19.2
Hong Kong	159	3.5	225	4.5	156	3.3	1,095	3.0
South Korea	222	4.8	95	1.9	35	0.7	1,137	3.1
Taiwan	40	0.9	39	0.8	47	1.0	370	1.0
Total	1,338	29.1	954	19.1	1,164	24.8	9,623	26.4

ᵃ % of worldwide Japanese private foreign investment.

Source: Calculated from data presented in: Pacific Basin Economic Council/Japan National Committee, *Pacific Economic Community Statistics*, Tokyo 1982.

isation can be found in some individual branches, closer investigation shows that vertical specialisation emerges with regard to the sub-branches, as can be illustrated by the electronic equipment branch. Here the horizontal exchange between Japan and South Korea in the sub-branch of 'consumer electronics' is of considerable size. At the same time, however, South Korea still has to import the lion's share of technologically sophisticated industrial electronics, for which it relies heavily on Japanese suppliers.[85]

In other words, despite their tremendous success in industrialisation and export growth, the economies of the NICs under consideration are still not completely integrated, which means that they do not have at their disposal complete control over technologically complex production sequences. Their strategy of exporting processed final products has thus contributed to a considerable increase of import dependence on Japan, as a result of which there has been a rapid increase of the high Japanese trade surpluses with these countries (see Table 24). From the beginning of the 1970s until the beginning of the 1980s this trade surplus has increased by more than 400%; in 1984 it was at US$ 15 billion and thus accounted for almost half the entire Japanese trade surplus.

Moreover, the Pacific developing countries occupy a cardinal position as targets for Japanese private direct investments (compare Tables 25 and 26). Altogether in the years 1951 to 1980 they absorbed more than a quarter (26%) of such capital flows, the ASEAN countries alone absorbing nearly 20% (dominated by the high investment flows to Indonesia). Thus the developing countries of the Pacific basin attain a share of the total Japanese foreign investments which, in the case of most other industrial countries, is reached only by the aggregate of all developing countries. Consequently Japanese investments play an important role as a source of foreign capital in nearly all the countries under consideration (for the ASEAN countries, cf. Table 31 below). Particularly when judged by their cumulative amounts, Japanese investments in the ASEAN countries are still especially oriented to raw materials.[86] Nevertheless, serious changes in structure can be expected here, particularly tending towards an increasing importance for the

[85] Cf. Watanabe, 'Analysis', op. cit., p. 406 ff.

[86] 'Agriculture and Fisheries' and mining account for 56% of Japanese investments in the ASEAN countries (cumulative figures as of March 1977), whereas only 35% are accounted for by manufacturing industry. However, the country-specific deviations are quite strong; in Indonesia 71% and 24%, Malaysia 28% and 63% the Philippines 57% and 29%, Singapore 0% and 72% , Thailand 4% and 78%. Cf. M. Ikema, 'Japan's Economic Relations with ASEAN' in Garnaut, *ASEAN*, op. cit., p. 463.

Table 27. JAPAN'S BILATERAL OFFICIAL DEVELOPMENT
ASSISTANCE (ODA) TO PACIFIC DEVELOPING
COUNTRIES, 1978-81

	Average 1980-1		Average 1979-80		1978	
	US$m.	*%ᵃ*	*US$m.*	*%*	*US$m.*	*%*
Indonesia	403.7	17.0	287.1	15.1	227.6	14.9
Malaysia	80.1	3.4	70.3	3.7	48.0	3.1
Philippines	168.5	7.1	90.8	4.8	66.5	4.3
Singapore	–	–	–	–	3.6	0.2
Thailand	201.6	8.5	184.6	9.7	103.8	6.8
ASEAN	854.5	35.9	632.8	33.3	449.5	29.3
Hong Kong	–	–	–	–	0.7	0.0
South Korea	249.2	10.5	64.5	3.4	66.1	4.3
Taiwan	–	–	–	–	– 11.4	– 0.7
Total	1,103.7	46.4	697.3	36.7	504.9	32.9

ᵃ % of Japan's total bilateral ODA.

Sources: Calculated from data presented in: OECD, *Zusammenarbeit im Dienst der Entwicklung*, Paris 1982 and 1983; S. Sekiguchi, 'Japan's Regional Policies' in G. Boyd (ed.), *Region-Building in the Pacific*, New York 1982, p. 69.

manufacturing industry, above all towards know-how-intensive growth branches.[87]

Japan has concentrated its development assistance even more than its private direct investments on the Pacific area, which has recently become an increasing trend. In 1980/1, an average of 46% of the bilateral ODA payments fell to the Pacific developing countries under discussion here, and 36% fell to the ASEAN countries alone — of which nearly half went to Indonesia (compare Table 27).

5. *Political assessment: the view of major participants*

To recapitulate, we presented in Chapter III.2 various explanations of the regionalisation tendencies in international economic relations, thus enabling them to appear potentially advantageous. There were two primary considerations: on the one hand the process of sectoral structural adjustments, conflicting as it does with the domestic and foreign trade-oriented goals of the industrialised

[87] For more information see Laumer, *Direktinvestitionen*, op. cit., p. 37 ff.

nations, and on the other hand the obvious deterioration of the global North-South dialogue. Then in Chapter III.3 we discussed the great demand, primarily from Japan, for regional political coordination and harmonisation in the Pacific Basin, while Chapter III.4 emphasised the existence of a region which is highly inter-dependent economically as a pre-condition for economic coopera-tion of Pacific countries.

Thus we can say unequivocally that a high potential of coopera-tion in the Pacific area is not only indicated, theoretically; there is political and empirical evidence for it as well. The extent to which this potential can be explored in the future depends decisively on the economic and general political interests and attitudes of the countries involved. We have already frequently mentioned that Japan's positive attitude toward an intensification and formalization of cooperation can be considered as beyond dispute. Thus it is primarily the attitude of the United States as a further economic superpower, as well as that of the ASEAN countries as a cooperation unit that already exists which becomes of increasing importance. Let us now turn to both these aspects.

(*a*) *On the position of the USA*. The Pacific basin has recently gained considerable importance in public political discussions in the United States — not only as a regional centre of gravity concerning economic interdependences but going beyond that because it is here that the ambitions and the interests of three nuclear powers — the United States, the Soviet Union and the People's Republic of China collide. It is obvious that all three are increasingly interested in the political and strategic importance of the Pacific area.

In the mean time, a number of politicians, academic and business leaders are of the opinion that there is a great discrepancy between the actual importance of the Pacific nations for American interests and the conceptually underdeveloped Pacific policy on the other hand: a discrepancy which should be eliminated. The political scien-tist R.O. Tilman has made a typical statement in this connection: 'America is a Pacific power, and America must be intimately involved in the affairs of the Pacific Basin . . . Given the realities of the geographic distribution of resources and populations, given the location of the strategically crucial sea routes from the Middle East, and given the political long-range importance of China, it is tempt-ing to argue that for America, the twenty-first century must belong to Asia, just as prior centuries belonged principally to Europe.'[88]

[88] R.O. Tilman, 'Asia, ASEAN, and America in the Eighties: The Agonies of Maturing Relationships', *Contemporary Southeast Asia*, vol. 1 (1981), p. 319.

Michael Mansfield, America's ambassador to Tokyo, said the same in fewer words: 'The United States is also a Pacific nation. We have, however, long directed our attention toward Europe — too long, in fact.'[89]

As early as the turn of the century John M. Hay, US Secretary of State from 1898 to 1905, recognised that the Atlantic as the 'Ocean of the Present' would at some time in the future give way to the Pacific as the 'Ocean of the Future'. Less than a century later, the question still stands: has the 'Pacific Future' actually started in the United States or has it at the very least moved closer? We will discuss this question more closely below, concentrating primarily on the economic aspects — without however, neglecting political considerations completely. Moreover, we must take into account that the relationship of the United States to the Pacific countries cannot be discussed independently of its relationship to Europe. This becomes particularly clear if we direct our attention to the economic area. The rise of the Pacific basin, which climbed up the ladder to become a world economic trade and finance centre of the first degree, is frequently considered a result of the very loss of growth dynamic in the 'mature' West European economies in the recent years. And there are further political connections. The controversies within the NATO alliance might in the long run create a climate in the United States from which a tendency to re-evaluate Asian-Pacific interests more positively might emerge. Up till the present, the Atlantic-European orientation of the United States has been absolutely dominant, but it could lose importance in future (even if only relatively) in favour of more intense efforts and initiatives toward cooperation in the Pacific.

A sentiment that is encountered time and again in the relevant literature as well as in political discussion in the United States is that US trade with the Pacific nations has been ahead of that with Western Europe in volume since the mid-1970s.[90] Of course this statement requires an exact interpretation, since its truth depends crucially on the regional delineations involved.

Table 28 gives more information on the relative importance of the West European and the Pacific countries as foreign trade partners

---

[89] M. Mansfield, 'Pacific Visions', *Perspectives* (East-West Center Magazine, Honolulu), Spring 1981, p. 13.

[90] Cf. for example B.K. Gordon, 'Asian Angst', *Foreign Policy*, no. 47 (summer 1982). p. 49: 'Americans recognize that East Asia and the Pacific region are vital to US security and no less important than Western Europe. Indeed, in business and economic terms, more of America's commerce currently flows across the Pacific than across the Atlantic.'

Table 28.   DEVELOPMENT OF U.S. REGIONAL STRUCTURE
OF FOREIGN TRADE, 1965/1975/1984

Share in US foreign trade		US export	US import	Total
Share of West European	1965	30.1	27.6	29.0
countries*a* in U S	1975	26.2	20.8	23.5
foreign trade	1984	25.2	21.4	22.9
Share of Pacific	1965	35.1 (14.7)*c*	42.0 (19.3)	38.2 (16.7)
countries*b* in U S	1975	38.4 (18.2)	45.9 (23.9)	42.1 (21.0)
foreign trade	1984	47.0 (25.6)	54.3 (34.6)	51.4 (31.1)

a Nine E.C. countries plus Austria, Finland, Iceland, Norway, Sweden, Spain, Switzerland.

b Japan, Canada, Australia, New Zealand, ASEAN countries, P.R. China, Taiwan, South
   Korea, Hong Kong and the South Pacific islands.

c Data in brackets exclude trade with Canada.

Sources: As Table 17.

of the United States. It allows us to draw the following conclusions
for the period 1965–80.

— While the countries of Western Europe maintained a relatively
strong position as the recipients of US exports (25%), US imports
from that area declined strongly in relative terms, from 28% to
21%. This signifies a considerable structural change, which furthermore was accomplished in an astonishingly short time for such a
major shift of relative trade positions. This naturally led to a reduction of the West European share of US total foreign trade (from
29% to 23%).

— The share of the Pacific countries (defined as Country Group II
in Fig. 1 plus the People's Republic of China) in total US foreign
trade increased by 9% to 51%, due primarily to the positive change
on the United States' export side. This leads to the conclusion that
the share of the Pacific countries is indeed considerably higher than
that of Western Europe, which it has obviously been at least since
1965.

— For the question under consideration here, however, it is far
more important to throw light on the development of the relations
of the United States with Pacific nations excluding Canada. It
would be absurd indeed to use the expansion or reduction of North
American continental trade between the United States and Canada
as an indicator for or against a Pacific orientation of the US economy. It can be seen now that this group of Pacific countries in a
narrow sense (excluding Canada), has experienced marked increases
on both the export and the import sides. Taken together, they have

achieved an increase in their share of US foreign trade from 17 to 31%, thus confirming that, at least in quantitative terms, the Pacific basin has surpassed the countries of Western Europe as a trade partner of the United States.[91]

The rapid expansion of trade with Japan is in no way a sufficient explanation for the development trend sketched above; otherwise it could legitimately be claimed that an area of trade interdependence called the Pacific basin was *de facto* of less importance than the bilateral exchange of goods between the United States and Japan. It is particularly noteworthy that the share of the Pacific developing countries in the foreign trade of the United States with the Pacific has doubled in the years between 1965 and 1984 (see Table 18). In absolute figures, the trade flows between the United States and the ASEAN countries are by now as great as its trade with West Germany. This means that the ASEAN countries as a group are the fifth most important trading partner of the United States, directly behind Mexico. [92]

Another factor closely related to the increasing importance of the Pacific basin for US foreign trade lies in the changes experienced by its domestic regional distribution of industrial production. For a long time a transition in industrial structure has been taking place particularly and increasingly in the growth branches of industry such as aircraft construction, computer construction, semiconductor and electronic industries, space industries, machine-tool production, petrochemicals etc., many of which have relocated to the South-West of the United States, the so-called 'Sun Belt'. The share held by the traditional industrial areas in the North-East in total US industrial production was 72% in the 1940s, but by the 1970s it had dropped to about 46%. Parallel to this development the relative importance of the ports on the West Coast increased from handling 16% of US foreign trade in 1967 to 24% in 1978. 'The shift of national US trade has occurred for a variety of reasons, but the emergence of the Asian economies certainly is the underlying factor.'[93]

---

[91] This simple analysis of shares is not to be confused with a causal explanation. It cannot be decided here if Western Europe's relative loss of importance as a US trading partner is the cause or the result of the strengthening position of the Pacific region. Likewise there may be no relationship at all between the two tendencies. The figures shown in Table 28 fall into a time period which does after all include the structural changes caused by two drastic oil price increases.
[92] Cf. J. Tokuyama, 'The Advantages of a Pacific Economic Basin', *Far Eastern Economic Review*, 23 March 1979.
[93] R. Ford, 'Port Activity in the Pacific Northwest' in A.S. Hoffman (ed.), *Japan and the Pacific Basin*, Paris 1980, p. 44.

This structural change of industrial locations has caused a reduction of the regional income disparities within the United States. On the other hand, the population shift towards the West and the South caused by this structural change has had a direct impact on the domestic political situation. The number of seats in the House of Representatives is allocated according to the population of each individual state; thus Midwestern and Northeastern states have lost a number of mandates, and with them political influence has shifted in favour of the South and the West. To what extent Pacific interests have thereby gained additional support from American political decision-makers will have to be considered later.

It would seem that the dynamic development of the Pacific basin has caused the United States to increase its participation in the political shaping of this area. 'Pacific optimism has become a growth industry in the US academically, politically and economically.'[94] At the moment, however, political interest is still concentrated on a relatively narrow group of individuals who, because of either their institutional affiliations or their individual preferences, have a particular affinity for the Pacific region.[95]

In 1979 the United States experienced a boom in Pacific-related activities in both Houses of Congress. Of great importance among these activities was first the publication of the Drysdale/Patrick report (see above), which had been commissioned by the chairman of the Senate Committee on Foreign Affairs, Senator John Glenn, and secondly a hearing on 'The Pacific Community Idea' before the Subcommittee for Asian and Pacific Affairs of the House of Representatives.

This Hearing had been initiated by Senator Lester L. Wolff with the specific intention of advancing the idea of economic cooperation in the Pacific "from the realm of theory to practice, from academic debate to concrete action".[96] The Heginbotham-Zagoria Mission took place in the autumn of the same year, in the course of which senior State Department officials attempted to sound out the reactions of the East Asian countries to the cooperation plans under discussion. Furthermore, the Joint Economic Committee as the advisory committee to the House of Representatives and the Senate commissioned the preparation of a compendium of economic inter-

---

[94] Opinion of D.K. Emmerson, quoted in *CAPS Newsletter* (Center for Asian and Pacific Studies at the University of Hawaii), vol. 1 (1982), no. 2, p. 7.
[95] Cf. M. Mansfield 'Prospects for a Pacific Community' in P.F. Hooper (ed.), *Building a Pacific Community*, Honolulu 1982, p. 88 ff.; C. Morrison, 'American Interest in the Pacific Community Concept' in *The Pacific Community Concept: Views from Eight Nations*, Tokyo 1980, p. 32 ff.
[96] Preface to 'The Pacific Community Idea', op. cit.

dependences among Pacific countries.[97] It was also in 1979 that the preparatory work on the founding of a Pan-Pacific Community Association was initiated by Senator Wolff. Because of the support of prominent politicians, the association was indeed founded one year later.

Thus the overall impression emerges that the Carter Administration was greatly interested in intensifying economic cooperation in the Pacific area, but at the same time did not develop political initiatives of its own. The State Department was obviously inclined to wait for the still uncertain first reactions of the ASEAN countries before integrating these reactions into its own policy decisions.

During the period of office of the Reagan Administration, there seems to be evidence of a strong personal representation of Pacific interests — which, however, has not yet led to any concrete action or further initiatives going beyond what has already taken place to strengthen the idea of the 'Pacific Community'. Of course any interpretation of the extent of the United States' Pacific engagement as being dependent on any prominent individual in the political arena or within the political parties would be superficial. The US position on Pacific economic co-operation is certainly not decisively influenced by the political affiliation of the Chairman of the Subcommittee on Asian and Pacific Affairs, be he Republican or Democrat, nor by the regional loyalty of a President from California. In the long run, basic economic lines of development and political interest areas will prevail over individual initiatives and activities.

In assessing this long-term basic position of the United States on efforts towards economic cooperation in the Pacific, the following points for and against may be cited in a political-economic perspective:[98]

The economic arguments in favour have already been discussed in connection with the rise of the Pacific countries as strong trading partners of the United States and the corresponding industrial structural changes towards the 'Sun Belt'. But another factor has to be considered — and this is essentially related to the political economy of North-South relations.[99] In the course of the preparatory discussions within the United Nations system on the political strategy for

[97] Published as *Pacific Region Interdependencies: A Compendium of Papers Submitted to the Joint Economic Committee*, Congress of the United States, Washington DC 1981.
[98] Cf. Morrison, 'American Interests', op. cit., p. 33 ff., and G. Boyd, 'A Pacific Regional Economic Order', *Asian Perspective*, vol. 7 (1983), p. 1 ff.
[99] Cf. Ch. Doran, 'US and Canadian Pacific Perspectives' in Boyd, *Region Building*, op. cit., p. 164 ff.; R.A. Scalapino, 'Pacific Prospects', *Washington Quarterly*, vol. 4 (1981), no. 4 p. 3.

the Third Developmental Decade, it became clear that politically responsible circles within the United States — together with those of other countries — feel that the global North-South dialogue has come to a halt.[100] From this point of view, any attempt to initiate regionalised discussions and negotiations between industrialised and developing nations must be considered especially attractive. Suitable prerequisites for such discussions can be found particularly in the Pacific area, since the ASEAN countries as well as the NICs of East Asia have always shown far more interest in discussing topical questions than in listening to each other's political rhetoric. There are, furthermore, common interests concerning raw materials and foreign trade policy which may be regarded as possibly opening the way to agreement.

A further point in favour seems to be gaining particular influence in the field of politics: it can be derived from the domestic dissatisfaction with the Asia and Pacific foreign policy of the United States up till now, which Robert Scalapino has characterised as the result of hasty adaptations to unexpected crises.[101] In the years following the Vietnam War till the late 1970s, the United States had to cope with political discussion on and about the experience it had been through; however, the political weather-chart changed at the beginning of the 1980s when many observers called for the development of a new concept of American engagement in Asia. Aside from the passing of time since the Vietnam War, particular mention was made of:

— the economically and ideologically weak position of the Soviet Union in the Pacific area (with the obvious exception of Indochina), despite its strengthened military presence;[102]

— the diplomatic and economic approchement between the United States and the People's Republic of China (opening of diplomatic relations in January 1979, reciprocal granting of the most-favoured-nation clause in February 1980, trade agreement on textiles in September 1980); and

---

[100] The authors agree with this diagnosis. It would, however, be a biased view to blame the developing countries exclusively without considering that their legitimate demands (e.g. for reduction of trade barriers) have been blocked by many industrial countries.
[101] Cf. R.A. Scalapino, 'Competitive Strategic Perceptions Underlying US Policy in Asia' in L. R. Vasey (ed.), *Pacific Asia and US Policies: A Political-Economic-Strategical Assessment*, Honolulu 1978, p. 1. Greene also finds a coherent strategy to be lacking and sees US Asian policy still 'on a somewhat fragmented course' (F. Greene, 'The United States and Asia in 1980', *Asian Survey*, vol. 21 [1981], p. 1).
[102] Cf. for more details Scalapino, 'Pacific Prospects', op. cit., p. 13 ff.

— the desire of the Pacific developing nations (again with the exception of Indochina) for an increasing political and economic presence of the United States in this region.

However, critical voices are also heard: The hopes for possible regional North-South compromises are confronted with the fear that the United States might be facing rising financial demands from the Pacific developing nations. The thesis of the necessity of a long-term concept of US policy in the Pacific is opposed by the view that plans for cooperation in the Pacific could magnify and concentrate essential questions affecting this heterogenous area which carries such a heavy burden bequeathed by its history: demands by the People's Republic of China for reunion with Taiwan, Hong Kong and Macao; increasing Japanese import competition and export success on other Pacific markets; the relationship between North and South Korea; the still unsolved question of Indochina; and the relationship of the ASEAN countries to Indochina and to the People's Republic of China. It is maintained that this accumulation of potential sources of political conflict would overtax any rational management of international relations and create new tensions. Moreover, the efforts towards regionalisation in the Pacific might also collide with the foreign trade interests of the United States, which are basically of a global character. And furthermore, the potential effects of economic cooperation in the Pacific on other Asian countries, particularly India and Pakistan, and the possible reactions of those countries must also be considered. Another issue which would weigh heavily could be termed 'the Latin American Dilemma': the inclusion of the Latin American countries bordering the Pacific, including Mexico, at too early a stage in the cooperation would be very likely to overtax the efforts at regional cooperation and might even completely cripple them. Excluding these countries, as well as India and Pakistan, would probably precipitate grave political conflicts, particularly when connected with preferential treatment of the developing countries of the Asian Pacific region and the ensuing discrimination working against the remaining Third World countries. Doubts would be cast on the inter-American cooperation efforts of the Organization of American States, and beyond this the relationships with all countries of the Third World would be sorely strained.

(b) *The position of the ASEAN countries.* Although the ASEAN countries are not major powers of the Pacific in either economic or political terms, their attitude towards plans to intensify Pacific economic cooperation will be particularly important in the future. One reason for this is that ASEAN is already in existence as a cooperation community and thus plays a special role. The second reason is the present tendency in Japanese and US political circles towards exercising their own political initiatives only with caution. Thus the ASEAN countries will play a pivotal role indeed in the progress of efforts towards cooperation, as the Japanese in particular judge the situation: 'If the ASEAN countries are not very much in favour of the idea, it will not materialise'[103] a quotation of the former Japanese Foreign Minister Okita. Kojima made an analogous statement: 'An ASEAN initiative would be most welcome since if the five Pacific advanced countries took the initiative, there would be trouble about membership from the beginning.'[104] This is especially true of every Japanese advance, so that Japan is at present exercising official restraint — due to its historical 'bad conscience' towards Southeast Asia and its present powerful economic position. The United States — for which the Pacific Basin is gaining in economic importance, although it is admittedly not of such vital interest as to Japan — is also now waiting for the reaction of the ASEAN countries.[105]

Table 17 above gave information on ASEAN's intensive trade interrelationships within the Pacific Basin. Tables 29 and 30 give a regional breakdown of the Pacific ASEAN foreign trade, which comprises 76% of exports and 68% of imports. Here the dominant position of Japan as a foreign trading partner is evident (ASEAN conducts about one quarter of its foreign trade exclusively with Japan). Foreign trade with the United States is hardly less extensive than the entire intra-ASEAN trade, in comparison with which the other industrial nations of the Pacific and the East Asian NICs take a less important place. This regionally concentrated foreign trade structure is basically true of all ASEAN countries, the two exceptions being the extremely high regional export concentration of Indonesia (88% — largely accounted for by petroleum) and the relatively low value for Thailand (55%).

Of course the ASEAN countries do not have anything approaching the importance as trading partners for the United State and Japan as the latter do for the former. In other words, there is an asymmetry of reciprocal vulnerability due to the varying intensity of trade diversifi-

---

[103] According to Pang Eng Fong, 'The Concept of a Pan-pacific Community and ASEAN: A View from Singapore' in *The Pacific Community Concept: Views from Eight Nations* (Proceedings of the Asian Dialogue at Oiso, Japan), Tokyo, 1980, p. 81.

[104] K. Kojima, comment in Garnaut, *ASEAN*, op. cit., p. 474.

[105] Cf. S. Uhalley, 'The "Pacific Community" Concept', paper presented at the Sixth Nakhodka Pacific Seminar, Aug. 19–24, 1981, p. 5.

Table 29. SHARE OF PACIFIC BASIN IN TOTAL EXPORTS OF ASEAN COUNTRIES, 1984 (%)

	1	2	3	4	5	1–5
	U.S.A.	Japan	Australia, Canada, New Zealand	Hong Kong, Korea, Taiwan, Papua-New Guinea	ASEAN	Pacific Basin
Indonesia	20.6	47.3	2.5	5.8	11.4	87.6
Malaysia	13.4	22.6	2.5	6.2	26.3	71.0
Philippines	38.5	19.6	3.4	8.9	9.8	80.2
Singapore	20.0	9.4	4.9	9.4	29.3	73.0
Thailand	17.2	13.0	3.0	7.2	14.0	54.6
ASEAN	19.7	24.4	3.4	7.4	20.5	75.5

Sources: IMF, Direction of Trade Statistics, *Yearbook 1981*; Ostasiatischer Verein, *Ostasien-Südasien-Südostasien, Wirtschaft 1981.*

Table 30. SHARE OF PACIFIC BASIN IN TOTAL IMPORTS OF ASEAN COUNTRIES, 1984 (%)

	1	2	3	4	5	1–5
	U.S.A.	Japan	Australia, Canada, New Zealand	Hong Kong, Korea, Taiwan, Papua-New Guinea	ASEAN	Pacific Basin
Indonesia	18.4	23.8	5.5	4.7	14.0	66.4
Malaysia	16.1	26.2	5.7	3.9	20.4	72.3
Philippines	26.9	13.4	3.7	9.3	11.4	64.7
Singapore	14.6	18.4	3.3	6.5	25.3	68.1
Thailand	13.4	26.8	3.4	6.4	13.7	63.7
ASEAN	16.5	21.6	4.3	5.9	19.4	67.6

Sources: As Table 29.

cation: 'Therefore the dependence is more a one-way relationship.'[106] The same basic pattern of a high Pacific regional concentration can be found in the area of private direct investments in the ASEAN countries (see Table 31). From a half up to more than three-quarters of all investments are from regional sources, and an increasing number of investors from NICs are gaining in importance: their investment activities in Thailand and Indonesia (in the latter case excluding the petroleum sector) are already more extensive than those of US investors.[107]

Applied to ASEAN, a careful interpretation of the above information enables us to conclude that factual economic interactions at least do not work against the attempt to institutionalise certain forms of economic cooperation. As regards the economic interdependences alone, there is indeed a firm supporting foundation. On the other hand, it is precisely this argument which is open to criticism and thus acquires an ambivalent meaning: does not the above empirical evidence point to a strong regional dependence, from which the ASEAN countries should free themselves as much as possible by means of export and import diversification, rather than institutionalising it — all the more so since ASEAN is a heavily export-oriented and world-market-dependent association of developing countries?[108] This question clearly indicates that intensive economic interaction is at best (but not in every case) a necessary condition for the success of cooperation; what it is not is a sufficient justification for its desirability. And of course the concepts of economic cooperation in the Pacific are related not only with economic, but also with a number of political problem areas thus considerably increasing the complexity of the entire area of decision-making 'The merits of the Pacific Community idea cannot be examined by its technocratic blueprints alone. Rather, the emphasis will have to be placed upon its political dimensions and implications.'[109] We will examine these aspects more closely below.

There is of course no official statement from the side of the ASEAN countries, but the comments of individual politicians and economists can be put together to form a preliminary though incomplete mosaic of opinion. Furthermore we have to take into account

---

[106] J. Wong, *ASEAN Economies in Perspective*, London/Basingstoke 1979, p. 19.
[107] Cf. for general information on this aspect L.T. Wells, Jr., *Third World Multinationals: The Rise of Foreign Investment from Developing Countries*, Cambridge, Mass./London 1983.
[108] Cf. A.O. Krueger, 'Regional and Global Approaches to Trade and Development Strategy' in Garnaut, *ASEAN*, op. cit., p. 44.
[109] N. Akrasanee *et al.*, *ASEAN and the Pacific Community: A Report*, Centre for Strategic and International Studies, Jakarta 1981, p. 26.

Table 31.   SHARE OF PACIFIC BASIN COUNTRIES IN CUMULATIVE PRIVATE FOREIGN INVESTMENT IN ASEAN COUNTRIES, AS OF END 1983 (%)

	Indonesia[a]	Malaysia[b]	Philippines	Singapore[e]	Thailand
Japan	25.0[a]	20.1	16.5	10.3	24.4
U.S.A.	37.0[a]	7.4	51.5	19.4	10.7
Canada	0.1	n.a.[c]	2.0	n.a.	n.a.
Australia	2.5	6.4	2.0	2.5	2.9
Hong Kong ⎫ South Korea ⎭	13.0	9.6	5.9[d]	13.6[d]	15.3[d]
Taiwan	2.2	12.2	0.8	10.9[f]	4.7
ASEAN					
Total	79.8	55.7	78.7	56.7	62.1

[a] Official Indonesian data exclude the petroleum sector and financial investments. Data for Japan and the U.S.A. are based on estimates which H. Laumer has undertaken including these sectors (as of end 1982). Other data cover 1967–March 1983.
[b] 1978–1983.
[c] Not available.
[d] Excluding South Korea.
[e] As of end 1981.
[f] Only Malaysia.

Sources: ESCAP, *Patterns and Impact of Foreign Investment in the ESCAP Region*, Bangkok 1985; UNIDO, *Industrial Development Review Malaysia*, Dec. 15. 545, July 1985; Laumer, *Direktinvestitionen*, op. cit., pp. 43 and 70. N. Akrasanee, *ASEAN and the Pacific Economic Co-operation: A Survey of Issues of Interdependence* (ESCAP, Development Planning Division), August 1980, p. 13; D.-S. Ahn, *Gemeinschaftsunternehmungen in Entwicklungsländern. Joint Ventures als Entwicklungsinstrument in den ASEAN-Staaten*, Tübingen 1981, p. 361 ff.; Laumer, *Direktinvestitionen*, op. cit., pp. 43 and 70.

the fact that there is no homogenous ASEAN position concerning the setting of regional priorities for external economic relations; rather, the varying political, cultural and economic starting conditions are translated into divergent assessments and objectives. Thus in Singapore, with its relatively advanced industrialisation and capability to meet international competition, there may be a greater willingness to accept plans for cooperation in the Pacific than, for example, in Indonesia, a country which has already slowed down ASEAN's internal moves toward integration in order to protect its infant industries.[110] Nevertheless, in the following paragraphs, we will not mention specifically the particular national goals of the countries involved. Rather, some general arguments will be presented, which are being discussed in all ASEAN countries at present, although with varying intensity.

Fears are often voiced that a larger Pacific cooperation organisation could have a detrimental effect on the integration efforts taking place within ASEAN.[111] Here we must refer to the consolidation period within ASEAN which at present is still in progress. ASEAN was founded in 1967 after the political turbulence of the early 1960's and the failures of ASA and Maphilindo.[112] However, for nearly a decade economic cooperation only existed on paper, until it gained momentum from the agreement to set up joint ASEAN industrial projects, as well as from the conclusion of a preferential tariff agreement in early 1977. In both areas, progress in integration still runs short of expectations. The five joint projects in the industrial sector have already triggered off controversy on purchase commitments, market chances and prices in an early phase of planning, which has led to Singapore's withdrawal from its own intended project.[113] As for the tariff preferences granted, these have admittedly

[110] While Soesastro has identified 'a great deal of reservation towards the idea' of Pacific economic cooperation in the case of Indonesia, Tan believes 'that Singapore would gain from increased contact with, knowledge and awareness of economic events and trends in the Pacific Community', adding immediately, however, that 'the economic and political significance of ASEAN to Singapore would be accorded priority consideration in her appraisal of the Pacific Community concept' (Akrasanee *et al., ASEAN,* op. cit., pp. 25 and 37).

[111] Cf. A.H. Zakaria, 'The Pacific Basin and ASEAN: Problems and Prospects', *Contemporary Southeast Asia,* vol. 2 (1981), p. 336; R.M. Nicholas, 'ASEAN and the Pacific Community Debate: Much Ado about Something', *Asian Survey,* vol. 21 (1981), p. 1206.

[112] Cf. on this R. Machetzki, 'International and Supranational Problems of Political Regionalism in South-East Asia' in B. Dahm and W. Draguhn (eds), *Politics, Society and Economy in the ASEAN States,* Wiesbaden 1975, p. 19 ff.

[113] For details cf. A. Kraft, *Aspekte der regionalen wirtschaftlichen Integration zwischen Entwicklungsländern. Das Beispiel der ASEAN,* Wiesbaden 1982, p. 219 ff.

been extended considerably, but they are — to a great extent — applied in the case of such items which are either characterised by low tariffs, or neither produced nor traded at all, cf. Chapter II.A(3*b*).

Thus it is easily understandable that the ASEAN countries give more importance and priority to the continuation and intensification of their own integration process. Furthermore, they are afraid that their internal allocation and distribution problems would be overlaid and magnified by the conflicts to be expected within an even larger cooperation organisation. 'A regional community that undermines the strength and cohesion of ASEAN as a sub-regional entity is clearly not in the interest of ASEAN.'[114]

There is an additional politico-psychological factor at work here. No matter what their content, all plans for Pacific cooperation have hitherto borne the stigma of being presented by those very countries (Japan and the United States) which in the past have time and again turned Southeast Asia into a theatre for their own political interests. Many representatives of ASEAN see the danger of institutionalising renewed dominant power relationships[115] in front of this backdrop, particularly since the demand for 'leadership of the United States and Japan' has already been explicitly mentioned.[116]

These fears strike at the very nucleus of the concept of economic cooperation in the Pacific which, among other things, has indeed been put forward with the claim that it represents a model arrangement for North-South relationships. We have already mentioned the ambivalent character of regionalised North-South relationships, which rests on two assumptions: on the one hand, that regionally specific potentials of mutual interests and agreements may be effectively utilised, but, on the other, that so-called 'changing majorities' would be created between industrialised and developing nations, which could lead to a process of desolidarisation within the 'Group of 77'. Thus in the relevant literature too the regionalisation strategy is a controversial topic. While Streeten and a number of representatives of ASEAN identify the principal danger as being 'that some of the weaker and poorer countries are bound to suffer, inequalities to be increased and the cry of neocolonialism to be raised

---

114 Akrasanee *et al.*, *ASEAN*, op. cit., p. 13
115 Cf. T. Watanabe, 'Pan-Pacific Solidarity without Domination' in *Pacific Region Interdependencies*, op. cit.; M. Ghazali Shafie, 'Toward a Pacific Basin Community: A Malaysian Perception' in *Pacific Region Interdependencies*, op. cit.
116 Drysdale and Patrick, op. cit., p. 24. 'The Americans seem to advocate a leading role for the United States in OPTAD. Is the Pacific Basin concept, therefore, a thinly disguised veil to allow for the continued predominance of "Northern" countries over "Southern" countries?' (Zakaria, *Pacific Basin*, op. cit., p. 336 ff.)

again', [117] other authors emphasise the positive aspects and believe that 'in the relations between industrialised and developing nations . . . interregional relationships [could] contribute more to the decrease of tensions and problems than the strengthening of the bloc of industrialised nations, and consequently of the bloc of developing nations.' [118]

At the same time, considerations of this nature — i.e. those which place particular importance on the political economy of North-South relations, which certainly plays a role for the ASEAN countries — should not be overestimated. The position of the ASEAN countries on plans for cooperation in the Pacific will most likely be determined by the extent of the advantages the ASEAN countries can themelves gain from participation. In this connection, two aspects frequently reappear: the political question concerning the relationship of the ASEAN countries to Indochina and the economic question of binding concessions on the part of the industrialised Pacific countries concerning development assistance and foreign trade policy.

ASEAN would certainly assume a far more positive attitude if the tense relationships to the countries of Indochina could be relaxed or eased through economic cooperation in the Pacific, particularly since it is these countries with which ASEAN would like to reach a *modus vivendi*. However, the proposed plans are almost diametrically opposed to these goals. As has already been mentioned, only those countries committed to a market-oriented economy are supposed to cooperate under American-Japanese leadership, and, contrary to occasional lip-service, this would necessarily imply the exclusion of the countries of Indochina. Accordingly the Malaysian Minister of the Interior has already recognised the danger 'of a bloc mentality inherent in the Pacific Basin concept'. [119] Thus Indochina's hard front position would only become stronger against the ASEAN countries which have been branded from the very begin-

---

[117] P.P. Streeten, 'Approaches to a New International Economic Order', *World Development*, vol. 10 (1982), p. 5.

[118] K. Esser and J. Wiemann, *Schwerpunktländer in der Dritten Welt. Konsequenzen für die Südbeziehungen der Bundersrepublik Deutschland*, Berlin 1981, p. 75. The authors are opposed to a cooperation model 'based on special arrangements with countries with which industrialised nations have particularly diversified relations . . . . For dissociation of the 'Fourth World' would be more conducive to the creation of conflict than it would be to that of order and stability' (op. cit., p. 73). However, their policy recommendations tend towards the conclusion of comprehensive bilateral cooperation agreements between industrialised countries and key countries (so-called 'threshold countries') of the Third World.

[119] Ghazali Shafie, 'Toward a Pacific Basin Community . . . .', op. cit., p. 75.

ning of their cooperation as vehicles of neocolonial US interests.[120]

It remains to be asked if the ASEAN countries can at least expect substantial concessions in the development and foreign trade policy of the Pacific industrialised countries, thus making a more intensive cooperation attractive. There would indeed be enough starting points: 'Are they [the industrial nations of the Pacific] willing to provide special treatment by reducing protectionist trade policies, helping stabilise the export earnings of the developing countries, untying foreign aid, agreeing to equal participation in the management of common programmes and exploitation of resources . . ., and establishing fair codes of conduct for the transnational corporations . . . which will practically dominate the implementation of the economic cooperation among the member-countries?'[121] The ASEAN countries give priority to the demand for tariff preferences, as well as for a system serving to stablise export earnings on raw materials (analogous to the EC's STABEX System). While the latter proposal has met with agreement in principle,[122] at least in Japan although without coming close to actual realisation, tariff preferences and other measures facilitating market access still remain illusory. In particular, the United States, as one of the most important global trading powers, is not in a position to offer preferences to certain developing countries of the Pacific and thus necessarily discriminate against other developing countries. The strong position of Latin America as a US trading partner (especially Mexico, with which the United States has a larger foreign trade volume than with all the ASEAN countries put together) testifies to this. (Compare also Chapter III.5.(*a*).

The ASEAN countries are obviously well aware that cooperation is merely an instrument for obtaining specific goals and not a purpose in itself. What, however, are the goals which ASEAN can attain *only* within the framework of a Pacific cooperation organisation? As long as the Pacific industrial nations are not prepared to

---

[120] Cf. F.H. Golay, 'National Economic Priorities and International Coalitions' in G.J. Pauker *et al., Diversity and Development in Southeast Asia*, New York 1977, p. 110. The Soviet assessment of Pacific cooperation plans can be found in Y. Bandura, 'The Pacific Community — A Brain Child of Imperialist Diplomacy', *International Affairs* (Moscow), no. 6/1980, p. 63 ff.; and A. Chernyshov, 'The Pacific: Problems of International Security and Cooperation', *International Affairs* (Moscow), no. 11/1977, p. 78 ff.

[121] A. Widjaja, 'Toward a Pacific Basin Community in the '80s: An Indonesian Perspective' in *The Pacific Community Concept*, op. cit., p.62; cf. also G.P. Sicat, 'ASEAN and the Pacific Region' in Hooper, *Building. . . .*, op. cit., p. 59 ff.

[122] Cf. Y. Yasuba, 'The Impact of ASEAN on the Asia-Pacific Region' in Garnaut, *ASEAN*, op. cit., p. 87; G. Boyd, 'ASEAN Regional Policies' in Boyd, *Region Building. . . .* op. cit., p. 97.

state the price (in the form of concessions in their development policy and foreign trade policy) which they would be prepared to pay for successful regionalisation of the Pacific economy, it is difficult to perceive such goals. Thus one cannot expect initiatives to be launched by ASEAN in the near future. 'As for ASEAN, it would seem premature for it to even consider taking an active or leading role in the formation of a Pacific community, whatever its magnitude in membership will be.'[123]

(c) *Conclusions and perspectives.* In spite of its undeniable operational vagueness and the many political obstacles at present impeding its realisation, the idea of institutional consolidation of a Pacific Basin Community is undoubtedly giving strong impetus to the shaping of economic relations in the Pacific Basin. Barnett calls it — suitably enough — 'amorphous dynamism'.[124] Some time will probably have to pass before the economic dynamics of the Pacific area can bring to birth a suitable form of economic cooperation, and it may be true, as the Pacific Basin Cooperation Study Group assumes, that this is indeed a task for the beginning of the twenty-first century. Certainly the countries involved are well advised to plan for a strategy of small progressive steps towards economic cooperation and not for the short-term completion of spectacular agreements, for which the problems are altogether too complex. Particular emphasis must be placed on aspects of economic distribution; because these have so often been disregarded or postponed, many regional efforts towards cooperation between developing countries have collapsed. In the case of cooperation efforts comprising industrialised as well as developing countries, the distribution aspects are probably even more important. Thus not only Drysdale and Patrick but also Kojima are probably correct to begin their plans with the transfer of financial resources, with trade-related structural changes, and with a code of conduct for private direct investments, i.e. with problem dimensions which touch directly on issues of the distribution of economic benefits. Of course, these are precisely the problem fields for which one should not be over-optimistic or expect short-term successes.

The adjacent region of South Asia seems at present to be going in the opposite direction — towards spectacular political action lacking in substance. Only three years after a first initiative started by Bangladesh, a common declaration proclaiming the founding of

---

[123] Sicat, *ASEAN*, op. cit., p. 57.
[124] R.W. Barnett, 'Introduction and Summary: The Concept of Community' in *Pacific Region Interdependencies*, op. cit., p. 5.

SARC — South Asian Regional Cooperation[125] — was formulated at a meeting of foreign ministers in New Delhi in August 1983. With this declaration, economic cooperation was prematurely advanced to the sensitive level of governmental responsibility, although severe political conflicts lie concealed beneath the calm surface and still occasionally break out between some of the countries involved.[126] Furthermore, the economic interrelationships are sorely burdened by the dominant position of India. Thus it is not astonishing that the most important area of potential cooperation, namely all questions connected with trade relationships, was completely excluded.

Two general statements may be made for the Pacific Basin which, in contrast to the nations of South Asia, has become a world economic power of the first degree. However the intended forms of cooperation are to be judged, these statements are unlikely to provoke opposition:

(i) The economic interdependences (trade flows, real capital and financial capital flows) will increase at a rate higher than the world average.[127] As a *factual* integration area, the Pacific Basin is at the moment only at the beginning of a turbulent development when seen historically. This is true regardless of the possible creation of a new Pacific organisation along the lines of OPTAD.

(ii) If — in either the foreseeable or the more distant future — economic policy cooperation should be realised, even if only in the form of selective measures of coordination, this would indeed have decisive consequences for the future distribution of roles in the world economy. For the economy of the European Community in particular, there would probably be an increased danger that it would no longer be able to maintain its already weakening competitive position.

6. *Economic development of the Pacific Basin in a European perspective*

There is little reason to prepare long lists of detailed measures to be taken against the Pacific challenge by Japan and the East and Southeast Asian NICs. A strategy following such lines would be in

---

[125] Cf. D. Braun, *Südasien zwischen Konflikten und Zusammenarbeit. Der Ansatz der South Asian Regional Cooperation (SARC)*, Ebenhausen, December 1983.
[126] Bangladesh, Bhutan, India, the Maldives, Nepal, Pakistan, Sri Lanka.
[127] Cf. also R. Machetzki, 'Tendenzen der wirtschaftlichen Entwicklung und Kooperation im pazifischen Raum', *Südostasien aktuell*, January 1984, p. 83.

danger of even increasing or reinforcing the already existing European protectionism.[128] It should also not be forgotten that the viewpoint of the Pacific countries is a wide-ranging one in which individual European countries are losing ground *vis-à-vis* the collective importance of the EC. Meanwhile, national egotism in Europe has been increasing so that success in liberalising the domestic market of the EC is in marked contrast to the lack of progress made in the conception of a common European foreign policy. It is precisely in this area that considerable parts of the necessary European strategies will have to be focused: 'The main reason why Europe is being left behind can be found in the fact that Europeans are preoccupied with national initiatives and jealousies, instead of joining together for one great common effort.'[129]

European particularism all too often impedes the solidarity of the EC in important questions in relation to Japan and the whole Pacific community. Market studies and the analysis of technological developments are pursued by individual member-states, and cooperation at the European level does not seem to be thought necessary. Individual and national segmentations are in contrast to the harmonisation of norms and standards, as well as customs formalities right across Europe. A public procurement policy valid for all of Europe is still far from attainment — although the innovative importance of such a policy for regaining competitiveness in peak technology can hardly be overstated. And the question has to be raised whether in the face of new world-wide dimensions a national competition policy oriented only to each national market will help to reinforce and secure Europe's competitiveness against the Pacific region. Furthermore, the EC will no longer be able merely to watch the global activities of the large Japanese trading houses (*Sogo shosha*), but will have to create its own efficient distribution structures on a worldwide basis. There are still many barriers impeding rationalised large-scale production in certain specific branches that will have to be removed before they will be able to take up competition with Japan. In addition, if large future-oriented research projects are aimed at keeping up with the technological developments of United

---

[128] In this connection we refer to the impressive lecture given by Eberhard Rhein, Chief of Cabinet to EC Commissioner Haferkamp, on the occasion of the Symposium on 'The Pacific Region: Its growing political-strategic and economic importance' organised by the Planning Unit of the West German Foreign Ministry. Many of Rhein's points agree in principle with those to be found below (cf. also E. Rhein, 'Die Bedeutung des Pazifischen Raumes für Europa', *EG-Magazin*, no. 2/Feb. 1984 (published by Commission of the European Communities).

[129] Horst Ehmke, 'Westeuropa in der Weltwirtschaft and die EG', *Frankfurter Rundschau*, 18 Feb. 1984.

States and Japan, they can only be planned at a European level for only the EC — and no individual European nation — has the necessary research and industrial capacity, as well as the required market size, at its disposal. Laurent Fabius, France's former prime minister and former minister of industry and research, has stated that 'the present electronic revolution is the first technological revolution which does not come out of Europe but out of the Pacific region. Our countries are too small to bear by themselves the burden of the necessary investments and to finance the colossal research tasks involved.'[130]

This of course should not mean that the development of modern technology is to be governed by bureaucracies of a national or even supranational scope. Not even in Japan have technological developments been completely steered by the bureaucracy; but Japanese government and private business have cooperated on the basis of a common positive attitude towards technology.

There are certainly a number of further examples which could be cited to illustrate that many grave problems of our time can no longer be solved at the level of the individual country. Thus it is clear that the shift in the centre of gravity of the world economy towards the Pacific, in conjunction with the absolute necessity for Europe to carry out far-reaching structural changes and regain technological competitiveness, must lead to the utmost effort being directed towards the creation of a Europe with one homogenous domestic market. This ultimately means that Europeans must reflect on the actual goal of European unity and economic cooperation.

We must also note a second aspect closely connected to the above. European provincialism which cannot 'look over the fence' and does not understand how to use experience it has gathered from all over the world should now — finally — be abandoned. This means that Europeans must finally pull themselves together and occupy themselves more intensively than before with the Pacific area — its culture, economy, politics and technology, and with its people and history. They must make an effort to achieve a higher profile in the East Asian-Pacific area for their personnel and their goods than has been the case hitherto.

One basic prerequisite for this will be getting to know Japan in particular and the other Pacific countries better than in the past: their strengths, their weaknesses, their economic and sociopolitical goals and priorities, their structural changes, and their marketing efforts on national and international markets. It is still difficult for Europeans to coordinate, not to mention harmonise, the idea of

[130] Cf. *Die Zeit*, Hamburg, 10 Feb. 1984.

Japan as a land of contemplation and aestheticism, of group-oriented relationships and basic closeness to nature, a land of temples and gardens, of Kabuki and No, with the idea of its relentless competition, its impressive heavy industry, its technological progress and steadily increasing number of robots, its huge cities and the numerous other results of its powerful economic growth.

Much too little has been done to bring about any changes in Europe in overcoming the language barrier. One only needs to compare the number of Japanese students of European languages with that of European students majoring in Japanese, and the number of Japanese who travel abroad every year with the number of foreigners who visit Japan.

Overcoming European half-heartedness and provincialism will indeed take time. But on a national level much can and must be done without delay, and this not only in connection with the creation of a homogenous market in Europe. European educational and social policies face the challenge of coping with the economic and technological tasks of our age by supporting talented scientists and high-level research. Otherwise the link-up to the American and Japanese industrial superpowers will be completely missed. Furthermore, attitudes towards work, technological progress, structural changes, adaptation, individual and social welfare, and the relationship of the state to the economy, have to be thoroughly re-examined.

Anyone who finds this list too demanding should remember that the growth of the Pacific area to a centre of the world economy marks a change of historic dimensions — one that can be compared to the rise of the continental European nations as competitors of England in the second half of the nineteenth century, which deprived England of its position as the 'world's workshop'. The economic fate of Europe today is still open to change, but time is of the essence.

PACIFIC ECONOMIC COOPERATION CONFERENCE, BALI, INDONESIA, NOV. 21–23, 1983: TASK FORCE REPORT

1. *Summary report*

1. The work of the four Pacific Economic Cooperation Conference Task Forces underlines the interest of countries in the Pacific region in tackling major trade and development problems, in the context of their own strong trade growth and development ambitions. Pacific economies haved a greater commitment to outward looking development strategies than is common to the international community generally and they have a substantial neighbourly interest in cooperation. The interest of Pacific countries in regional action is nonetheless consistent with, and may well improve the potential for, action on a broader multilateral basis especially given the rapid growth of the importance of these countries in the world economy.

2. Although the world economy has been seriously shaken by the effects of the oil crises and prolonged recession in industrial countries, the Pacific stands out as a region in which there has been generally effective adjustment to these problems in the world economy and in which economic growth has continued to be impressive. The promise and performance of the economies in this region has reinforced the increasingly widespread view that the centre of world economic power is shifting from the Atlantic to the Pacific area, and this trend is likely to continue for many years to come.

3. Four Pacific Task Forces were set up by the Bangkok Pacific Economic Cooperation Conference to study the important trade and investment/technology interests of Pacific countries and to report upon them to the next Pacific Economic Cooperation Conference to be held in Indonesia. The work of these Task Forces (on Agricultural and Renewable Resource Goods Trade; Minerals and Energy Trade; Manufactured Goods Trade; and Investment and Technology Transfer) was based at leading institutions in Thailand, Australia, Korea, and Japan. The Task Forces involved leading figures from throughout the region and included officials, business people and researchers in the mode that has emerged and proven idtself in fostering the practice of Pacific economic cooperation through the Canberra and Bangkok Conferences.

4. The Task Forces observe that the strong regional concentration in all trade and investment flows within the Pacific warrant more serious effort at regional cooperation and consultation on trade and investment issues. The concentration of trade interests in the region reflects the rapid industrial growth of regional economies, a pattern of resource endowments encouraging complementary trade and economic relationship, and important transport and other cost advantages in trading among relatively proximate

groups of countries, especially in minerals and energy products. An important fact is that, for agricultural and mineral products, the supply capacity
within the Pacific region offers adequate potential for meeting the bulk of
present or prospective demand requirements and for providing a large
measure of regional food and resource trade security.

5. The Task Forces address a wide range of issues and problems. National
policies affecting industrial and agricultural production and development,
and the exploration, development and investment regimes operating in
minerals and energy producing countries, are considered alongside matters
related more directly to international markets and trade flows. The importance of the interaction between different issues addressed is emphasised in
the work of the Task Forces.

6. Two major conflusions emerge from review of Task Force Reports.
First, all Task Forces identify the need for improved information exchange
in their respective fields of study. Such exchanges, within the framework of
Pacific Economic Cooperation Conference activities, will deepen understanding of critical issues and differing national perspectives and provide
the base for the development of agendas for policy action. Second, the Task
Forces stress the importance of fostering a climate among Pacific countries
that encouraged specific coordinated policy actions to achieve trade and
development abjectives. The Task Forces also identify some major priorities for cooperation among Pacific countries in their approach to trade
policy problems and in their efforts at mobilising investment, technology
and other resources for the purposes of regional development.

7. The Task Forces suggest approaches to promote greater information
exchange, consultation and understanding in the following areas:

— In the area of agricultural and renewable resource goods trade, the
evaluation of national policies and practices relating to production,
management, conservation and trade was seen as likely to encourage
cooperative policy action in the longer term.

— On Pacific minerals and energy matters, relevant government officials
and independent researchers, together with industry representatives from
producer and consumer countries, could usefully provide regular and comprehensive assessments of market conditions, anticipate supply/demand
movements, and longer term influences of technological changes on
resources and energy demand as well as commenting on policies directly
affecting trade.

— Consultation on general conditions affecting manufactured goods
trade, and for the monitoring of policies and programs affecting the structure of industrial growth, could be helpful in avoiding industrial policy
strategies which are costly in the use of national and regional resources and
have been evident in many countries.

— The exchange of information and discussion of various policies affecting
foreign investment and technology transfer could strengthen further what
was seen to be a generally favourable investment and development climate
on the Pacific region.

8. Steps that might be taken to implement these objectives are set out in the paper on institutional developments. Consultative arrangements in these fields are seen as important in developing the practice of cooperation and ecouraging a policy climate favourable to Pacific trade and economic growth. Consultation and information exchange in each area could be very useful, whether or not other more comprehensive policy steps or institutional developments are immediately possible, since they would serve to strengthen policy approaches and improve information about market opportunities in the longer term. The arrangements would not require elaborate institutional development, but, as it is suggested in the work of the Task Forces, should be built upon the bases already established through the Pacific Economic Cooperation Conference and its Task Force activities, in conjunction with established organisations such as PBEC.

9. Because of the particular trade and development needs of the Pacific region, and the growth in the importance of the Pacific economy in the world economy, the Task Force work suggests a more active role for the governments of the region on trade policy. Pacific countries have a clear and common interest in measures aimed at halting protectionist trends and the 'beggar-thy-neighbour' trade deals that are now a disturbing feature of regional and world trade policy. They also have a longer term interest in engineering comprehensive negotiations, within the GATT most-favoured-nation framework, on agricultural and renewable resource goods trade, processed raw material trade, and manufactured goods trade.

10. Progress on these issues depends heavily on:

— careful preparation of an agenda for negotiation staged over a period of time, and

— encompassing a sufficiently wide range of interests so that the benefits of cooperation are shared by all countries.

11. An immediate step to improve the trade policy climate could involve the encouragement of a commitment by Pacific countries for standstill on protectionist measures. A moratorium on new trade barriers would be simply the first step in signalling the start of a longer process of purposeful trade negotiations initiated by Pacific countries and conducted on a non-discriminatory basis. Though significant trade liberalisation may not be possible at this time, it is desirable to start the process, and to develop adequate public support for it, now.

12. The Task Forces stress the importance of freer trade in the GATT framework to the interests of Pacific countries and specified an agenda for trade negotiations which Pacific countries could consider over the longer term. Among the items on the agenda for study and negotiation in the near future, Task Forces listed the following:

— The removal of non-tariff trade barriers (such as voluntary export restraints, and orderly marketing agreements) on agricultural products and labour-intensive manufactured goods, and other manufactured goods.

— Tariff reduction and the removal of restrictions on trade in food items, such as meat, diary products, oilseeds; tropical zone products, such as rubber, coconut and bananas; and certain fisheries and lumber items.

— The extension of the General System of Preferences for agricultural, fisheries, and forest product exports from developing countries, including ASEAN, and negotiation of the graduation problem.

— The liberalisation of all GATT-sanctioned quotas on agricultural imports, particulary among the developed countries.

— Seeking a redrafting of the United States PL 480 to make to more of a food aid delivery service than a market share enforcement mechanism.

— Codification, harmonization and liberalisation of agricultural, fisheries and forestry trade-irritants, such as quantitative, labelling and phyto-sanitary requirements.

— The renegotiation of commodity arrangements, such as the Multi-Fibre Agreement, to capture their original purpose of orderly marketing.

— The reduction of tariff escalation affecting trade in processed raw materials (including food, industrial raw materials, and metals) and the eventual removal of tariff and quota restrictions on trade in these commodities.

— Restraint on export promotion subsidies, dumping, countervailing duties, and industry subsidies.

— More open government tendering procedures for both commodities and services.

13. The Task Forces are conscious that success in encouraging a process of trade negotiation over time would require important domestic and other policy initiatives. These included the need for industrial adjustment assistance, the development of policies which enhanced food security, and the redirection of industrial policies more broadly. Arrangements for consultation, information exchange, and policy review were seen as helpful to facilitating changes in the direction of domestic policy in ways that would be helpful to trade policy cooperation over the longer term.

14. The Pacific Economic Cooperation Conference could usefully call for a standstill on protectionist measures and for the exploration of an agenda for trade negotiations within a GATT-most favoured nation framework. With careful preparation over the next year, Pacific governments could be encouraged to make the urgent commitment to calling a standstill on protectionist measures and to initiate a longer term process of negotiations on trade barriers.

15. An underlying theme in the work of the Task Forces is the interest in promoting further Pacific economic growth and development. A major concern over the coming decades is to ensure that the trade and other foreign economic policies, and broader development strategies, facilitate a marked elevation of the income levels of the poorer countries of the region.

16. The role of foreign direct investment in promoting regional economic development is also given attention in the work of the Task Forces. While

the climate for foreign investment in minerals and energy exploration and production and in manufacturing activity in the Western and Northern Pacific is good relative to other parts of the world, there is an important need to maintain, and improve upon, this situation. In arrangements for consultation and exchange of information in the minerals and energy, industrial trade, and investment, high priority should be attached to discussion of issues affecting the investment climate and, as a first step, consideration could be given to some aspects of the Charter on International Investment prepared and endorsed by PBEC.

17. These trade and investment issues are critical to the trade and development interests of all the countries of the Pacific region, both rich and poor alike. But an important element in the Task Force work stresses the particular interest of the Pacific countries as a whole in directing resources towards, and framing policies which assisted, the special needs of the poorer countries in Southeast Asia and the Pacific. Among the problems deserving of further study is the structure of incentives to technology transfer and effective mechanism for technology transfer.

18. There are a number of ways in which cooperative policy action in the Pacific would assist the aim of enhancing economic growth and development:

— The poorer countries in the Pacific have a larger agricultural base than other Pacific countries. The development of new aid and technical cooperation programs to foster agricultural development, and the proper husbanding of renewable resources (such as forests and fisheries) was identified as an important priority. The reopening of discussions between Japan and the ASEAN countries on the potential implementation of particular commodity STABEX-like schemes and their finding is also important in this context.

— To many of the poorer Pacific countries, minerals and energy trade and production are of special importance. Improved availability of international or regional funds for compensatory finance could ease the problems of some developing countries, permit a longer-term perspective on their resource development and revenue objectives, and make other forms of economic cooperation within the Pacific more attractive to those countries. While the provision of international compensatory finance should desirably be at a multilateral rather than a regional level, an effective regional commitment to ensuring that such arrangements were adequate would obviously facilitate regional cooperative action more broadly. The existing regional focus of European compensatory finance arrangements suggests a case for exploring a regional scheme along similar lines in the Pacific area.

— Substantial new commitments can be made to financing development in the poorer Pacific countries, via established institutions such as the Asian Development Bank or through the strengthening and development of new institutions, as suggested in the Report of the Investment Task Force.

— Trade measures should be directed at serving the interests of the developing countries in the Pacific and aimed at expanding markets for agricultural and lalbour-intensive goods in particular. These trade measures would need to cover the issues set our in Paragraph 12(*c*) but might also encompass the extension of marketing assistance and services to promote trade development.

19. Hence a crucial third element, alongside:

— calling a halt to protectionist measures and

— initiating a process of trade negotiation, must be

— the commitment of new resources, both public and private, targeted at the development of the poorer countries in the region.

It is critical to preparation for successful government level Pacific initiatives that Japan declare its willingness substantially to underwrite regional economic security in this way. The United States, Canada, Australia, New Zealand and Korea must also be prepared to contribute, but, Japan's role is critical.

20. These substantive policy interests and the actions recommended by the Task Forces towards their implementation can only be undertaken effectively if there is a careful step-by-step approach. The necessary institutional developments and follow up are discussed in the accompanying paper on institutional arrangements.

2. *Report on institutional aspects*

1. The idea of regional economic cooperation in the Pacific area has undergone a process of maturation during the past decade and a half. There is a growing consensus today that a systematic arrangement for multilateral consultation would enable the various governments of the region to cooperate more effectively in trade and economic matters, and to formulate their respective national economic policies in a mutually beneficial way.

2. Proposals to give an institutional form to regional economic interdependence began to take shape during the 1960s. One of the earliest formulations for Pacific area economic cooperation was the proposal for a Pacific Free Trade Area outlined by Prof. Kiyoshi Kojima of Japan. One outcome of this initiative was the implementation of a series of Pacific Trade and Development (PAFTAD) Conferences, comprising primarily regional economists. International business organization such as the Pacific Basin Economic Council (PBEC) have actively supported the idea of regional economic cooperation.

3. In the 1970s, greater attention was paid to the problems and potential benefits of a growing, interdependent, regional economy. In 1979, an Organisation for Pacific Trade and Development (OPTAD) was proposed by Professor Hugh Patrick of Yale University and Peter Drysdale of Australian National University in their report of the US Senate Foreign Relations Committee. The report recommended the creation of an inter-governmental consultative organisation which would serve as a multilateral official forum for cooperation and coordination in matters of economic and trade policy. The OPTAD plan, although not officially adopted by the governments, has

provided a useful reference in the subsequent discussion of the desirability and feasibility of institutional arrangements for Pacific economic cooperation.

4. The most important collective effort to deal with the issues relating to regional economic interdependence has been the Pacific Economic Cooperation Conference (PECC), of which the first meeting was held in Canberra in September 1980. The prime motivators of the Pacific Community Seminar, as the 1980 Canberra meeting was called, were Sir John Crawford of Australia and Dr Saburo Okita of Japan. The Canberra Seminar was attended by delegations of three from each of eleven countries (the five Pacific OECD countries, five ASEAN countries and the Republic of Korea) as well as a joint delegation from Pacific island states (one each from Papua-New Guinea, Fiji and Tonga). Typically, each country delegation included one senior government official, one business leader, and one academic or professional member. Representatives of the Asian Development Bank (ADB), PBEC and PAFTAD were also present at the meeting.

5. The seminar focussed on the rationale, the format and the agenda of a new consultative system. The rationale dealt largely with the events and challenges arising from rapidly increasing regional economic interdependence. The format favored was similar to the one adopted for the seminar which emphasised the importance of a tripartite participation of the government, business and academic sectors. It recommended that 'a standing committee of about twenty-five persons be established to coordinate an expansion of information exchange within the region and to set up Task Forces to undertake major studies of a number of issues for regional cooperation'.

6. A prime responsibility of the committee was to be 'to establish Task Forces in agreed areas to explore substantive issues for regional economic cooperation, review their reports and transmit them to governments'. The subject matter of Task Force activity was illustrated in the following list of topics: 'trade (including market access problems and structural adjustment associated with industrialisation in the developing countries); direct investment (including guidelines for investors and harmonization of foreign investment policies); energy (including access to market assurance of continued supply, alternative forms, conservation and research exchanges); Pacific marine resources; and international services such as transportation, communication, and education exchanges.' The recommendations of the Canberra conference were not implemented immediately because of an implied need for official governmental endorsement and commitment.

7. The Second Pacific Economic Cooperation Conference (PECC) was held in Bangkok, on June 3–5, 1982. The Bangkok meeting, hosted by Dr Thanat Khoman, Deputy Prime Minister of Thailand, was attended by some sixty participants and observers from twelve countries and international organisations such as OECD and UN ESCAP. As in the Canberra seminar, each country was represented by a tripartite delegation of the government, business and academic sectors who participated in the conference, the academic group was invited to attend a two-day preparatory

meeting at ESCAP, out of which came four papers drafted to reflect the consensus of their views on the main issues that face the Pacific region on trade, investment, commodity problems, and institutional structure for consultation and consensus-forming in the Pacific region. These papers were presented at the opening session of the conference and provided the main basis for discussion in the next two days.

8. The Conference concluded that Pacific economic cooperation at the immediate stage should take the form of a series of tripartite consultative meetings to review matters of common concern to the Pacific Basin Countries, and to pass on recommendations to the respective governments and relevant organisations. The Conference agreed to set up a Standing Committee which was to be responsible for the organisation of the next conference and Four Task Forces, one each on trade in manufactures, trade in agricultural products, trade in minerals, and investment and technology transfer. The Task Forces were to prepare substantive reports to be reviewed by the next PEC Conference to be held in Indonesia. It was emphasised that, in the preparation of the reports, the tripartite views should be fully reflected. This was to be achieved by organising various forms of national as well as international meetings, consultations, and review committees as an essential part of the report preparation.

9. In accordance with the decision of the Bangkok Conference, four Task Forces were established, with a lead institute having responsibility to coordinate the activities of each Task Force. They were to address the following four topics: Minerals and Energy Trade, which is coordinated by the Australian National University; Investment and Technology Transfer, which is coordinated by the Japan Special Committee for Pacific Cooperation; Trade in Manufactured Goods, which is coordinated by the Korea Development Institute (KDI); and Trade in Agricultural and Renewable Resource Goods, which is coordinated by the Pacific Cooperation Committee of Thailand.

10. On November 1 and 2, the coordinators of the Task Forces met in Hong Kong to review and discuss the preparatory work and progress made by each of the four Task Forces. At the meeting, the Task Force Coordinators also discussed the schedule and plans for overall PECC activities. The meeting agreed that the activities of the four Task Forces needed to be closely coordinated and linked to activities of the Standing Committee. The Task Force coordinators also adopted an interConference schedule for the activities of the Task Forces and the Standing Committee.

11. Major PECC activities leading up to the Bali Conference are described below:

— The first draft of each Task Force was completed by April 1983 to be presented to the inter-Conference Standing Committee meeting.

— The Standing Committee meeting was held in Bangkok on May 23–24, 1983, to review the progress reports of the four Task Forces and make preparations for the Bali Conference schedule for November 21–23, 1983. The Standing Committee also authorised the convening of a second meeting of the Task Force Coordinators to be held in Seoul in September, 1983.

— Each Task Force convened a workshop during the months June to August 1983. The workshops were attended by the respective International Advisors who reviewed the background papers prepared by the Task Forces and assisted in the drafting of summary reports.

— The second meeting of the Task Force Coordinators was held in Seoul, on September 24–26, 1983, to prepare an integrated report of the Task Forces and to finalise preparations for the Bali Conference. The meeting also adopted a report on 'Suggested Institutional Arrangements for the Future', which is presented in the section that follows.

— The summary reports, together with the integrated report and the background papers, were distributed, together with the background papers, to members of the Standing Committee in advance of the November PEC Conference.

— Prior to the Bali PEC Conference, the Standing Committee met to review and deliberate on the summary reports of the Task Forces to be presented to the Conference.

12. The present three-tier format of Conference/Standing Committee/ Task Forces has effectively served the PECC purpose of formulating means and methods for promoting regional economic cooperation. Building on the strength of the present framework, limited modifications might be introduced for greater institutional effectiveness and flexibility. The proposed framework envisages an arrangement involving five components: the Conference, the Standing Committee, the Task Forces, a Coordinating Group and national committees. It is important that 'national committees' be established in those countries where they have not yet been formed. Where necessary, the existing national committees should be strengthened and vitalised.

13. The PEC Conference considers and reviews the progress of Pacific economic cooperation, including the work of its Task Forces, and reaches such conclusions and makes such recommendations as it deems appropriate. In particular, it establishes future agenda for the Task Forces and receives their reports. Each participating country is represented at the Conference by a tripartite delegation of the government, business and academic sectors. Additional participants in the Conference will include members of the Standing Committee and the Coordination Group, and representatives of international and regional organizations. Other individuals and observers may be invited by the Standing Committee. The Conference is held at regular intervals of 12 to 18 months. The place and dates of each Conference are to be decided by the Conference before the one that precedes it.

14. The Standing Committee directs and monitors Task Force activities and makes necessary decisions concerning the participation in and the agenda of the next Conference. The Standing Committee also transmits conclusions and recommendations as appropriate to governments and other organisations. It will also make recommendations concerning the site

and time of the Conference that follows the next Conference. The national committee of each of the participating countries will be represented by a Standing Committee member. The Chairman of the Pacific Basin Economic Council (PBEC) or his designated representative, and the Chairman of the Steering Committee of the Pacific Trade and Development Conference (PAFTAD), may also be invited to participate in the Standing Committee meetings. The Standing Committee member of the host country of the next scheduled Conference will serve as its chairman.

15. Task Forces will be sponsored and organized by institutions in different countries of the region. They will develop information on the need, opportunities and methods for regional cooperation in several subject areas. Participation in Task Force activities from all Pacific countries is encouraged, including those countries not represented in the Standing Committee.

16. Each Task Force will review the state of affairs in the subject area it is concerned with and report its findings and suggested actions to the Conference through the Standing Committee. The Coordinating Group will informally review the draft Task Force reports and prepare a Report on Issues for Pacific Cooperation which integrates the findings of the The Task Forces and incorporates other materials as appropriate.

17. The second phase of the Task Forces activities begins after the Standing Committee and PECC have finished their review and critique of the draft reports. The Task Force activities will be based on guidelines provided by the PECC and the Standing Committee. Based on these guidelines, the Task Forces may be requested to extend their initial analysis, address gaps in the initial effort, and promote change consistent with Task Force findings. In this latter instance, the Task Forces may seek involvement of other organisations active in Pacific affairs. It may also contribute to the establishment of a more permanent forum for exchange of information and action on issues relating to Pacific cooperation.

18. During the 1982–3 inter-Conference period, the coordinators of the Task Forces have functioned as a *de facto* working group which coordinated the PECC activities on behalf of the Standing Committee. the Standing Committee may formalise this arrangement by appointing a Coordinating Committee whose main function is to plan overall PECC activities and coordinate work among the Task Forces on behalf of the Standing Committee. The Coordinating Group will be chaired by a representative of the next PECC host country which will also provide its secretariat services. The Coordinating Group will place particular emphasis on the integration of Task Force findings and the development of an action program to advance the interests of Pacific economic cooperation.

19. PECC and the Task Forces will be assisted and supported in their activities by the 'national committees', which are to be established in the respective participating countries. National Pacific Cooperation Committees are organised on a tripartite basis and to serve as a focal point within each country pertaining to the activities of the PECC. They will seek the

support of the government and to involve as wide a range of participation as possible. They are expected to nominate the country's Standing Committee member as well as participants to the PEC Conference.

20. The host country of the next PEC Conference will provide the secretariat service for the Standing Committee and the Coordinating Group as well as the next PEC Conference.

BIBLIOGRAPHY

Abegglen, J., and A. Etori, 'Japans Technologie heute', *Spektrum der Wissenschaft*, April 1981, p 30 ff.

Ahn, D.-S., *Gemeinschaftsunternehmungen in Entwicklungsländern. Joint Ventures als Entwicklungsinstrument in den ASEAN-Staaten*, Tübingen 1981.

Akrasanee, N. *et al.*, *ASEAN and the Pacific Community. A Report* (Centre for Strategic and International Studies), Jakarta 1981.

Akrasanee, N., *ASEAN and Pacific Economic Co-operation: A Survey of Issues of Interdependence* (ESCAP, Development Planning Division), August 1980.

——, *'Thailand and ASEAN Economic Cooperation'* (Institute of Southeast Asian Studies; — ASEAN Economic Research Unit, *Current Issues*, no. 12), Singapore 1980.

——, *Industrial Sector in the Thai Economy* (Thai University Research Association, Research Report, no. 1), Bangkok, November 1980.

——, and H.Ch. Rieger (eds), *ASEAN–EEC Economic Relations* (Institute of Southeast Asian Studies), Singapore 1982.

Anjaria, S.J. *et al.*, *Developments in International Trade Policy* (IMF Occasional Paper, no. 16), 2nd imp., Washington, July 1983.

Ariff, M., 'Malaysia's Trade and Industrialization Strategy with Special Reference to ASEAN Industrial Co-operation' in R. Garnaut, (ed.), *ASEAN in a Changing Pacific and World Economy*, Canberra 1980, p. 280 ff.

Arndt, H.W., 'ASEAN Industrial Projects' in *Asia Pacific Community*, no 3/1978, p. 117 ff.

Balassa, B., 'The Tokyo Round and the Developing Countries' *Journal of World Trade Law*, vol. 14 (1980), p. 93 ff.

——, The 'New Protectionism' and the International Economy', *Journal of World Trade Law*, vol. 12 (1978), p 409 ff.

——, and M. Sharpston, 'Export Subsidies by Developing Countries: Issues of Policy', *Commercial Policy Issues*, November 1977, p. 13 ff.

Baldwin, R.E., and T. Murray, 'MFN Tariff Reduction and Developing Country Trade Benefits Under the GSP', *Economic Journal*, vol. 87 (1977), p. 33 ff.

Ball, M.M., 'Regionalism and the Pacific Commonwealth', *Pacific Affairs*, vol. 46 (1973), p. 232 ff.

Bandura, Y., 'The Pacific Community — A Brainchild of Imperialist Diplomacy', *International Affairs*, no. 6/1980, p. 63 ff.

Banks, G., 'The Economics and Politics of Countertrade', *The World Economy*, vol. 6 (1983), p. 159 ff.

Barnett, R.W., 'Introduction and Summary: The Concept of Community' in *Pacific Region Interdependencies: A Compendium of Papers Submitted to the Joint Economic Committee* (Congress of the United States), Washington DC 1981.

Bautista, R.M., *The 1981–85 Tariff Changes and Effective Protection of Manufacturing Industries* (University of the Philippines School of Economics Discussion Paper no. 8213), August 1982.
——, 'Trade Strategies and Industrial Development in the Philippines: With Special Reference to Regional Trade Preferences' in R. Garnaut (ed.), *ASEAN in a Changing Pacific and World Economy*, Canberra 1980, p. 175 ff.

Becker, H., 'Die Internationalisierung des japanischen Yen', in *Geld in Japan* (OAG series 'Japan Modern', vol. 2), Berlin 1981, p. 203 ff.

Behrmann, J.N., 'International Sectoral Integration: An Alternative Approach to Free Trade', *Journal of World Trade Law*, vol. 6 (1972), p. 269 ff.

Bhagwati, J.N., 'Compensation for Trade Protectionism' in K. Haq (ed.), *Dialogue for a New Order*, New York 1980, p. 75 ff.

Böttcher, E., *Kooperation und Demokratie in der Wirtschaft*, Tübingen 1974.

Boyd, G., 'A Pacific Regional Economic Order', *Asian Perspective*, vol. 7 (1983), p. 1 ff.
——, 'Transpacific Policies' in G. Boyd (ed.), *Region Building in the Pacific*, New York 1982, p. 1 ff.
——, 'ASEAN Regional Policies' in G. Boyd (ed.), *Region Building in the Pacific*, New York 1982, p. 78 ff.

Braun, D., *Südasien zwischen Konflikten und Zusammenarbeit. Der Ansatz der South Asian Regional Cooperation (SARC)* (Stiftung Wissenschaft und Politik), Ebenhausen, December 1983.

Bretzfelder, R. and H. Friedenberg, 'State Differences in Per Capita Personal Income Growth in the Seventies', in *Survey of Current Business* (US Department of Commerce), August 1979, p. 25 ff.

Brown, H. (ed.), *China Among the Nations of the Pacific*, Boulder, Colorado 1982.

Bull, H. (ed.), *Asia and the Western Pacific: Towards a New International Order*, Melbourne 1975

Bundesverband der Deutschen Industrie, *Administrative Importbeschränkungen in Japan. Zur Wirkung tarifärer und nichttarifarer Handelshemmnisse*, Cologne, March 1982.

Center for Strategic and International Studies (ed.), *Asia Pacific in the 1980s: Toward Greater Symmetry in Economic Interdependence*, Jakarta 1980

Chang, K.-Y., 'Building the Pacific Community: An Incrementalist Approach', *Issues Studies: A Journal of China Studies and International Affairs*, February 1983, p. 39 ff.

Cherneyshov, A., 'The Pacific: Problems of International Security and Cooperation', *International Affairs*, 11/1977, p. 78 ff.

Chia Siow Yue, 'ASEAN and the Pacific Economic Community', Southeast Asian Affairs (Institute of Southeast Asian Studies), Singapore 1981.
——, 'Singapore's Trade and Development Strategy, and ASEAN Economic Cooperation, with Special Reference to the ASEAN Common Approach to Foreign Economic Relations' in R. Garnaut (ed.), *ASEAN*

in a Changing Pacific and World Economy, Canberra 1980, p. 241 ff.

Chong Li Choy, *Open Self-Reliant Regionalism: Power for ASEAN's Development*, Institute of Southeast Asian Studies, Singapore 1981.

Clausen, A.W., 'Global Interdependence in the 1980.' (Remarks before the Yomiuri International Economic Society), Tokyo, 13 January 1982.

Cline, R.S. and M.W., 'The Communist Five and the Capitalist Ten Socio-Economic Systems in Asia', *Journal of East-Asian Affairs*, vol. 2 (1982), p. 1 ff.

Cline, W.R. (ed.), *Trade Policy in the 1980s*, Washington DC 1983.

——, *'Reciprocity': A New Approach to World Trade Policy*, Washington DC 1982.

Corbet, H., 'Importance of Being Earnest about Further GATT Negotiations', *The World Economy*, vol. 2 (1979), p. 319 ff.

Council for Economic Planning and Development, Republic of China, *Taiwan Statistical Data Book 1985*.

Crawford, J. and S. Okita (eds), *Raw Materials and Pacific Economic Integration*, London 1978.

—— and G. Seow (eds), *Pacific Economic Cop-Operation: Suggestions for Action*, London 1981.

Curzon, G., *Multilateral Commercial Diplomacy*, London 1965.

Dahm, B. and W. Draguhn (eds), *Politics, Society and Economy in the ASEAN States*, Wiesbaden 1975.

Dalrymple, F.R., 'The Pacific Basin Community Concept', *Indonesian Quarterly*, vol. 9 (1981), no. 4, p. 43 ff.

Dam, K.W., *The GATT Law and International Economic Organization*, Chicago 1970.

Davies, D., 'The Pacific Community: Hands Across the Sea', *Far Eastern Economic Review*, 19 Feb 1980.

De Rosa, D.A., 'Trade and Protection in the Asian Developing Region', *Asian Development Review*, vol. 4 (1986), no. 1, p. 27ff.

Diaz-Alejandro, C.F., 'Comment' in W.R. Cline (ed.), *Trade Policy in the 1980s*, Washington DC 1983, p. 305 ff.

Dohnanyi, K. von, *Japanische Strategien und das deutsche Führungsdefizit*, Munich 1969.

Donges, J.B., *Aussenwirtschafts-und Entwicklungspolitik*, Berlin 1981.

Donowaki, M., 'The Pacific Basin Community — A Japanese Overview', *Asia Pacific Community*, no. 15/1982, p. 15 ff.

Doran, C., 'US and Canadian Pacific Perspectives,' in G. Boyd (ed.), *Region Building in the Pacific*, New York 1982, p. 162 ff.

Downen, R.L. and B.J. Dickson (eds), *The Emerging Pacific Community. A Regional Perspective*, Boulder, Colo. 1984.

Drysdale, P., 'The Proposal for an Organization for Pacific Trade and Development Revisited', *Asian Survey*, vol. 23 (1983), p. 1293 ff.

——, 'Japan, Australia, New Zealand: The Prospect for Western Pacific Economic Integration', *Economic Record*, vol. 45 (1969), p. 321 ff.

——, 'Pacific Economic Integration: An Australian View', in K. Kojima (ed.), *Pacific Trade and Development*, Tokyo 1968.

—— and H. Patrick, *An Asian-Pacific Regional Economic Organization: An Exploratory Concept Paper*, US Government Printing Office, Congressional Research Service, Washington DC 1979.

Dunn, L. *et al.*, *In the Kingdom of the Blind: A Report on Protectionism and the Asian-Pacific Region*, London 1983.

Duscha, W., 'Die Integrationsbestrebungen der ASEAN — Abriss einer Bestandsaufnahme zu Beginn der 80er Jahre', *Internationales Asienforum*, vol. 13 (1982), p. 331 ff.

Dymock, P. and D. Vogt, 'Protectionist Pressures in the U.S. Congress', *Journal of World Trade Law*, vol. 17 (1983), p. 496 ff.

Economic Planning Agency (Japanese Government), *Economic Survey of Japan 1980/81*, Tokyo 1981.

Economist Intelligence Unit, *The ASEAN, Hong Kong, South Korea and Taiwan Economies. Their Structure amd Outlook into the 1980s*, London 1980.

Edwards, J., 'Moulding a New Community', *Far Eastern Economic Review*, 22 Aug. 1980.

Ehmke, H., 'Westeuropa in der Weltwirtschaft und die EG', *Frankfurter Rundschau*, 18 Feb 1984.

Eli, M., *Wirtschaftliche Entwicklungsperspektiven der Republik Korea*, Hamburg 1979

ESCAP, *Patterns and Impact of Foreign Investment in the ESCAP Region*, Bangkok 1985.

——, 'The Case History of Successful Export Policies: The Republic of Korea', Document E/ESCAP/Trade/TOPMMT/5, 12 May 1986.

Esser, K. and J. Wiemann, *Schwerpunktländer in der Dritten Welt. Konsequenzen für die Südbeziehungen der Bundesrepublik Deutschland*, Berlin 1981.

Ester, H., 'Slow Start in the Pacific', *Far Eastern Economic Review*, 26 Sept. 1980.

Farran, A., 'Energy, Politics and Pacific Basin Development', *Asia Pacific Community*, no. 15/1982, p. 83 ff.

Fifield, R.H., 'ASEAN and the Pacific Community, in *Asia Pacific Community*, no. 11/1981, p. 14 ff.

Ford, R., 'Port Activity in the Pacific Northwest', in A.S. Hoffman (ed.), *Japan and the Pacific Basin*, Atlantic Institute for International Affairs, Paris 1980, p. 43 ff.

Frank, J., 'The "Graduation" Issue for LDCs', *Journal of World Trade Law*, vol. 13 (1979), p. 289 ff.

Fraser, M., 'Australia and the Pacific Community Concept' in: Crawford, J. and G. Seow (eds), *Pacific Economic Co-Operation: Suggestions for Action*, London 1981, p. 88 ff.

Friedrich, B., S.-J. Park and R. Wiegelmann, *Entwicklungspolitik der EG*, Frankfurt 1980.

Fujiwara, J., 'Japan-Southeast Asia Cooperation in the 1980s', *Asia Pacific Community*, no. 13/1981, p. 1 ff.

Gälli, A., *Neue Wachstumsmärkte in Fernost. Acht Länder auf der Schwelle zur Wirtschaftsmacht*, Munich 1983.

166   *Bibliography*

——, *Taiwan: Ökonomische Fakten und Trends*, Munich 1980.
Garnaut, R. (ed.), *ASEAN in a Changing Pacific and World Economy*, Canberra 1980.
GATT, Document L/5517/Add. 5, 5 Dec. 1983.
GATT, *The Tokyo Round of Multilateral Trade Negotiations*, vol. II, Geneva 1980.
Gelber, H.S., 'Australia, the Pacific and the United States in the 1980s', *Comparative Strategy*, vol. 3 (1981), P. 97 ff.
Ghazali Shafie, M., 'Toward a Pacific Basin Community: A Malaysian Perception', in *Pacific Region Interdependencies. A Compendium of Papers Submitted to the Joint Economic Committee*, Congress of the United States, Washington DC 1981, p. 71 ff.
Gilpin, R., 'Three Models of the Future', *International Organization*, vol. 29 (1975), p. 73 ff.
Glaubitt, K., and B. Lageman, *Arabische Integrationsexperimente. Der Sudan als Bewährungsfeld arabischer Produktions- und Entwicklungsintegration*, Tübingen/Basel 1980.
—— and W. Lütkenhorst, *Elemente einer neuen Weltwirtschaftsordnung*, Tübingen/Basel 1979
Global Strategy for Growth (A Report on North-South Issues by a Study Group under the Chairmanship of Lord McFadzean of Kelvinside), London 1981.
Golay, F.H., 'National Economic Priorities and International Coalitions', in Pauker, G.J. *et al.*, *Diversity and Development in Southeast Asia*, New York 1977, p. 89 ff.
Gordon, B.K., 'Asian Angst', in *Foreign Policy*, no. 47 (1982), p. 49 ff.
——, 'Japan and the Pacific Basin Proposal', in *Korea and World Affairs*, vol. 5 (1981), no. 2, p. 268 ff.
——, 'Japan, the United States, and Southeast Asia,' *Foreign Affairs*, vol. 56 (1977/8), p. 579 ff.
Greene, F., 'The United States and Asia in 1980', *Asian Survey*, vol. 21 (1981), p. 1 ff.
Haddad, W.W., 'Japan, the Fukuda Doctrine, and ASEAN', *Contemporary Southeast Asia*, vol. 2 (1980), p. 10 ff.
Hager, W., 'Protectionism and Autonomy: How to Preserve Free Trade in Europe', *International Affairs*, vol. 58 (1981/2), p. 413 ff.
——, 'Free Trade Means Destabilization', *Intereconomics*, vol. 19 (1984), p. 28 ff.
Hall, K.O., 'Strengthening Third World Negotiating Capacity', in K. Haq (ed.), *Dialogue for a New Order*, New York 1980, p. 45 ff.
Han, S.-J., 'The Politics of Pacific Cooperation', *Asian Survey*, vol. 23 (1983), p. 1281 ff.
——, (ed.), *Community-Building in the Pacific Region: Issues and Opportunities*, Asiatic Research Center, Korea University, Seoul 1981.
Haq, K. (ed.), *Dialogue for a New Order*, New York 1980.
Haq, M. ul, 'North-South Dialogue — Is there a Future?' K. Haq (ed.), *Dialogue for a New Order*, New York 1980, p. 270 ff.
Harris, S. and B. Bridges, *European Interests in ASEAN*, London 1983.

Haubold, E., 'Der Westen verliert Anziehungskraft', in *Frankfurter Allgemeine Zeitung*, 22 Feb. 1982.

Hax, K., *Japan. Wirtschaftsmacht des Fernen Ostens*, Cologne/Opladen 1961.

Hemmer, H.-R., *Wirtschaftsprobleme der Entwicklungsländer*, Munich 1978.

Hernádi, A., *Japan and the Pacific Region*, Hungarian Scientific Council for World Economy, Budapest 1982.

——, 'Development Strategies and Economic Policy in the Pacific Region', *Asia Pacific Community*, no. 13 (1981), p. 68 ff.

——, 'Pacific Region as a Growth Sub-Center and Japan's Role', *Asia Pacific Community*, no. 5 (1979), p. 109 ff.

Hesse, H., 'Zum Konzept einer Handelsanpassungspolitik', in G. Bombach *et al.* (eds), *Probleme der Wettbewerbstheorie und — politik*, Tübingen 1976, p. 341 ff.

Höpker, W., 'Die Pazifische Herausforderung. Kooperation und Konfrontation um das Meer der Zukunft', *Beiträge zur Konfliktforschung*, vol. 9 (1979), p. 33 ff.

Hoffman, A.S. (ed.), *Japan and the Pacific Basin*, Atlantic Institute for International Affairs, Paris 1980.

Hofheinz, R.,Jr., and K.E.Calder, *The Eastasia Edge*, London 1982.

Hong, W.T., 'Export Growth and Transformation of Industrial Structure' (paper presented at the International Forum on Industrial Planning and Trade Policies), Seoul 1–12 June 1982.

Hooper, P.F. (ed.), *Building a Pacific Community*, Honolulu 1982.

Ichimura, S., 'Japan and Southeast Asia', *Asian Survey*, vol. 20 (1980), p. 754 ff.

Ikema, M., 'Japan's Economic Relations with ASEAN', in R. Garnaut (ed.), *ASEAN in a Changing Pacific and World Economy*, Canberra 1980, p. 453 ff.

ILO, *Employment, Trade and North-South Co-operation*, Geneva 1981.

IMF, Direction of Trade Statistics, *Yearbook 1985*.

Institute of Asian Studies/Deutsche Industrie- und Handelskammer in Japan (eds), *Wirtschaftspartner Japan*, Hamburg 1980.

Investment Incentive Programs of the Pacific Basin, ed. by International Business Education Program, Graduate School of Business Administration, University of Southern California, Los Angeles 1983.

Jackson, J.H., 'GATT Machinery and the Tokyo Round Agreements' in W.R. Cline (ed.), *Trade Policy in the 1980s*, Washington, DC, 1983, p. 159 ff.

Jaeger, F., *Welthandel und Wachstum. Chance für die Dritte und Vierte Welt?*, Diessenhofen 1977.

Japan Center for International Exchange (ed.), *The Pacific Community Concept: Views from Eight Nations*, Tokyo 1980.

Johannson, J.K., and R.S. Spich, 'Trade Interdependence in the Pacific Rim Basin and the E.C.: A Comparative Analysis', *Journal of Common Market Studies*, vol. 20 (1981),p. 41 ff.

Jorgensen-Dahl, A., 'Extra-Regional Influences on Regional Cooperation in S.E. Asia', *Pacific Community*, vol. 8 (1977), p. 412 ff.

Jüttemeier, K.H., and R. Lammers, 'Subventionen in der Bundesrepublik Deutschland' (*Kieler Diskussionsbeiträge*, nos. 63/64) Kiel, Nov. 1979.

Kahn, H., *World Economic Development. 1979 and Beyond*, New York 1979.

Kanahele, G.S., and M. Haas, 'Prospects for a Pacific Community', *Pacific Community*, Oct. 1975, p. 83 ff.

Kawai, S., 'Future Japan — ASEAN Economic Cooperation', *Asia Pacific Community*, no. 10 (1980), p. 98 ff.

Kelkar, V.L., 'GATT, Export Subsidies and Developing Countries', *Journal of World Trade Law*, vol. 14 (1980), p. 368 ff.

Kirby, S., *Towards the Pacific Century: Economic Development in the Pacific Basin* (Economist Intelligence Unit, Special Report no. 137), London 1983.

Kitamura, H., 'Asian-Pacific Economic Cooperation: The Role of Governments', *Asia Pacific Community*, no. 18 (1982), p. 17 ff.

——, 'International Division of Labor and Industrial Adjustment: Relevance of Theory to Policy Analysis', *The Developing Economies*, vol. 18 (1980), p. 377 ff.

Kleinjans, E., 'Thoughts on a Pacific Community' (Paper presented at the Asian/Pacific Round Table, 11 May 1980), Washington DC.

Koekkoek, K.A., 'On the Case for Graduation', *Intereconomics*, vol. 18 (1983), p. 225 ff.

Körner, H., 'The New Protectionism and the Third World', *Intereconomics*, vol. 17 (1982), p. 179 ff.

—— et al., *Industrielle Arbeitsteilung zwischen Industrie- und Entwicklungsländern und Strukturanpassung*, Munich 1981.

Kojima, K., 'A New Capitalism for a New International Economic Order', *Hitotsubashi Journal of Economics*, June 1981, p. 1 ff.

——, 'Economic Cooperation in a Pacific Community', *Asia Pacific Community*, no. 12 (1981), p. 1 ff.

——, *Economic Cooperation in a Pacific Community* (Japan Institute of International Affairs), Tokyo 1980.

——, 'Comment' in R. Garnaut (ed.), *ASEAN in a Changing Pacific and World Economy*, Canberra 1980, p. 135 ff.

——, *Direct Foreign Investment*, London 1978.

——, *Japan and a Pacific Free Trade Area*, London 1971.

——, 'Asian Developing Countries and PAFTA: Development, Aid and Trade Preferences', *Hitotsubashi Journal of Economics*, June 1969, p. 1 ff.

——, 'Japan's Interest in the Pacific Trade Expansion: PAFTA Re-Considered', *Hitotsubashi Journal of Economics*, June 1968, p. 1 ff.

—— (ed.), *Pacific Trade and Development*, Tokyo 1968

——, 'A Pacific Economic Community and Asian Developing Countries', *Hitotsubashi Journal of Economics*, June 1966, p. 17 ff.

——, 'Japan's Interest in Pacific Trade Expansion' in Kojima (ed.), *Pacific Trade and Development*, Tokyo 1968.

Korea Development Institute, 'Tariff Policy: Present Status and Reform

Plan', Seoul, July 1982 (mimeo, in Korean).
Krämer, H.R., 'Probleme der Regionalisierung des internationalen Handels' in H. Giersch and H.-D. Haas (eds), *Probleme der weltwirtschaftlichen Arbeitsteilung*, Berlin 1974, p. 555 ff.
——, *Formen und Methoden der internationalen wirtschaftlichen Integration. Versuch einer Systematik*, Tübingen 1969.
Kraft, A., *Aspekte der regionalen wirtschaftlichen Integration zwischen Entwicklungsländern. Das Beispiel der ASEAN*, Wiesbaden 1982.
Kraus, W., 'Pazifische Zusammenarbeit und Europäische Gemeinschaft. Zur Frage der Europäischen Position gegenüber der weltwirtschaftlichen und weltpolitischen Schwerpunktbildung im pazifischen Raum', *Aussenpolitik*, 35 (1984), p. 190 ff.
——, *Die japanische Herausforderung: Fernöstliche Mentalität und Strategie*, Berlin 1982.
——, 'Wirtschaftliche Integrationsbestrebungen in Ostasien', *Internationales Asienforum*, 1 (1970), p. 408 ff.
—— and W. Lütkenhorst, 'Atlantische Gegenwart — Pazifische Zukunft? Anmerkungen zur wirtschafts- und außenpolitischen Orientierung der USA', in *Asien*, no. 10/Jan. 1984, p. 5 ff.
Krause, L.B., *US Economic Policy toward the Association of Southeast Asian Nations. Meeting the Japanese Challenge*, Washington DC 1982.
——, 'The Pacific Economy in an Interdependent World: A New Institution for the Pacific Basin', in J. Crawford and G. Seow (eds), *Pacific Economic Co-operation: Suggestions for Action*, London 1981, p. 128 ff.
——, and S. Sekiguchi, *Economic Interaction in the Pacific Basin*, Washington DC 1980.
Krishnamurti, R., 'Multilateral Trade Negotiations and the Developing Countries', *Third World Quarterly*, vol. 2 (1980), p. 251 ff.
Krueger, A.O., 'Regional and Global Approaches to Trade and Development Strategy' in R. Garnaut (ed.), *ASEAN in a Changing Pacific and World Economy*, Caberra 1980, p. 21 ff.
Kuo, Sh.W.Y., G. Ranis, and J.H.C. Fei, *The Taiwan Success Story*, Boulder, Colo. 1981.
Lai Fung-wai, F., *Without a Vision: Japan's Relations with ASEAN* (National University of Singapore, Occasional Paper no. 40), Singapore 1981.
Langhammer, R.J., 'Sectoral Profiles of Import Licensing in Selected Developing Countries and their Impact on North-South and South-South Trade Flows' *Konjunkturpolitik*, vol. 29 (1980), p. 21 ff.
Laumer, H. (ed.), 'Wachstumsmarkt Südostasien. Chancen und Risiken unternehmerischer Kooperation' (papers presented at a conference of the Ifo-Institute , 19–21 Oct. 1983), Munich, 1984.
——, *Die Direktinvestitionen der japanischen Wirtschaft in den Schwellenländern Ost- und Südostasiens*, Munich 1984.
——, ' "Sogo Shosha": Japans multinationale Handelsunternehmen — weltweit ohne Pendant', *Ifo-Studien*, nos 3/4, 1981.
——, 'Japans Wirtschaft in den achtziger Jahren — Perspektiven, Chancen, Risiken', *Ifo-Dokumentation*, Munich 1981.

Lee Poh Ping, 'Reflections on the Pacific Community Concept', *Asia Pacific Community*, no. 8 (1980), p. 35 ff.

Leontief, W., *et al.*, *Die Zukunft der Weltwirtschaft. Bericht der Vereinten Nationen*, Stuttgart 1977.

List, F., *Das nationale System der politischen Ökonomie*, Basel/Tübingen 1959 (reprint of 1841 original).

Lizano, E. 'Integration of Less Developed Areas and of Areas on Different Levels of Development', in F. Machlup (ed.), *Economic Integration: Worldwide, Regional, Sectoral*, London/Basingstoke 1976, p. 275 ff.

Lörcher, S., 'Sozialversicherung, Altersversorgung, Rentensystem' in M. Pohl (ed.), *Japan 1979/80. Politik und Wirtschaft*, Hamburg 1980, p. 81 ff.

Logue, T.J., 'Trade and Telecommunications in the Pacific: Bridges between East and West', Honolulu, Sept. 1981 (mimeo).

Lorenz, D., 'International Division of Labour versus Closer Cooperation? With Special Regard to ASEAN-EEC Economic Relations' (paper presented at Third Conference on ASEAN-EEC Economic Relations, 26–28 Oct. 1983, Bangkok) rev. version, January 1984.

——, 'Ursachen und Konsequenzen des Neomerkantilismus' in A. Woll (ed.), *Internationale Anpassungsprozesse*, Berlin 1981, p. 9 ff.

——, 'On the Crisis of the "Liberalization Policy" in the Economics of Interdependence', *Intereconomics*, vol. 13 (1978), p. 169 ff.

Low, P., 'The Definition of "Export Subsidies" in GATT', *Journal of World Trade Law*, vol. 16 (1982), p. 375 ff.

Lütkenhorst, W., 'Handelsförderung und Handelsbarrieren in den Ländern Südostasiens' in H. Laumer (ed.), *Wachstumsmarkt Südostasien. Chancen und Risiken unternehmerischer Kooperation* (papers presented at a Conference of the Ifo-Institute 19–21 Oct. 1983), Munich 1984, p. 265 ff.

——, 'GATT Between Self-Destruction and Reform', *Intereconomics*, no. 4 (1984).

——, *Trade Policy Approaches of Pacific Basin Developing Countries* (Institut für Entwicklungsforschung und Entwicklungspolitik, Materialien und kleine Schriften no. 96), Bochum 1984.

——, 'Pacific Basin Interdependencies — A Case for Large-Scale Economic Cooperation?', *Intereconomics*, vol. 18 (1983), p. 28 ff.

——, 'Die ASEAN-Staaten und Konzepte einer pazifischen Wirtschaftskooperation', in A. Woll, K. Glaubitt and H.-B. Schäfer (eds), *Nationale Entwicklung und internationale Zusammenarbeit — Herausforderung ökonomischer Forschung*, Berlin 1983, p. 259 ff.

——, *Zielbegründung und Entwicklungspolitik. Das Grundbedürfnisziel in methodologisch-theoretischer Perspektive*, Tübingen 1982.

——, *Konzepte einer wirtschaftlichen Kooperation zwischen Industrie- und Entwicklungsländern im pazifischen Raum. Eine Problemskizze zur Diskussion weltwirtschaftlicher Regionalisierungstendenzen* (Institut für Entwicklungsforschung und Entwicklungspolitik, Materialien und kleine Schriften no. 92), Bochum 1982.

Machetzki, R., 'Tendenzen der wirtschaftlichen Entwicklung und

Kooperation im pazifischen Raum', *Südostasien Aktuell*, Jan. 1984, p. 66 ff.
——, 'International and Supranational Problems of Political Regionalism in South-East Asia' in B. Dahm and W. Draguhn (eds), *Politics, Society and Economy in the ASEAN States*, Wiesbaden 1975, p. 17 ff.
Macrae, N., 'Pacific Century, 1975–2075?', *The Economist*, 4 Jan. 1975.
Majid, M., 'Regional Security through Trade and Investment', *Contemporary Southeast Asia*, vol. 2 (1980), p. 30 ff.
Malmgren, H.B., 'Threats to the Multilateral System' in W.R. Cline (ed.), *Trade Policy in the 1980s*, Washington DC 1983, p. 189 ff.
Mansfield, M., 'Prospects for a Pacific Community, in P.F. Hooper (ed.), *Building a Pacific Community*, Honolulu 1982, p. 85 ff.
——, 'Pacific Visions', *Perspectives* (East-West Center, Honolulu), Spring 1981, p. 12 ff.
Martin, J.V., Jr., 'Management of Bilateral Economic Relations by Japan and Australia', *Asia Pacific Community*, no. 13 (1981), p. 113 ff.
Mayrzedt, H., 'Einige Perspektiven der Regionalisierung des Nord-Süd-Dialogs', *Aussenwirtschaft*, 36 (1981), p. 143 ff.
——, *et al.*, *Perspektiven des Nord-Süd-Dialogs und internationale Verhandlungsmechanismen*, Cologne 1981.
Miller, E.B., 'Soviet Partizipation in the Emerging Pacific Basin Economy: The Role of "Border Trade"', *Asian Survey*, vol. 21 (1981), p. 565 ff.
Miller, J.D.B., 'A Pacific Economic Community: Problems and Possibilities', *Asia Pacific Community*, no. 9 (1980), p. 10 ff.
Ministry for Foreign Affairs, *Löhne in Japan*, Tokyo, June 1979.
Ministry of International Trade and Industry, *White Paper on International Trade 1981*, Tokyo 1981.
Minx, E., *Von der Liberalisierungs- zur Wettbewerbspolitik*, Berlin/New York 1980.
de Miramon, J., 'Countertrade: A Modernized Barter System', *OECD Observer*, no. 114 (1982), p. 12 ff.
Morrison, C.E., 'American Interests in the Concept of a Pacific Basin Community' in J. Crawford and G. Seow (eds), *Pacific Economic Cooperation: Suggestions for Action*, London 1981, p. 114 ff.
——, 'American Interest in the Pacific Community Concept' in Japan Center for International Exchange (ed.), *The Pacific Community Concept: Views from Eight Nations*, Tokyo 1980, p. 32 ff.
Morris-Suzuki, T., 'Japan and the Pacific Basin Community', *The World Today*, vol. 37 (1981), p. 454 ff.
Müller, U., 'Die Gefährdung der GATT-Ordnung', *Wirtschaftsdienst*, 62 (1982), p. 254 ff.
Müller-Godeffroy, H., *et al.*, *Der neue Protektionismus*, Bonn 1983.
Nakajima, N., 'Pacific Basin Cooperation Concept and Japan's Options', *Asia Pacific Community*, no. 9 (1980), p. 1 ff.
Nakajo, S., 'Japanese Direct Investment in Asian Newly Industrializing Countries and Intra-Firm Division of Labor', *The Developing Economies*, vol. 18 (1980), p. 463 ff.
Naya, S., 'Japan's Role in ASEAN Economic Development', *Asia Pacific*

Community, no. 1 (1978), p. 34 ff.

Nicholas, R.M., 'ASEAN and the Pacific Community Debate: Much Ado About Something?', *Asian Survey*, vol. 21 (1981), p. 1197 ff.

Nishikawa, S., and H. Shimada, 'Employment and Unemployment: 1970 to 1975', *Keio Business Review*, no. 13 (1974), p. 43 ff.

Nowzad, R., *The Rise in Protectionism* (IMF Pamphlet Series no. 24), Washington DC 1978.

Oborne, M.W., and N. Fourt, *Pacific Basin Economic Cooperation*, (OECD Development Centre Studies), Paris 1983.

Ochel, W., *Die Entwicklungsländer in der Weltwirtschaft*, Cologne 1982.

OECD, *The Impact of the Newly Industrializing Countries on Production and Trade in Manufactures*, Paris 1979.

——, *Interfutures: Facing the Future*, Paris 1979.

Okita, S., 'The Future of Pacific Basin Cooperation', *Asien*, no. 1 (1981), p. 53 ff.

——, 'A View on the Pacific Basin Cooperation Concept', (Japan Institute of International Affairs), Tokyo, May 1981 (mimeo).

——, *The Developing Economies and Japan*, Tokyo 1980.

Okochi, K., 'Lebensumstände und Beschäftigungsverhältnisse älterer Leute in Japan', in W. Kraus, *Humanisierung der Arbeitswelt. Gestaltungsmöglichkeiten in Japan und in der Bundesrepublik Deutschland*, Tübingen 1979, p. 185 ff.

Olsen, E.A., 'Changing US-interests in Northeast Asia', *World Affairs*, vol. 143 (1980), p. 346 ff.

Ooi Guat Tin, *The ASEAN Preferential Trading Arrangements* (PTA): *An Analysis of Potential Effects of Intra-ASEAN Trade* (Institute of Southeast Asian Studies, ASEAN ERU, Research Notes and Discussions Paper no. 26), Singapore 1981.

Outters-Jaeger, J., *The Development Impact of Barter in Developing Countries* (OECD), Paris 1979.

Pacific Basin Cooperation Study Group, *Report on the Pacific Basin Cooperation Concept*, Tokyo, 11 May 1980.

Pacific Basin Economic Council/Japan National Committee, *Pacific Economic Community Statistics*, Tokyo 1982.

The Pacific Community Idea: Hearings before the Subcommittee on Asian and Pacific Affairs of the Committee on Foreign Affairs (House of Representatives, 96th Congress, 1st Session), US Government Printing Office, Washington DC 1979.

Pacific Economic Cooperation Conference, *Issues for Pacific Economic Cooperation* (A Report by the Task Forces), Bali, Indonesia, 21–23 Nov. 1983.

Pacific Economic Cooperation Conference Task Force on Trade in Manufactured Goods, Report of Findings, Seoul, Sept. 1983 (mimeo).

Pacific Forum (ed.), *Increasing the Scope for Private Investment in the Emerging Pacific Economic Community*, Honolulu 1981.

——, *Strengthening Pacific Area Economic Cooperation*, Honolulu 1980.

Pacific Region Interdependencies: A Compendium of Papers Submitted to the Joint Economic Committee (Congress of the United States), Washington DC 1981.

Pang Eng Fong, 'The Concept of a Pan-Pacific Community and ASEAN: A View from Singapore' in Japan Center for International Exchange (ed.), *The Pacific Community Concept: Views from Eight Nations*, Tokyo 1980, p. 77 ff.

Ping, L.P., 'Reflections on the Pacific Community Concept', *Asia Pacific Community*, no. 8 (1980), p. 35 ff.

Pitt, M.M., 'Alternative Trade Strategies and Employment in Indonesia' in A.O. Krueger *et al.* (eds), *Trade and Employment in Developing Countries*, vol. 1: Individual Studies, Chicago/London 1981, p. 181 ff.

Polomka, P., 'The Pacific Community Idea: An Australian Perspective', *Contemporary Southeast Asia*, June 1983, p. 27 ff.

Prospects for Closer Economic Cooperation in the Asian-Pacific Area (Asian Club, Occasional Paper A–5), Tokyo 1981.

Quick, R., *Exportselbstbeschränkungen und Art. XIX GATT*, Cologne 1983.

Reich, R.B., 'Beyond Free Trade', *Foreign Affairs*, vol. 61 (1983), p. 773 ff.

Reiter, K., *Regionale wirtschaftliche Zusammenarbeit von Staaten der Dritten Welt. Eine theoretische und empirische Analyse der ASEAN*, Saarbrücken 1983.

Republic of the Philippines, Tariff Commission, *Tariff Profiles in ASEAN*, vol. I., Manila, January 1979.

Rhein, E., 'Die pazifische Herausforderung: Gefahren und Chancen für Europa', *Europa-Archiv*, vol. 39 (1984), p. 101 ff.

——, 'Die Bedeutung des pazifischen Raumes für Europa', *EG-Magazin*, no. 2/Feb. 1984.

Rothschild, K.W.; 'Aussenhandelstheorie, Aussenhandelspolitik und Anpassungsdruck', *Kyklos*, vol. 32 (1979), p. 47 ff.

Rothstein, R.L., *The Weak in the World of the Strong: The Developing Countries in the International System*. New York 1977.

Sandhu, K., 'The Pacific Basin Concept: A View from ASEAN' in J. Crawford, and G. Seow (eds), *Pacific Economic Co-Operation*, London, 1981, p. 176 ff.

Sapir, A., 'Trade Benefits Under the EEC Generalized System of Preferences', *European Economic Review*, vol. 25 (1981), p. 339 ff.

Sautter, H., *Regionalisierung und komparative Vorteile im internationalen Handel*, Tübingen 1983.

——, ' "Soziale Marktwirtschaft" als Ordnungsprinzip für die Wirtschaftsbeziehungen zwischen Entwicklungs-und Industrieländern' in O. Issing (ed.), *Zukunftsprobleme der sozialen Marktwirtschaft*, Berlin 1981, p. 633 ff.

——, 'Regionalisierungstendenzen im Welthandel zwischen 1938 und 1970', in H. Giersch, and H.-D. Haas (eds), *Probleme der weltwirtschaftlichen Arbeitsteilung*, Berlin 1974, p. 573 ff.

Savage, I. R., and A. Deutsch, 'A Statistical Model of the Gross Analysis of Transaction Flows', *Econometrica*, vol. 28 (1960), p. 551 ff.

Saxonhouse, G.R., 'The Micro and Macroeconomics of Foreign Sales to

Japan' in W.R. Cline (ed.), *Trade Policy in the 1980s*, Washington DC 1983, p. 259 ff.

Scalapino, R.A., 'Pacific Prospects', *The Washington Quarterly*, vol. 4 (1981), no. 4, p. 3 ff.

——, 'Competitive Strategic Perceptions Underlying US Policy in Asia', in L.R. Vasey (ed.), *Pacific Asia and US Policies: A Political-Economic-Strategical Assessment*, Honolulu 1978, S. 1 ff.

Schatz, K.W., and F. Wolter, 'Internationale Arbeitsteilung mit Entwicklungsländern und strukturelle Anpassungserfordernisse in Industrieländern — Der Fall der westdeutschen Wirtschaft' in S. Borner (ed.) *Produktionsverlagerung und industrieller Strukturwandel*, Bern 1980, p. 97 ff.

Schmidt, P.-G., 'Das Welttextilabkommen — Hydra des Protektionismus?' *Wirtschaftsdienst*, 61 (1981), p. 446 ff.

Schmiegelow, H., *Japans Aussenwirtschaftspolitik. Merkantilistisch, liberal oder funktionell*, Hamburg 1981.

Schultz, S. *et al.*, *Wirtschaftliche Verflechtung der Bundesrepublik Deutschland mit den Entwicklungsländern*, Baden-Baden 1980.

Sekiguchi, S., 'Japan's Regional Policies' in G. Boyd (ed.), *Region Building in the Pacific*, New York 1982, p. 53 ff.

Shimada, H., *The Japanese Employment System* (Japanese Industrial Relations Series, Japan Institute of Labour), Tokyo 1980.

Shinohara, M., New Targets and Redifinition of Economic Cooperation — in the Asia-Pacific Region', *Asia Pacific Community*, no. 18 (1982), p. 1 ff.

——, 'Trade and Industrial Adjustments in the Asia-Pacific Region and Japan', *Asian Economies*, no. 39 (1981), p. 5 ff.

——, 'Emerging Industrial Adjustment in Asia-Pacific Area', *Asia Pacific Community*, no. 11 (1981), p. 1 ff.

Sicat, G.P., 'Trade and Industrial Policies in ASEAN Countries' (paper presented at International Forum on Industrial Planning and Trade Policies, Seoul, 1–12 June 1982).

——, 'ASEAN and the Pacific Region' in P.F. Hooper (ed.), *Building a Pacific Community*, Honolulu 1982, p. 49 ff.

——, 'ASEAN and the Pacific Region', in J. Crawford, and G. Seow (eds), *Pacific Economic Co-Operation*. London 1981, p. 216 ff.

Sihotang, K., *Private ausländische Direktinvestitionen in Indonesien: 1870–1980* (Bochumer Materialien zur Entwicklungsforschung und Entwicklungspolitik, no. 26), Stuttgart 1983.

Sinha, R., 'Japan and ASEAN: a special relationship', *The World Today*, 1982, p. 483 ff.

Sneider, R.L., and M. Borthwick, 'Institutions for Pacific Regional Cooperation', *Asian Survey*, vol. 23 (1983), p. 1245 ff.

Soesastro, H., 'ASEAN and the Political Economy of Pacific Cooperation', *Asian Survey*, vol. 23 (1983), p. 1255 ff.

——, *Institutional Aspects of ASEAN Pacific Economic Co-operation*, ESCAP-Document DP/EGAPEC/11, Bangkok, 2 June 1982.

——, 'The Pacific Community Idea: Much Ado About Nothing?', *Asian*

Perspective, vol. 5 (1981), no. 1, p. 1 ff.
——, 'Economic Relations in the Asia Pacific Region', *Indonesian Quarterly*, vol. 7 (1979), no. 4, p. 28 ff.
——, and S.-J. Han (eds), *Pacific Economic Cooperation: The Next Phase* (Centre for Strategic and International Studies), Jakarta 1983.
Sopiee, N., *ASEAN and the Pacific Basin Concept: Four Questions and Five Imperatives*, Williamsburg, Va. Nov. 1980.
Stecher, B., *Zum Stand der internationalen Handelspolitik nach der Tokio-Runde* (Kieler Diskussionsbeiträge no. 69), Kiel, August 1980.
Streeten, P., 'What New International Economic Order?,' in U.E. Simonis (ed.), *Ordnungspolitische Fragen zum Nord-Süd-Konflikt*, Berlin 1983, p. 79 ff.
——, 'Approaches to a New International Economic Order', *World Development*, vol. 10 (1982), p. 1 ff.
Streit, M.E., 'Anpassungsverhalten ökonomischer Systeme', *Wirtschaftsdienst*, 61 (1981), p. 515 ff.
Tambunlertchai, S., and J.Yamazawa, 'Manufactured Export Promotion: The Case of Thailand' (paper presented at a Conference on Trade and Industrial Cooperation in East and South-east Asia, Institute of Developing Economies, Tokyo, 8–9 March 1983).
Tan, G., *Trade Liberalization in ASEAN* (Institute of Southeast Asian Studies, ASEAN ERU, Research Notes and Discussion Papers no. 32), Singapore 1982.
Tanaka, T., 'The Patterns of International Specialization among Asian Countries and the Future of Japanese Industry', *The Developing Economies*, vol. 18 (1980), p. 412 ff.
Tien-tung Hsueh, 'Hong Kong's Model of Economic Development' in Tzong-Biau Lin, R.P.L. Lee and U. E. Simonis (eds), *Hong Kong: Economic, Social and Political Studies in Development*, New York 1979, p. 9 ff.
Tilman, R.O., 'Asia, ASEAN, and America in the Eighties: The Agonies of Maturing Relationships', *Contemporary Southeast Asia*, vol. 2 (1981), p. 308 ff.
Timberman, D.G., 'In Search of a Pacific Basin Community', *Asian Survey*, vol. 21 (1981), p. 579 ff.
Tokuyama, J., 'The Advantages of a Pacific Economic Basin', *Far Eastern Economic Review*, 23 March 1979.
Tumbocon-Haresco, R., 'Turning an Economy on Taxes', *ASEAN Business Quarterly*, 2nd Quarter 1981, p. 23 ff.
Tumlir, J., 'International Economic Order — Can the Trend be Reversed?', *The World Economy*, vol. 5 (1982), p. 30 ff.
Uhalley, S., 'The "Pacific Community" Concept' (paper presented to the 6th Nakhodka Pacific Seminar, 19–24 August 1981, mimeo).
Uhlig, C.. 'Die neue Weltwirtschaftsordnung aus ordnungstheoretischer und ordnungspolitischer Sicht' in U.E. Simonis (ed.), *Ordnungspolitische Fragen des Nord-Süd-Konfliktes*, Berlin 1983, p. 43 ff.
——, 'Kooperation als Instrument zur Integration der Entwicklungsländer in die Weltwirtschaft', in K. Ringer, *et al.* (eds), *Perspektiven der*

Entwicklungspolitik, Tübingen 1981, p. 369 ff.

UNCTAD, *Protectionism, Trade Relations and Structural Adjustment*, Report by UNCTAD Secretariat (TD/274), 7 Jan. 1983.

——, *Industrial Development Review: Malaysia*, July 1985.

UNIDO, *Export Processing Zones in Developing Countries* (UNIDO Working Papers on Structural Changes no. 19), August 1980.

——, *Industrial Redeployment Tendencies and Opportunities in the Federal Republic of Germany* (UNIDO Working Papers on Structural Changes no. 5), November 1978.

United Nations, *World Economic Survey 1983*, New York 1983.

——, *Transnational Corporations in World Development: A Re-Examination*, New York 1978.

Vance, C., 'American Foreign Policy for the Pacific Nations', *International Security*, vol. 5 (Winter 1980/1), p. 3 ff.

Vermont, R., 'L'avènement du Pacifique', *Politique Etrangère*, March 1981, p. 625 ff.

Vondran, R., 'Japanische Wirtschaftserfolge — Schicksal oder Motivation für die übrigen Industriestaaten', *Ifo-Dokumentation*, Munich 1981.

Walsh, J.I., 'Countertrade: Not just for East-West any more', *Journal of World Trade Law*, vol. 17 (1983), p. 3 ff.

Wanandi, J., 'Pacific Economic Cooperation: An Indonesian View', *Asian Survey*, vol. 23 (1983), p. 1271 ff.

——, 'Indonesia and the Pacific Community' in *Pacific Region Interdependencies: A Compendium of Papers Submitted to the Joint Economic Committee* (Congress of the United States), Washington DC 1981, p. 81 ff.

Wang, Y.K., 'Export Assistance Regimes in the Pacific Asian Developing Countries — the Cases of South Korea, Taiwan, the Philippines and Thailand' (paper presented at the Pacific Cooperation Task Force Workshop on Trade in Manufactured Goods, Seoul, 28–30 June 1983).

Watanabe, T., 'Pan-Pacific Solidarity Without Domination' in *Pacific Region Interdependencies: A Compendium of Papers Submitted to the Joint Economic Committee* (Congress of the United States), Washington DC 1981, p. 68 ff.

——, 'An Analysis of Economic Interdependence among the Asian NICs, the ASEAN Nations, and Japan', *The Developing Economies*, vol. 18 (1980), p. 393 ff.

Wells, L.T, Jr., *Third World Multinationals: The Rise of Foreign Investment from Developing Countries*, Cambridge, Mass./London 1983.

Wells, R.J.G., 'ASEAN Commodity Trade', *Asia Pacific Community*, no. 13 (1981), p. 50 ff. ·

Whitlam, E.G., *A Pacific Community*, Cambridge, Mass./London 1981.

Widjaja, A., 'Toward Pacific Basin Community in the 1980s', *Indonesian Quarterly*, vol. 8 (1980), no. 3, p. 71 ff.

——, 'Toward a Pacific Basin Community in the 80s: An Indonesian Perspective' in Japan Center for International Exchange (ed.), *The Pacific Community Concept: Views from Eight Nations*, Tokyo 1980, p. 57 ff.

Wionczek, M.S., 'Pacific Trade and Development Cooperation with Latin America', *Asia Pacific Community*, no. 9 (1980), p. 21 ff.

Wolf, M., 'Managed Trade in Practice: Implications of the Textile Agreements' in W.R. Cline (ed.), *Trade Policy in the 1980s,* Washington DC 1983, p. 455 ff.

Wolff, A.W. 'Need for New GATT Rules to Govern Safeguard Actions' in W.R. Cline (ed.), *Trade Policy in the 1980s*, Washington DC 1983, p. 363 ff.

Wong, J., *ASEAN Economies in Perspective*, London/Basingstoke 1979.

Yah, L.C., 'The Economic Development of the Members of the Association of Southeast Asian Nations (ASEAN)' in J. Lozoya and A.K. Bhattacharya (eds), *Asia and the New International Economic Order*, New York 1981, p. 174 ff.

——, 'ASEAN's External Trade: Intra-ASEAN and Extra-ASEAN Cooperation', *ASEAN Business Quarterly*, no. 4 (1979), p. 9 ff.

Yasuba, Y., 'The Impact of ASEAN on the Asia-Pacific Region', in R. Garnaut (ed.), *ASEAN in a Changing Pacific and World Economy*, Canberra 1980, p. 73 ff.

Yasushi, H., 'How to Make a Concept Real — The Idea of Pacific Basin Cooperation', *Japan Quarterly*, vol. 27 (1980), p. 471 ff.

Yeats, A.S., *Trade Barriers Facing Developing Countries,* London 1979.

Yoffie, D.B., and R.O. Keohane, 'Responding to the "New Protectionism"': Strategies for the Advanced Developing Countries in the Pacific Basin' in W. Hong and L.B. Krause (eds), *Trade and Growth of the Advanced Developing Countries in the Pacific Basin*, Seoul 1981, p. 560 ff.

Yu, G.T. (ed.), *Intra-Asian International Relations*, Boulder, Colo. 1977.

Yung Chul Park, 'Export-led Development: The Korean Experience 1960-78', in E. Lee (ed.), *Export-led Industrialization and Development*, Singapore 1981, p. 79 ff.

Zakaria, A.H., 'The Pacific Basin and ASEAN. Problems and Prospects', *Contemporary Southeast Asia*, vol. 2 (1981), p. 332 ff.

Zimpel, U.H., 'Exportieren nach Indonesien' in Deutsch-Indonesische Industrie- und Handelskammer/Institut für Asienkunde (eds), *Wirtschaftspartner Indonesien*, Jakarta 1979, p. 171 ff.

INDEX

179